THE
MEDITERRANEAN WORLD

The Classical Mediterranean World

Edited by

WILLIAM H. McNEILL

and

JEAN W. SEDLAR

New York
OXFORD UNIVERSITY PRESS
London 1969 Toronto

Library of Congress Catalogue Card Number: 68-8409
This reprint, 1974
Printed in the United States of America

Preface

The readings in this volume were chosen to emphasize the distinctive character of ancient Greek (or Hellenic) civilization and to show how it met and mingled with other cultural strands as it expanded eastward and westward beyond the confines of the Aegean basin where it arose.

The book opens with selections which illustrate the two central realities of ancient Greek life: the polis or city-state as a basic institution (exemplified in poems by Tyrtaeus and Solon); and the idea of natural law—that the processes of physical nature (described by Anaxagoras), like those of human society (expressed in Aeschylus' *Prometheus*), were governed by fixed laws. The excerpts from Herodotus and Thucydides which follow show how these ideals met with brilliant and unexpected success in the wars against Persia, then with grinding disaster in the Peloponnesian War fifty years later. The subsequent passages from Plato's dialogues demonstrate how a sensitive and highly intellectual man—or two men, Plato himself and his mentor Socrates—tried to construct a new basis for personal and public life after the former naïve identification between each individual citizen and his polis had ceased to suffice.

The readings in Section II illustrate how Greek ideas met and combined with diverse elements of Near Eastern culture in the period following the conquests of Alexander. The Rosetta stone, the Second Book of Maccabees, the writings of Philo Judaeus, and the New Testament all provide clear examples of cultural intermingling. But the weakening and eventual bankruptcy of the Greek rationalistic tradition can be sensed in the selections from Lucian, Plotinus, the Gnostics, and the Manichaeans. Lucian, the pagan, mocks; but the others, in their different ways, all yearn for salvation and escape from a world that, to Herodotus and his predecessors, had seemed so full of interesting and surprising things.

The readings in Section III present some Roman reactions to the Greek civilization encountered after Rome became the overlord, first of Greece itself, then of the entire Mediterranean basin. Lucretius' enthusiasm, Augustus' indifference, Juvenal's distaste, and Marcus Aurelius' conversion to the Greek cultural inheritance illustrate the range of Roman responses. Finally, in the *Confessions* of that great North African theologian, St. Augustine, many of the strands displayed by earlier authors are reconciled—or at least combined.

In surveying the thousand-year period covered by this volume, the historian faces numerous questions. What happened to the Greek idea of freedom, expressed so eloquently by Herodotus, and to the concept of citizenship expounded by Tyrtaeus, Solon, and Pericles (as transcribed by Thucydides)? What became of Greek rationalism, the notion of natural law, and the fifth-century B.C. Greek view of the private and public goals of human life? How did the close-knit, "totalitarian" polis of sixth- and fifth-century Greece compare with the Near Eastern religious sects and, above all, with the Christian church that arose in Roman times? To what degree did these religious associations serve the same psychological and social purposes that the polis had served in the time of Pericles?

Finally, how did Greek, or Graeco-Roman, civilization act and react upon the immemorial ways and wisdom of the Near East? In one sense, Near Eastern institutions and values won a great victory; for Graeco-Roman civilization undeniably adapted itself to the two great ruling forms of the region: bureaucratic empire and monotheism. From this viewpoint, true Hellenism spanned little more than a century; and the handful of little Greek city-states who defeated mighty Persia won merely a brief reprieve before being incorporated into another vast, bureaucratically organized empire. But it can also be argued that the ideas and ideals that found expression in fifth- and fourth-century Greece were so durable and attractive that they survived the subsequent decline of rationalism and political freedom and lived on to transform later civilizations.

This process of diffusion and transformation of Hellenic culture may perhaps best be understood as one of initial cultural differentiation between Greece and the neighboring Near Eastern world, followed by intermingling and a variegated, though in time reasonably coherent, recombination of elements originally separate and opposed. But the problem of Hellenism has exercised the imagination of historians and philosophers from the time of St. Augustine onward—if not before—and no unity of opinion can be expected now. Only the importance of the period is uncontested; for it was from the confrontation and blending of Greek and Near Eastern cultures that Western civilization emerged.

Chicago, Illinois W.H.M.
January 1969

Editorial Note

In contrast to the first two books of this series, the present volume covers a period from which many important texts have survived virtually complete. Moreover, in Greek and Latin—unlike Babylonian or Egyptian—the fundamental meanings of words are not subject to dispute. Thus the system of scholarly annotation frequently employed in the earlier volumes—brackets to indicate proposed restorations; parentheses enclosing explanatory interpolations; and italics or question marks identifying doubtful translations—is little in evidence here. Exceptions are Anaxagoras' fragments and the Rosetta decree, where lacunae appeared in the originals, and the Manichaean texts. These last, translated from the Coptic and Parthian languages, represent an area of linguistic and religious scholarship which is comparatively recent, and for which the available texts are rare and in generally poor condition.

The editors are responsible for the introductions and footnotes, which seek to place the various selections in historical context and make them more easily comprehensible to the nonspecialist. In many instances, material provided by the translator has been a source of valuable information for the notes; but notes reprinted verbatim are followed by "(tr.)." The texts themselves have been reproduced exactly as they stand in the sources indicated, except for the cuts made necessary by limitations of space. No attempt has been made either to standardize spelling as between British and American usage or to adopt a consistent system of transliteration.

Contents

I CLASSICAL GREECE

II EASTERN HELLENISM

Maps

I

Classical Greece

CLASSICAL GREECE
0
100 Miles
THRACE
MACEDONIA
ILLYRIS
EPIRUS
THESSALY
CHALCIDICE
PHRYGIA
MYSIA
TROAS
AEOLIS
ASIA
LYDIA
MINOR
IONIA
CARIA
SPORADES
CYCLADES
DOLOPIA
MALIS
AETOLIA
ACARNANIA
LOCRIS
PHOCIS
BOEOTIA
EUBOEA
ATTICA
ACHAIA
ELIS
ARCADIA
ARGOLIS
PELOPONNESUS
MESSENIA
LACONIA
Epidamnus
Pella
Pydna
Potidaea
Stagira
Eion
Amphipolis
Philippi
Abdera
Byzantium
Propontis
Hebrus R.
Strymon R.
Haliacmon R.
Aous R.
Peneus R.
MT. OLYMPUS
VALE OF TEMPE
MT. ATHOS
MT. PELION
THASOS
LEMNOS
Sestos
Lampsacus
Hellespont
Abydos
Ilium (Troy)
Pergamum
LESBOS
Phocaea
Hermus R.
Sardis
CHIOS
Clazomenae
Ephesus
SAMOS
C. MYCALE
Maeander R.
Priene
Miletus
Halicarnassus
COS
RHODES
CORCYRA
Corcyra
Pharsalus
C. of Actium
Thermopylae
LEUCAS
Delphi
Naupactus
Chalcis
Thebes
Plataea
Eleusis
Marathon
Carystus
Gulf of Corinth
Megara
Athens
Sicyon
Corinth
Aegina
SALAMIS
AEGINA
Mycenae
Argos
Elis
Olympia
Sparta
Pylos
CEPHALLENIA
ZACYNTHOS
SCYROS
ANDROS
DELOS
NAXOS
MELOS
Aegean
Sea
Ionian
Sea

Introduction to Tyrtaeus

The ordinary citizen-soldier formed the backbone of all armies in the classical age of Greece. Fighting was both a duty and a privilege of citizenship, restricted to those who could afford to furnish their own equipment. Although some Greek city-states maintained a few picked troops in constant readiness for emergencies, the levy of citizens formed the main body of the army in time of war. The soldiers received only rudimentary training, and fought with uncomplicated weapons. War in ancient Greece was not a semi-permanent state of affairs, requiring a professional standing army, but an interruption of the normal course of events. Campaigns were generally short; wars often consisted of a single battle. Pursuit of a defeated enemy was limited, and usually did not involve laying waste the enemy's territory.

Land battles in Greece were fought almost exclusively by heavily armed foot-soldiers, called hoplites. The hoplites on each side were organized into a phalanx—a close-order formation in several ranks. On his left arm each soldier carried a round shield about three feet across, covering most of his body, while his right hand grasped a spear seven or eight feet long which was wielded overhand. In battle, the two opposing phalanxes met with clashing shields, their impact heightened by the speed of the charge. If the first clash was not decided by the superior weight and momentum of one phalanx over the other, spear fighting continued, with the men in the ranks behind supplying fighters as those in the front line fell.

The success of the phalanx in battle depended partly on the skill of those in the front line wielding their spears, partly on the cohesiveness of the ranks and the readiness of the men in back to step forward to fill gaps in the front line. Since his own right side was exposed, each hoplite depended for protection upon his neighbor's shield. Under such circumstances, individual courage and steadfastness were of supreme importance for the success of the entire army. Greek generals therefore sought to fire the patriotism of the soldiers and steel them for an intense, if brief, effort.

Tyrtaeus' poems attempt to arouse the citizen-soldier's pride in his city and to contrast the honor of a hero's death with the ignominy of flight. Little is known of Tyrtaeus himself, and only fragments of his works have survived. He was active in Sparta—the city whose army was pre-eminent in Greece for three centuries owing to its superior training, discipline, and maneuverability. Probably he lived in the second half of the seventh century B.C.; the military tactics described in his poems presuppose the phalanx organization and express the values shared by the Greeks of that time. Later tradition records that Tyrtaeus was a lame Athenian schoolmaster whom the Spartans appointed as their general on the instructions of the Delphic oracle; but this may be merely a reflection of the later Greek view that militaristic Sparta was incapable of producing poets.

TYRTAEUS: TWO POEMS

Fragment 6.7

Death is the last proof of valor for him who falls in the front ranks
For his country at war bravely giving his life.
But to forsake one's town, and to leave one's fat fields behind him,
Begging while roaming the lands,—nothing is harder than that;
Trudging from place to place with his mother and tottering father,
And with his children small, and with the bride of his youth.
For disliked he will be and always a stranger among those
To whose cities he comes, driven by dire distress.
Shame does he bring on his kindred, belying his noble demeanor,
No disgrace is he spared, no humiliation left out.
This is the fate of the wayfaring man, no honor enjoys he,
And no name for himself nor for his heirs that he leaves.
Therefore let's fight for this land with ardor, and for our children

University of Chicago College History Staff, *History of Western Civilization,* Topic II, pp. 1-4, trans. by C. W. Mackauer (with some phrases from an earlier translation by Livio Stecchini). Used by permission of the College of the University of Chicago.

Let's die, and our life let us not spare any more.
Fight, young heroes, and cling in close formation together,
Don't think of shameful flight, don't cause a break in the line.
But make mighty and strong your will in your heart, and your courage;
Don't be lovers of life while you are fighting with men.
And the elder among you whose knees are nimble no longer,
—Don't run away and leave them, who are older, behind.
For a shame would it be when a hero, slain in his exploit,
Should lie in front of the young, one who is older than they,
White already his head and graying the hair of his whiskers,
Breathing his life's last breath into the dust of the earth;
Bloody he holds in his hands his bowels and covers them fumbling,
—What a disgrace for the eyes and how revolting to see!
And his body is robbed of its armor. But for a young man
All is becoming as long as he is blooming in youth.
He is admired by men, he is loved by women his life long;
Glory will be his share, if he should fall in a fight.
Therefore each should stay where he stands, both his legs well asunder,
Pressing his feet to the ground, biting his lip with his teeth.

Fragment 8

Since you are Heracles'[1] children, the god's who was never defeated,
Be of good cheer, for Zeus[2] is not yet losing his might.
Don't be afraid of the numbers of men, don't run in a panic;
Straight in the enemies' face each man thrusting his shield,
Scorn your own life with haughty disdain, but cherish and welcome
Like the rays of the sun death's livid arrows of doom.
For familiar to you with his tears and his horrors is Ares,[3]
And of sorrowful war well have you learned every mood;

1. Heracles (Hercules), the mythical hero famous for his gigantic strength, was supposedly also an ancestor of the Greeks.
2. Zeus was the chief of the gods in Greek mythology.
3. Ares, the god of war, was known for his bloodthirstiness.

You have been with the victors and you have been with the vanquished,
More than your share you endured of the surprises of war.
Of those heroes who cling in close formation together,
Fighting the foe with their swords, taking their place in the front,
Few are killed in the battle, and saved are the masses behind them;
But if the champions yield, courage breaks down with them all.
Nobody reaches the end when he tells of the woes that are waiting
For the cur who runs cowardly off from the field;
Easy it is to pierce from behind the back of the man who
Turns and flees in the stark horrors of merciless war.
Shame is the lot of the man whose body is stretched in the field's dust
And in his cowardly back quivers the shaft of the spear.
No, each man should stay where he stands, both his legs well asunder,
Pressing his feet to the ground, biting his lip with his teeth,
Thighs and legs below and breast and shoulders above them
Hidden behind the broad spread of the shield in his fist.
And he should boldly brandish his vigorous spear in his right hand,
Shaking the crest of his helm crowning the top of his head.
So should he learn how to fight by braving the danger of battle,
Never should he with his shield yield to the rain of the darts,
But he should jump on his foe and wound his man with his mighty
Spear or his sword and then kill his opponent at once.
Foot he should set against foot, and shield he should press with his own shield
Crest he should press against crest, helmet press against helm,
Chest should he squeeze against chest, and so should he fight with his rival,
Grasping the haft of his sword or the long shaft of his spear.—
And you, men without armor, hurl deftly your stones at the foemen,

Ducking quickly again under the rims of the shields,
Javelins also dart with careful aim at the enemies,
Always gathering around those who are heavily armed.

Introduction to Solon

Solon, the greatest legislator of classical Greece, was born about 639 B.C. into a family of Athenian nobility. His first profession was that of merchant: he appears to have made money and gained a reputation for integrity as well. Sometime before 600 B.C. he was a prime mover in urging the Athenians to capture the strategically located island of Salamis from Megara, a rival city. Some fragments survive of a patriotic poem he wrote to inspire his countrymen to fight for Salamis. Few details are known of Solon's early career; but it is evident that he was among the most prominent citizens of Athens.

Athens in Solon's day had become polarized into opposing parties of rich and poor. The laws favored the rich, who had become progressively richer while the poor sank into debt and slavery. The Athenian state had reached a point of crisis where both sides recognized the need for accommodation: the rich, to avoid a violent revolution in which they might be expropriated; the poor, to gain by peaceful means some share in the benefits and the regulation of society. Both parties agreed to accept Solon as mediator in this conflict—the rich no doubt soothed by his noble antecedents, the poor trusting in his reputation for integrity. Elected to the office of archon, he was given dictatorial powers to revise the Athenian constitution.

Solon sought to readjust social and economic conditions so as to maintain a balance of power among the various segments of society. Thus he gave something to each party, but undue advantage to none. He divided the population into four economic groups: those in the upper groups paid the highest taxes, but in return became eligible for the chief offices of state. As a check upon the oligarchy of wealth, he established an Assembly composed of six thousand members chosen in the most democratic way possible—by lot from among all free citizens. Solon liberated the Attic peasantry from serfdom, thereby creating that class of farmer-proprietors which later became the mainstay of the Athenian state. He altered the coinage and the law of inheritance, opened Athenian citizenship to aliens, and legislated on manners and morals. His laws applied equally to all citizens. It is a rare tribute to his wisdom that the majority of his regulations were still in force at Athens five centuries later.

The following poetic fragments almost certainly antedate Solon's legislative activity. Their allusions to the evils of disharmony and the fearful results of unbridled arrogance refer unmistakably to the condition of Athenian society prior to his reforms. His conception of Fate is a frequently recurring theme in Greek thought—notably in the works of the great dramatists of the fifth century B.C. Fate to Solon was a kind of natural (or divine) law which decreed that excessive pride inevitably leads to downfall. One object of his constitution was certainly to protect Athens from that fatal consequence.

SOLON: TWO POEMS

Eunomy

Our city never shall be destroyed, by Zeus' decree
And by the will of the blessed immortal gods:
For, as a high-spirited guardian, Pallas Athena[1]
Of the mighty father holds her hands over it.
But the citizens themselves are fain to ruin the great city in
    their madness,
Lured by their insane pursuit of wealth,
Unjust is the mind of the people's leaders, who are bound
To suffer many troubles through their great hybris.[2]
For they do not know how to restrain insolence
Nor decently to enjoy the present feast.
. . . .
Rich they are, giving in to deeds of injustice.
. . . .

University of Chicago College History Staff, *History of Western Civilization*, Topic II, pp. 5-9, trans. by Livio Stecchini. Used by permission of the College of the University of Chicago.

1. Athena, the goddess of wisdom and war, was the patron deity of Athens.
2. Hybris is the Greek term for excessive pride. In Greek mythology hybris ranked as an offense against the gods, who often avenged themselves by arranging for the offender's downfall.

With no respect for sacred goods or public
They steal and grasp everywhere
Nor leave they untouched the holy foundations of Right,
Who in silence witnesses their present actions and past
And in time shall come, for sure, to take revenge.
Inexorable this festering sore already spreads to the whole city,
And quickly she has fallen into wretched servitude,
Which wakes up civil strife and dormant war,
That destroys the lovely youth of many.
For, through the factions in which the unjust thrive,
Our beloved city is soon consumed by her haters.
These are the evils loose upon the people:
Of the poor, many, sold, in shameful chains,
Take the road leading to a foreign land,

. . . .

Thus the public evil reaches each man at home;
Barred gates do not hold it;
It leaps over high fences, it never misses,
Even if one flees to the house's innermost corner.
This is what my heart bids me to teach the Athenians:
That dysnomy brings many evils to the city,
But eunomy makes all things orderly and fitting,
And often puts fetters on the unjust ones;
She smooths the uneven, quiets insolence, destroys hybris,
And sears the budding flowers of Ate;[3]
It rights crooked judgments, softens arrogance,
Quiets the zeal of opposing factions,
Stills the bile of vexing discord. Under its rule
All is even-fitting and full of wisdom everywhere.

On Justice

Noble daughters of Memory and Olympian Zeus,
Pierian Muses,[4] lend ear to my prayer,

3. Ate, a daughter of Zeus, originally personified guilty love with an evil result. Later she was regarded as a goddess of Fate and the avenger of unrighteousness.

4. The Muses were originally the nymphs of springs whose waters gave inspiration, later the nine goddesses of the various types of poetry, art, and science. Pieria is a district in Macedonia, one of the earliest seats of worship of the Muses.

Grant me from the blessed gods prosperity,
And from all men always to have a good name;
And so to be sweet to friends, bitter to enemies,
Admired by those and frightening to these.
Riches I do want to have but unjustly I do not wish
To possess them: Right is certain to come with time.
God-given wealth comes to man a lasting thing,
Solid from deep bottom to the crown.
That which men acquire by hybris, comes not
In the order of things, but is dragged against will,
Forced by unjust deeds. Soon with it mingles Ate:
She starts from little, as does fire,
At first a paltry thing, a ruin at the end.
For, the works of hybris do not endure for men,
But Zeus brings everything to its proper end: Sudden,
As spring wind quickly scatters clouds
And from the deep stirs the many waves
Of barren sea, and on wheat-growing land
Tears down the fair works of husbandry, reaches high heaven,
Seat of the gods, sets the sky clear again to view:
The sun's might shines forth over the fecund earth
In beauty, and nothing more of the clouds is seen,—
So comes Zeus' retribution: not at each stroke,
As mortal man, turns he quick to anger;
Yet ever steadily he sees him who conceals
A heart of guilt, and this surely is revealed in the end.
Some pay at once, some later. If they themselves escape,
And the gods' doom meets them not in its pursuit,
It, for sure, will return a second time: the innocent children
Will pay for their deeds, or the distant progeny.
We mortal men, alike good and bad, cling to this notion,
That the opinion each has of himself will always be,
Till something befalls us; then we lament.
Before then we rejoice, agape at hollow hopes.
He who is weighed down by painful sicknesses
Harbors the thought how one day he will be whole.
One who is a coward, thinks he will prove a hero.
Another, of no pleasing aspect, thinks he will be beautiful.

One without money suffers the toils of want,
But believes for certain he shall come to wealth.
Each man strives for his goal: one roams upon the sea, the home of the fishes,
On ships, wishing to take home some gain,
Tossed by the grievous winds,
Sparing no danger to his life.
Another cuts the plant-bearing earth and slaves all the year round,—
I mean those who work with the curved plough.
Another, skilled in the art of Athena and Hephaestus[5]
Master of crafts, contrives a living with his hands,
And another, trained by the gifts of Olympian Muses,
By knowing the measure of the delightful art.
Another is made a seer by his lord, far-shooting Apollo;[6]
He may tell from afar the evils coming to a man,
Against whom the gods are plotting; but in no way the fated things
Can be guarded off by augury or by sacred offerings.
Others, having the skill of the Healer[7] rich in drugs,
Are physicians. For these too there is no clear outcome:
At times from little ache there springs a big pain
That none can heal with soothing drugs;
And on one who is beset with frightful sicknesses
It is enough to lay one's hands, and he is whole.
Fate indeed to mortal men brings both good and ill,
Nor can the gifts of immortal gods be shunned.
Indeed any enterprise has risk:
No one can tell the end by the beginning.
Nay, one who tries to practice good
Unsuspecting falls into great and sore disaster,[8]
But to him who practices ill, god allows
That, freed from folly, he end all things in luck.

5. Hephaestus was the god of fire and of the crafts which required fire for their execution. Athena was the patron of cleverness and inventiveness.

6. Apollo was the god of light and of order, justice, and legality.

7. Aesculapius, the god of medicine and healing.

8. Ate. See note 3 above.

Of wealth no clear limit is set to men.
For those of us who enjoy the greatest riches
Strive twice as hard. Who can satisfy all?
It is true, gains are immortals' gift to mortals;
But out of them there springs up Ate
Whom Zeus sends in retribution, to some soon, to some later.

Introduction to Anaxagoras

The Greeks, like the Mesopotamians and Egyptians before them, cherished various legends attributing the origin and regulation of the world to the actions of gods and goddesses. But unlike their predecessors, the Greeks eventually became dissatisfied with these myths and sought an alternative explanation of nature. This step was taken first in a few Greek cities of Ionia—a narrow strip of coastline in western Asia Minor. The Ionians were a prosperous trading people maintaining extensive contacts with Egypt, Crete, and inland Asia Minor. Undoubtedly they became acquainted with the two great myth-systems of the ancient Near East—the Egyptian and the Mesopotamian—and noticed the divergencies between these foreign myths and their own. Perhaps the differences appeared irreconcilable, and thus cast discredit upon all myths. In any event, Greek society had not developed a powerful priesthood capable of explaining and harmonizing the differences. By the sixth century B.C. certain Ionian thinkers had begun groping toward a non-mythological explanation of the origin and nature of the world.

Like the old myth-makers, these first scientist-philosophers sought to reduce the varied phenomena of the visible world to a rational and coherent system. The significant novelty was that the philosophers eliminated anthropomorphism—deities who ruled by their personal will—in favor of a world operating according to its own internal laws. Nonetheless, the new philosophical cosmologies were indebted to certain aspects of the myths; and even the myths sometimes explained events in terms of impersonal natural forces. In the epics of Homer, for instance, the gods themselves are subject to the workings of Fate. The poems of Hesiod (*ca.* 800 B.C.), which trace the ancestry of the Greek gods back to the beginning of the world, describe an original chaos which separated itself into earth and sky. The astrologers of Babylonia and Egypt believed that certain conjunctions of the stars produced definite and predictable results on earth, though they also claimed that the gods could interfere with the process.

No complete works have survived from any of the Greek philosophers before Plato. Modern reconstructions of their views must be compiled from scattered remarks and quotations in later authors, and are necessarily somewhat tentative. Plato and Aristotle gave occasional attention to the opinions of their predecessors; but Aristotle's pupil Theophrastus (373-287 B.C.) was the first to write a systematic history of philosophy. Theophrastus' works—which were the standard authorities on philosophy in the ancient world—survive only in certain excerpts collected in Hellenistic times. Quotations from a few of the pre-Socratic philosophers have come down to us in the writings of Simplicius, a Neo-Platonist of the sixth century A.D. It is from Simplicius that we have the majority of the extant fragments of Anaxagoras.

Anaxagoras, who lived from about 500 to 428 B.C., was already the product of a century of philosophical speculation about the nature of the universe. Born in Clazomenae in Asia Minor, he seems to have spent most of his active life in Athens, where he was a friend of the statesman Pericles. At an uncertain date the Athenians brought Anaxagoras to trial on a charge of impiety. The details of the case are unknown, though afterwards the philosopher apparently left Athens and resided for the remainder of his life in Lampsacus on the Hellespont. He wrote only one short book, setting forth all his opinions with great brevity. The extant remains of this work comprise only about one thousand words. But they show clearly that he wrote later than Parmenides or Zeno and probably after Empedocles, for his opinions indicate familiarity with theirs.

Anaxagoras denied the primacy of a single element or combination of elements, like the water of Thales or the four substances of Empedocles. Likewise he rejected Parmenides' conception of the ultimate substance as immoveable, continuous, limited Being. None of these, to his mind, satisfactorily explained the origin of change. To avoid the apparent absurdity of stating that things are created out of nothing, Anaxagoras concluded that the original mixture contained everything, and that matter is infinitely divisible, since this is the only way that even the smallest particles can contain a portion of everything. But to account for the origin of the visible world he presupposed the existence of clumps of matter, or seeds, which form the basic constituents of things.

The motive force in Anaxagoras' system was Mind (*Nous*). Mind bore many of the qualities of an abstract principle; but it was nonetheless material. To the fifth-century Greeks, the ultimate criterion of reality was extension in space. Mind, however, was regarded as a particularly fine and pure sort of matter. Anaxagoras apparently thought that it was distributed discontinuously throughout the universe, since he stated that there could be larger and smaller quantities of it. He believed that Mind owed its power to its fineness and to the fact that, though present within the mixture of elements, it was unmixed. It is not clear from Anaxagoras' extant fragments how Mind imparted the original motion to things. Evidently at first the quantity of matter in motion was small, but then progressively increased. The result was a vortex—a whirling action which by its immense speed produced the separation of the elements.

It is remarkable how closely Anaxagoras' conception of the vortex resembles modern theories about the origin of the universe. Indeed, a number of Greek scientific theories—the atomic system of Democritus is another example—have much in common with modern ideas. The ancient Greeks, of course, lacked any precise instruments for the observation and measurement of phenomena, and modern science has corrected many of their errors. But it was the Greeks who produced the idea of natural law—that change occurs according to a fixed and recurring pattern accessible to reason and apart from the will of personalized supernatural figures. As attempts to fit the observed facts of nature into an organized system operating according to its own laws, the work of Anaxagoras and his fellow philosophers marks the beginning of scientific method.

ANAXAGORAS: FRAGMENTS

1 All things were together,[1] in number and in smallness without limit, for the small, too, was without limit.[2] And as long as all things were together no one of them could be clearly distinguished, because of their smallness. Yes, and air and

Trans. by Charles M. Bakewell, in his *Source Book in Ancient Philosophy*, New York: Charles Scribner's Sons, 1907, pp. 49-53.

1. I.e., in the beginning.

2. I.e., there is no ultimate entity (for example, atoms) to which all visible phenomena can be reduced.

ether, both being infinite, dominated all things,[3] for they are the biggest things in the universe both in quantity and in size.

3 For there is no least of what is small: there is always a still smaller. For it is impossible that that which is should cease to be by being divided. On the other hand there is always a still larger than the large. And [the large] is equal to the small in number [of portions].[4] In itself, however, each thing is both large and small.

4 And this being so one must suppose that many things and of all sorts coexist in all [the worlds][5] that are brought together—seeds of all things,[6] having all sorts of forms and colors and savors. And (in all these worlds)[7] men have been put together, and all animals that have life; and these men possess inhabited cities and tilled fields, as we do; and they have a sun and moon and other heavenly bodies, as we have; and their earth brings forth many plants and of all sorts, the most serviceable of which they garner and use for their sustenance. This then is the view that I have put forward with regard to the differentiation [of the primal mixture],—that it takes place not with us alone but also elsewhere.

Before these things were differentiated, when all things were still together, there was not even any color clearly distinguishable, for the mixture of all things prevented it—of the moist and the dry, the warm and the cold, the bright and the dark.[8] (And there was much earth too in the mixture)[9] and an endless multitude of seeds, no one like another.

3. In Greek popular belief, the sky was a solid hemisphere like a bowl; the earth was a round, flat plate on which the sky rested. The gap between earth and sky was filled by air near the earth's surface and by ether above.

Anaxagoras apparently takes air and ether as the equivalents of hot and cold, which form two distinctive masses. Thus ether is the rare, hot, and dry; air (or mist) the dense, cold, and wet.

4. Because all things are infinitely divisible.

5. Or: the world. It is uncertain whether Anaxagoras taught that more than one world existed contemporaneously.

6. Anaxagoras assumes a tendency of matter to coagulate, although it is infinitely divisible.

7. Or: all parts of the world (if only one world is assumed).

8. The notion of opposites was basic to the cosmological systems of some of Anaxagoras' predecessors, especially Heraclitus, who had shown that one of a pair of opposites cannot exist without the other. According to Aristotle,

5 We must know that when these things are separated one from another the whole is neither more nor less [than it was before], for it is impossible that there should be more than the whole, but the whole is always equal to itself.

6 And since the parts of the great and of the small are equal in number, this is another reason for holding that all things are in everything. Nor is it possible for one of the parts to exist in isolation from the rest, but everything includes a portion of everything.[10] Since it is impossible that there should be any least part no portion can be isolated, or come to be by itself, but as at the beginning, so now, all things are together. And in everything that has been differentiated, in what is largest as in what is smallest, many things are contained, and an equal number.

7 And so we cannot know either by word or by deed the number of the things that have been differentiated.

8 Nor are the things that exist in one and the same world isolated, or chopped off from one another as with a hatchet—the warm from the cold or the cold from the warm.

9 . . . while these things are thus swirling around and becoming differentiated by force and velocity. And the velocity gives the force. But their velocity is not to be compared to the velocity of anything in our present world. It is in every way many times as swift.

10 For how could hair come from what is not hair, flesh from what is not flesh?[11]

11 In everything there is a portion of everything except Mind. There are some things in which there is Mind also.

12 All other things contain a portion of everything, but Mind is infinite and self-ruled and is mixed with nothing. For if it did not exist by itself, but were mixed with anything else,

---

Anaxagoras taught that things are generated out of their opposites—e.g. hot is produced from cold and vice versa—proving that the opposites must have been present in each other all the time.

9. This clause seems not to belong here; the text may be corrupt.

10. The difference among various kinds of seeds is not in the number of their components, but in their proportions: everything is characterized by whatever it has most of.

11. This sentence suggests that in addition to opposites like hot and cold Anaxagoras also considered natural substances like hair, flesh, and bone as primary elements.

it would contain a portion of all things. . . . For in everything there is a portion of everything, as I have said above. And in that case the things mixed with it would prevent it from having power over anything else such as it now has, being alone and by itself. For it is the thinnest of all things and the purest, and it possesses all knowledge and the greatest power. And whatsoever things are alive, the largest as well as the smallest, over all is Mind the ruler. And over the whole revolving universe Mind held sway, so that it caused it to revolve in the beginning. The revolution first began in a small area; now it extends over a larger space, and it will extend still farther. And Mind knows all things, whether mixed together, or differentiated and separate. Mind also regulated all things,—what they were to be, what they were [but are not now], and what they are; and Mind regulated the revolution in which revolve the stars, the sun and the moon, and the air and the ether that are differentiated [from the primal mixture]. And it is this revolution that caused the differentiation. The dense is differentiated from the rare, the warm from the cold, the light from the dark, the dry from the moist;[12] and there are many portions of many things. Nothing, however, is altogether differentiated and distinct from anything else, excepting only Mind. And all Mind, whether greater or smaller, is alike. Nothing else, however, is like anything else. But whatever portions are predominant in each individual thing, these it has always been taken to be, because they were the most conspicuous things.

13 And when Mind began to set things in motion there was a differentiation of all that was in motion, and whatever Mind set in motion was all separated; and when things were set in motion and separated the revolution caused them to be much more separated.

14 And Mind, which is eternal, is most assuredly now also where all other things are—in the surrounding mass, in the things that have been differentiated, and in the things that are being differentiated.

15 The dense and the moist, the cold and the dark, crowded

12. Anaxagoras assumes that like attracts like and that in a vortex the heavy elements tend toward the center, the light ones toward the circumference.

together where the earth now is;[13] the rare, the warm, the dry, and the bright travelled out into the far-off ether.

16 And from these as they were differentiated the earth was fashioned. For from the clouds water is separated off, from the water, earth; and from the earth stones are solidified by the influence of the cold, and they travel out still farther from the water.

17 We Greeks are wrong in using the expressions "to come into being" and "to be destroyed," for no thing comes into being or is destroyed. Rather, a thing is mixed with or separated from already existing things. And so it would be more accurate to say, instead of origin, commingling; instead of destruction, dissolution.

21 Because of the weakness of our senses we are unable to discern the truth.[14]

13. For instance, air was solidified into clouds, from which came water; from water earth was produced; from earth, stones.
14. This is reminiscent of Parmenides' opposition of the Way of Truth (i.e., Reason) to the Way of the Senses, which are deceptive.

Introduction to Aeschylus

The poet Aeschylus is the earliest Greek dramatist of whom any complete works have survived. About eighty plays by him are mentioned in classical sources; of these, seven have been preserved entire, together with fragments of others. Apart from his work, little is known of the poet's life. His traditional birth-date, 525 B.C., has been obtained by subtracting forty years from the date of his first victory in the drama competitions held at the Dionysia festivals. We know that he fought in the infantry at the battle of Marathon (490 B.C.), and possibly at Salamis (480 B.C.) and Plataea (479 B.C.) as well. He was the dominant figure in Athenian literature in his generation, and played a major role in the development of Greek tragedy.

Greek tragic drama is an outgrowth of the dithyramb—the

choral song and dance performed in honor of Dionysus, the god of vegetation and especially of the vine. Numerous legends clustered around the name of Dionysus. He was supposed to have been a miraculous child, then a beautiful and strong young man who first conquered all enemies, but through his excess pride suffered defeat and death. His death proved redemptive; like the vegetation which he symbolized, Dionysus died only to be reborn. The dithyramb was a lament on his death, performed in front of the altar where a goat representing him was sacrified. The chorus—fifty men dressed as satyrs, with the heads and bodies of men and the legs of goats—sang of some incident in the life of the god. This "goat-song" was thus a very specialized art form, bound by religious conventions and performed only at the Dionysia festival.

The first step in the development of the drama out of the dithyramb was the introduction of an actor to play against the chorus—an innovation supposedly made in the sixth century B.C. by the playwright Thespis (from which the adjective "thespian"). Phrynicus (*ca.* 600 B.C.?) was reputedly the first dramatist to take his subject matter from myths unconnected with the history of Dionysus. By the time of Aeschylus, the conventions of Greek tragedy had been fairly well established. The dramatists always wrote in poetry, often in verses of complex rhythm. The plays consisted of speeches and songs separated by dialogues and choral interludes sung to the accompaniment of musical instruments. The actors and members of the chorus were all male, wearing masks that stylized the predominant features of the character they portrayed. They expressed emotion through a broad range of gestures and mimicry rather than by facial expressions, which in any case could scarcely have been visible to most of the audience in the large outdoor theaters. Action was not portrayed, but narrated: deeds of passion and violence occurred offstage and were subsequently recounted by the actors. The movements both of actors and chorus were stately and rhythmical, the atmosphere restrained and dignified.

Aeschylus' *Prometheus Bound* is the first play of a trilogy based upon the myths of Prometheus' encounter with Zeus. Prometheus was originally a petty demon, one of the dwarf-like phallic deities connected with primitive mystery-religion. He was a patron of potters and smiths; the chief feature of his worship was a torchlight procession which wound through the potters' quarter of Athens on the occasion of the Prometheia festival. Prometheus shared an altar with the god Hephaestus, who was a younger deity but also a patron of smiths. Many of the same legends were associated with both gods, who were supposed to have been initiators of human culture and to have taught mankind the use of fire.

Prometheus in Aeschylus' play is a Titan—a member of the godly dynasty defeated in war by Zeus, and therefore liable to the conqueror's revenge. In the poet's hands Prometheus has become a dark and majestic figure. As a potter he knew how to form men out of clay; now he wished to put the fire of life inside them, as soul. Zeus, of course, could not tolerate such presumption; he responded by removing all fire from the earth. But Prometheus knew that fire could be produced by rubbing the soft wood of a hollow reed with a fire-stick; thus he stole fire back to earth.

Zeus in *Prometheus Bound* is the supreme tyrant who works his will through Might and Force without regard for justice. As an absolute monarch, he proposes to destroy the human race. Prometheus is a minor deity who dares to resist the tyrant's will. Even the gods are powerless to aid him. In the play Prometheus' visitors seek to impress upon him the folly of his stubborn if heroic stance. To be sure, Zeus cannot destroy the Titan, who is a god and therefore eternal; but he can punish him. He orders Prometheus chained to a rock, tortured, and finally cast down into Tartarus, deep inside the earth. With this the play ends.

But *Prometheus Bound* has a sequel, called *The Unbinding of Prometheus,* from which enough fragments have survived to enable us to reconstruct in outline the further course of the tragedy. The key to the outcome is that Prometheus is the "fore-thinker"—he knows the future. In the second play, he makes clear that he possesses a secret which can topple Zeus from his throne. The chief of all the gods cannot afford to remain ignorant of this. The secret is that the sea-nymph Thetis, whom Zeus intends to marry, is fated to bear a son greater than its father. Prometheus arranges to have the secret revealed to Zeus, who promptly presents the nymph to another of her suitors. In return Zeus releases Prometheus from his bonds, restores his dignities, and establishes in his honor the Prometheia festival. In the third play of the trilogy, peace is concluded and solemnly celebrated.

It is possible to regard the *Prometheus* trilogy as no more than an artistic re-weaving of old legends. But it can also be taken to represent the victory of intellect over brute force. We know that Aeschylus detested tyranny; in another of his plays, *The Persians,* he attributes the Greek victory over Persia at Salamis to the superiority of unfettered minds over slavish obedience. Prometheus, like

Greece, is vastly inferior to his opponent in sheer might. His advantage lies in superior knowledge. He cannot destroy the tyrant; but like the Greeks of Marathon and Salamis, he can humiliate him and bring him to terms.

AESCHYLUS: FROM PROMETHEUS BOUND

(MIGHT *and* FORCE[1] *enter, bearing the figure of the Titan* PROMETHEUS. HEPHAESTUS, *with chains and tools, accompanies them.*)

MIGHT

We stand upon the borders of the earth; this is
The Scythian track,[2] a wilderness where none has walked.
Hephaestus, you must now attend to the commands
Our Father gave you. Curb this villain to the crags
That thrust and loom above us, make him prisoner
In bonds of adamant[3] whose grip he cannot break.
It was your prize[4] he stole and brought to men—the gift
Of fire which strengthens all their arts; for an offense
So great as this he must atone before the gods,
That he may learn to bear the sovereignty of Zeus
With patience and to be man's champion no more.

HEPHAESTUS

Embodied Might and Force, you have fulfilled your task
As Zeus ordained, and nothing keeps you here. But I
Have not the will to show a kinsman violence,
To bind a god against the storm-whipped chasm walls.

From *Prometheus Bound*, trans. by Warren D. Anderson, Indianapolis: Bobbs-Merrill, 1963, pp. 3-5, 7-15, 20-26.

1. Might (*Kratos*) and Force (*Bia*) are here personified as the attendants of Zeus, or demons.
2. Scythia was the region north of the Black Sea, then inhabited by nomadic peoples.
3. The hardest known substance.
4. Zeus had given the custody of fire to Hephaestus.

Yet must I summon up that will, and do the deed;
It would be perilous to slight the Father's word.

(*Carrying his tools, he moves reluctantly toward* PROMETHEUS.)

O child of guiding Themis,[5] nobly daring heart,
Against your will and mine I now must nail you fast
With bolts of bronze upon this peak far off from men,
Where neither form nor voice of man can ever come.
Beneath the flaming brightness of the sun your skin
Shall blacken; you shall wait in longing for the night
With her mantle of stars to cover that fierce radiance
Until the chill of dawn is scattered by new suns.
Forever shall each hour bring round its pain to weigh
Upon your heart, since no man born can set you free.
Thus have you been rewarded for befriending man.
A god, you did not shrink before the wrath of gods
But gave their privilege to man, beyond man's right.
For that you must stand sentinel on this bleak rock,
Set stiffly upright and unsleeping at your post.
And you will pour out ceaseless lamentations, all
In vain. Compassion will not move the mind of Zeus:
All monarchs new to power show brutality.

MIGHT

Now do your work—enough of useless pitying.
How can you fail to loathe this god whom all gods hate,
Who has betrayed to man the prize that was your right?

HEPHAESTUS

The ties of kin and fellowship are strangely close.

MIGHT

I grant it; but to disobey the Father's word—
How can that be? How can that fill you with less dread?

5. In the traditional mythology, Themis was a child of Ge or Gaia (Earth). Aeschylus equates the two to make Ge-Themis the mother of Prometheus.

HEPHAESTUS

As always, you are pitiless and impudent.

MIGHT

It does no good to mourn this victim. You must cease
From wasting effort on unprofitable things.

HEPHAESTUS

How bitterly I hate my craftsman's cunning now!

MIGHT

You should not hate it, since the truth is simply told:
This present sorrow comes in no way from your skill.

HEPHAESTUS

And yet I would some other had received my gift.

MIGHT

All things are burdensome but one—to rule supreme
Among the gods; for none is free but Zeus alone.

HEPHAESTUS

Here is the proof. I see it and have no reply.

MIGHT

Here is the prisoner! Make haste to chain him, then;
Your Father could look down and see you idling here.

HEPHAESTUS

Then he could see me ready with the manacles.

(*Begins to fit them on.*)

[They rivet Prometheus to the rock.]

. . . .

HEPHAESTUS

Let us be gone: the chains are tight around his limbs. (*Exit.*)

MIGHT

Now this will teach you to be insolent and steal
The gods' high privilege for creatures of a day!
What help can mortals bring you in this suffering?
The name you bear in heaven is ill chosen—"he
Of foresight"![6] You yourself will need that foresight now,
For how will you get free from such strong workmanship?

(*Exit, with* FORCE.)

PROMETHEUS

Bright air of heaven, winging swiftness of the winds,
And river waters, surges of the open sea
With countless shining laughter, and Great Mother Earth,
And sun that looks on all things: be my witnesses.
See what a god must suffer at the hands of gods!

Behold these bitter torments
That will crush me down through the numberless years
I must yet endure,
This outrage the new chief lord of the blest
Has wrought for my pain—bondage most shameful!
Weep, heart, for the evil that weighs on you now
And still is to come: where shall these hardships
At last see the day of fulfillment?

But why speak thus? Of all that is to be I have
Exact foreknowledge, and no unforeseen distress
Will come to me. I must accept what fate has brought,
Bear it as lightly as I can, and recognize
No might can be the equal of Necessity.
Yet I must speak of my condition, though it be
Unspeakable. This yoke of suffering is mine
Because I granted mortal men prerogative:
I sought the source of fire by stealth and carried it
Within a hollow fennel reed. My gift to man
Has taught him every skill and been his great resource.

6. *Prometheia* in Greek means "forethought."

Such is the crime for which I pay the penalty,
Spread-eagled, pinned in chains beneath the open sky.

(THE DAUGHTERS OF OCEANUS[7] *enter as the* CHORUS, *taking a position above* PROMETHEUS. *They are near him but cannot yet be seen by him.*)

But now
What echo, what fragrance steals faint on my senses?
Is it of gods, or mortal, or mingled of both?[8]
Has someone come to this land at earth's limit
To gaze on my misfortune? With what purpose, then?
You see a god made captive, met with evil fate—
Hated by Zeus and counted an enemy
In the sight of every one of the gods
Who enter his courts, because
I have gone so far in my kindness to man.

(*He hears the* CHORUS. *They move down to a position in front of him as he speaks the next lines.*)

What is this rustle of birds that I hear
Close at hand? The air is alive
With the swift whirr and flutter of wings,
And all that draws near me brings terror.

CHORUS

You need fear nothing: We have come to you in friendship.
Wing to wing we raced together
Through the sky-track to these summits,
When our strongest pleas had scarcely won consent.
Swift was the wind's rush that bore me onward;
For clang of steel came through the depths of our sea-chambers

7. The god Oceanus personifies the great stream of water which was supposed to flow around the earth. Aeschylus makes him Prometheus' father-in-law.

8. I.e., beings halfway between gods and men; such are the daughters of Oceanus.

And the echo struck my heart free of all maiden shyness—
I sped forth unshod in my wingèd carriage.

PROMETHEUS

Behold my pain,
Daughters of Tethys[9] whose offspring are numberless,
Born of the stream that encircles the earth
With unresting waters, O children of
Father Oceanus,
And see in what cruel bonds I lie, pinned down and pierced,
Doomed to serve out on these sentinel cliffs
Such watching as no man could envy.

CHORUS

I see, Prometheus, and tears of sudden terror
Set a blinding mist before me
When I look upon your body
Worn down to wasted gauntness on these cliffs,
Outraged and maimed by these fetters of steel.
For now new helmsmen hold command upon Olympus:
New laws give Zeus unlawful power;
The Great Ones of old[10] he sends down to darkness.

PROMETHEUS

I would he had plunged me down beyond
Hades,[11] hall of the dead, and let Tartarus[12]
Take me forever
When once he had savagely fixed me in chains;
Then none, whether god or man, would be gloating
Over this outrage.
But now I am made the sport of the winds,
A thing for my enemies' laughter.

9. Wife of Oceanus.
10. Kronos and the Titans.
11. Hades is the God of the dead and Zeus' brother. In classical Greek usage, the name applies to the god rather than to the place over which he presided.
12. In Homer's *Iliad* Tartarus denotes a place of confinement for the Titans who had rebelled against Zeus. It was located as far below Hades as the earth is below heaven. In later mythology it became a place of punishment for wicked mortals after death, indistinguishable from Hades.

CHORUS

What god could be so hard of heart
That such distress should move him to joy?
All share your anger at the shame you suffer, all but Zeus;
For he is revengeful, still keeping his mind inflexibly
Set on oppressing the race of Uranus.[13] He will not rest
Till his spirit is glutted, unless by some cunning
He should be thrust from his firm dominion.

PROMETHEUS

I swear that although I am tortured and mocked
In merciless irons, he who presides
Among the blest shall have need of my aid
To show how the course he ponders will bring
The loss of scepter and privilege.
But he shall not hold me charmed in the spell
Of persuasion's honeyed words, nor shall threats
Ever force me to grovel in fear
And make known his fate. He must first set me free
From chains, and for these affronts he must prove
Willing to grant satisfaction.

CHORUS

Your heart is over-bold: you go
Too far in speaking out, and give
No ground before your bitter pains.
But mine is set trembling by terror's piercing shock:
I fear for what may come.
How are you ever to find safe harbor, sorrows
At an end? The son born of Kronos[14] is ever pitiless
And keeps his heart unyielding.

PROMETHEUS

Though he is harsh and limits all justice

13. Uranus was the first chief of the gods in Greek mythological history. He was displaced by his son Kronos, who was in turn displaced by Zeus. The "race of Uranus" means the Titans, the giant gods born to Uranus and Ge (Earth).
14. Zeus.

To his own secret judgments, still I believe
He will change that mood
One day when his strength lies broken thus.
Then will he subdue his unresting wrath
To join in a strong compact of friendship
And match my eagerness with his.

CHORUS

Speak out, and set before us now the whole account:
Upon what charge of guilt were you arraigned by Zeus
That he should treat you with such cruelty and shame?
Let it be told, unless the story wounds your heart.

PROMETHEUS

The very telling brings me pain, yet not to speak
Would be as painful: all is evil fortune here.
When first the gods began to feel a bitter hate
And stirrings of sedition rose within their midst—
One faction bent on driving Kronos from his throne
That Zeus might play the lord and master, while again
Another vowed that Zeus should never rule the gods—
I sought at once to give the Titans, who are born
Of Earth and Sky, such counsel as was best for them.
I could not: my proposal to use subtle means
They greeted with contempt. They plotted violence
And thought to gain an easy mastery through force,
Though more than once my mother Themis, who is hailed
As Gaia[15] too (one godhead known by many names),
Had prophesied to me the path of things to come—
How fate decreed that neither strength nor violence
But rather craftiness should bring the victory.
All this I set forth fully in my arguments,
Yet they would not so much as listen to a word.
It seemed then that no better course remained for me,
As matters stood, than to enlist my mother's aid
And take my stand with Zeus in mutual accord.

15. See note 5 above.

I counselled, and the black abyss of Tartarus
Closed over Kronos, that most ancient god, and all
His following. But though Zeus had received from me
Such services, the mighty master of the gods
Rewarded me thus evilly, with punishment;
For tyranny somehow contains within itself
The sickness of suspicion aimed against its friends.
  But I have not yet told you what you sought to know,
The cause of my mistreatment. This I shall make plain.
  No sooner was Zeus seated on his father's throne
Than straightway he allotted privilege among
The several gods, to each his duly ordered share
Of power. But to mortals in their misery
He paid no heed: his wish was to annihilate
Their race and then beget another in their stead.
To this design none made resistance—none but I:
I dared oppose it, and delivered mortal men
From sinking utterly destroyed to Hades' realm.
It is for this I bow beneath such suffering,
A painful fate to bear and pitiful to see.
I sought in mercy to give mortals preference:
For me, no mercy—ruthlessly have I been brought
To order, in this sight that brings disgrace on Zeus.

CHORUS

None but an iron heart, a nature hewn from rock,
Can fail to join with you in anger at such woe,
Prometheus. For myself I had no wish to see
What I have seen, and to behold it grieves my heart.

PROMETHEUS

To friends, indeed, the sight is truly piteous.

CHORUS

Surely you did not venture further deeds than these?

PROMETHEUS

Through me, the race of mortals turned their eyes from death.

CHORUS

What remedy did you devise against that spell?

PROMETHEUS

Dim hopes,[16] a tribe I brought to settle in their hearts.

CHORUS

A great and profitable service done to men.

PROMETHEUS

But I bestowed on them still more: the gift of fire!

CHORUS

Is flashing fire now theirs, these creatures of a day?

PROMETHEUS

—And with its aid they shall search out a hundred skills.

CHORUS

On such indictments, then, you were condemned by Zeus?

PROMETHEUS

Condemned to suffer endless outrage and abuse!

CHORUS

And has no limit been laid down for your ordeal?

PROMETHEUS

There is no end until such time as he decrees.

CHORUS

Can that time come? What hope is left? Can you not see
That you have erred? I take no pleasure in the charge;
To you it can bring only pain. But let the past
Be past, and seek some means of rescue from your trials.

16. Although the Greek word used here literally means "blind," Aeschylus seems to have in mind its figurative use as "dim" or "obscure."

PROMETHEUS

When you are free of grief, it is an easy thing
To counsel and admonish one who has been met
With evil fortune. All that came to pass, I knew.
Of my own choice—mistaken, I will not deny—
I brought man aid and brought distress upon myself.
Yet I did not expect to meet such punishment,
My body withering upon the soaring cliffs
Amid this waste and solitary wilderness.
But do not mourn the present sorrow that I bear:
Alight upon the earth and hear from me what fate
Will come, that you may know in full the whole account.
Believe my words and aid me in the suffering
That now is mine, for woe is ever wandering—
It settles now on one, now holds another fast.

CHORUS

We hear your call, and we answer it
Gladly, Prometheus. I come even now
From my lightning-swift courser with hastening step,
Leaving the high paths of the eagle's flight
To visit this land studded with rock; and I long
To hear to its end
The tale of your piteous trials.

(*The members of the* CHORUS *have taken their places at a distance from* PROMETHEUS. OCEANUS *enters riding a winged steed.*)

[He offers to aid his kinsman Prometheus; but Prometheus refuses for fear that Zeus will take revenge on Oceanus also.]

CHORUS

I mourn the evil
Of your ruinous fate, Prometheus,
And I bring offerings of tears shed
In a slow stream from these gentle eyes, these fountains
That have stained my cheek with sadness;
For this act of force is hateful

Wherein Zeus, by private sanction,
Shows his arrogant dominion
Over gods that once were mighty.

From every land now
Comes the clashing cry of sorrow:
For its splendor, for its brilliance
In time past, men mourn the honor
That was yours with your blood brothers;
And of those gone forth to settle
The domain of holy Asia[17]
There is none but suffers with you
In your lamentable fortune.

So they mourn who dwell at Colchis,[18]
Maidens unafraid in battle;
So mourn Scythia's thousands, gathered
In the earth's most distant regions
Round about Lake Maeotis;[19]

And the pride of fierce Arabia,[20]
Men who have a city hard by
Caucasus among the mountains,
Foemen storming like war galleys
Onward with whetted spear blade.

I had beheld till now no other god
Cast down into such distress
Save Atlas,[21] that most mighty of all beings,
Who groans under the firmament's weight

17. Asia, like Europa, was one of the daughters of Oceanus, named after the land over which she presided.

18. Colchis was a country at the eastern end of the Black Sea; Aeschylus thinks of it as being in Scythia. Colchis was known as a place for sorcery.

19. Now known as the Sea of Azov.

20. Possibly this is a corrupt reading; the geography seems not to fit.

21. Atlas was a Titan and the brother of Prometheus. After taking part in the Titans' battle against Zeus, he was condemned to support the vault of heaven on his shoulders.

He bears upon his shoulders.[22]

The sea laments with crash of wave
On wave, all its deeps cry out;
The darkened reaches of Hades groan in answer,
Earth's rivers with pure-flowing streams
Lament your grievous sorrows.

PROMETHEUS

You must not think that stubborn pride or haughtiness
Has kept me silent. It is care that wears away
My heart as I behold myself so foully used—
Though who but I determined, in the last resort,
Their privilege for these new gods? Yet I shall say
No more of this—you would already know the tale
That I might tell you. Listen rather to the griefs
Of mortal men, their helpless state before I placed
Intelligence within them and the use of mind.
And I shall speak from no desire to censure them
But only to make plain the kindness of my gifts.
At first, though they had power to see, they saw in vain
And hearing heard not. In the manner of such forms
As move through dreams, they spent their lives confusedly
With aimless actions. And they knew not how to build
With bricks for warmth, nor yet the craft of working wood:
Beneath the ground they made their homes, like swarming ants,
Within the farthest depths of caves where no light comes.
And they had no unfailing sign of winter, none
Of blossom-laden springtime or of summer rich
In fruit, but acted without plan in all they sought
To do until I taught them how the planets rise
And how the riddle of their settings might be read.[23]

22. The preceding five lines probably do not belong in the play. A sixth line which appears in the Greek text has been omitted from the translation as being particularly suspect.

23. Aeschylus refers to the relation of the seasons to the risings and settings of particular planets or constellations of stars. He mentions only three seasons, the traditional number; the first definite reference to autumn in Greek literature occurs only late in the fifth century B.C.

Likewise did number, subtlest of devices, come
Of my inventing; so came woven shapes of words,
Wherewith the mother of the Muses, Memory,[24]
Keeps all things. I was first to make the fierce wild ox
A slave to yoke and collar, so that it might take
The place of mortals where their work was heaviest;
Obedience to chariot-rein and trace I taught
The horse, chief crown of luxuries that vast wealth brings;
And none but I contrived the means for mariners
To course the pathways of the sea with wings of sail.
Such cunning things did I devise for mortals; yet
Unhappily I lack the cleverness to win
My own deliverance from present suffering.

CHORUS

Your wits are scattered by this untoward despair,
They wander. Like some bad physician taken sick,
You fall into despondency and cannot tell
What kind of remedy might make you whole again.

PROMETHEUS

(*Unheeding*) Your wonder will increase when I have told the rest,
Such skills and such contrivances did I devise.
The greatest boon was this: if ever men fell ill
They had no aid from healing mixtures one might take
In food or draughts, or use as ointments. So for lack
Of medicines their bodies withered up; but then
I taught them ways of mixing soothing remedies
That serve them now to ward off every form of ill.
I showed the plan of divination's many ways:
I was the first to judge which dreams should be fulfilled
In waking, and made known to men the mysteries
Of spoken omens and of portents travelers
May meet. In flight of taloned birds I carefully
Determined which are of good omen or of ill
By nature, with such habits and accustomed food

24. The Muses were the goddesses of the various arts, supposedly the inspirers of poets.

As mark their several kinds, the loves or enmities
They bear each other, and their resting in close flocks.
The entrails' smooth appearance I described as well
And showed what color they must have to please the gods,
Their varied symmetry in bladder and in lobe;
By burning offerings of limbs wrapped up in fat
And strips of loin I brought men knowledge of an art
Not fathomed easily, and I made plain the sense
Of tokens seen in fire that were till then obscure.
  Such were these gifts; but what of others lying hid
Beneath the earth, that are of service to mankind—
Of copper, iron, silver, gold? Would any claim
To have discovered them before me? None could make
That boast, I know, unless he wished to boast in vain.
In brief, the sum of the entire account is this:
All arts that men possess are from Prometheus' hand.

CHORUS

You must not go beyond all bounds in aiding men
And fail to heed your own unhappy state, for I
Am hopeful that one day when this imprisonment
Is ended, you will be as powerful as Zeus.

PROMETHEUS

These things are not yet thus ordained by Fate, who brings
Fulfillment. I must feel the weight of countless woes
Before I am delivered from my bondage here,
And skill is weaker than Necessity[25] by far.

CHORUS

And who then is the helmsman of Necessity?

PROMETHEUS

The triple Fates[26] and vigilant Erinyes.[27]

25. Necessity is not a deity but a personified abstraction, often associated with the Fates or other figures representing destiny.
26. Or *Moirai*, the three goddesses who determine human destiny. The singular, *Moira*, means "fate" in the abstract sense of one's lot in life.
27. The Erinyes were primeval spirits of retribution. Their specific function was to avenge blood-guilt, though here they play the role of cosmic powers.

CHORUS

But can it be that Zeus is their inferior?

PROMETHEUS

From destiny,[28] at least, he can have no escape.

CHORUS

What destiny is set for Zeus but endless rule?

PROMETHEUS

Your questions must not press so far; do not insist.

CHORUS

It surely is some solemn word you keep concealed.

PROMETHEUS

Another tale, and one that is on no account
To be made known. The veil of utmost secrecy
Must cover it, for only if I keep it safe
Shall I escape these shameful bonds and suffering.

CHORUS

Let not the war-strength of Zeus,
Lord of all things, turn its attack on my purpose,
Let me not fail
To draw near to the gods
In feasts of the ritual bull[29]
Slain where my father Oceanus' path
Flows endlessly,
Nor let my tongue give offence.
May I rather hold this truth
And keep it bright before me:

Sweet is life's course when we pass
All our days in confidence,
Making the spirit

28. Prometheus speaks here of destiny not as personified by Fates or Erinyes, but as an impersonal law to which even Zeus is subject.
29. On occasion lesser deities were thought of as sacrificing to greater ones

Strong with the splendor of happiness.
And I shudder to look on you now,
Crushed by this thousand-fold pain that has come because
You do not tremble at Zeus
And your private whim gives man
Too high a place, Prometheus.

O my friend, will that gift be repaid?
Tell me, where are your defenders?
Will they aid you, these short-lived creatures? Were you not
witness
To the feebleness, unavailing
As a dream, whose dragging fetters
Keep the race of mankind in its sightless captivity?
When Zeus has established his concord,
Man's will cannot transgress it.

. . . .

Introduction to Herodotus

Herodotus (*ca.* 484-425 B.C.) has traditionally been called the "Father of History." The title is inaccurate, for as a recorder of historical data he had many predecessors: the scribes of ancient Mesopotamia and Egypt; chroniclers of the Greek cities of Ionia; and Hecataeus of Miletus (late sixth century B.C.), the author of a part factual, part fabulous history of the Greek-speaking peoples. But the sixth-century Greek historians were little known to later ages, while the literature of the ancient Near East is a discovery of modern archaeology. The works of Herodotus are the earliest histories to be read continually from the Hellenistic period down to modern times.

Herodotus' declared intention in writing his history was "to preserve the memory of the past by putting on record the astonishing achievements both of our own and of the Asiatic peoples . . . [and] to show how the two races came into conflict."* Indeed, no

* First paragraph of Book One of the *Histories*.

other ancient historian attempted to cover so large a subject. Herodotus was an inveterate traveler. Born in Halicarnassus in Asia Minor, he seems to have visited most of the world then known to the Greeks—Persia, Babylonia, Scythia, Phoenicia, Egypt, and Italy. He recorded the legends and customs of many peoples, but remained noncommittal about the accuracy of his information. While proud to be a Greek, he described the habits of foreign peoples with admirable detachment, and gave credit even to Greece's arch-enemies, the Persians, for bravery and honor.

Herodotus' sources may have included some written Greek chronicles as well as the works of Hecataeus. But in the main he relied upon oral testimony gathered in the various places he visited. Some of his reports are therefore good stories rather than true ones; and his statistics cannot be taken seriously. Nonetheless, his descriptions of events occurring in his own lifetime—about which he could converse with eyewitnesses—have proved to be reasonably accurate.

Like all the literature of fifth-century Greece, the *Histories* were designed for oral recitation. Herodotus showed an astonishing mastery of prose style in an age when poetry was the nearly universal form of composition. Though his digressions were numerous, he wove them successfully into the main narrative, and never lost sight of his principal theme—the struggle of Greece with Persia. His *Histories* have a quality so strongly reminiscent of Homer that they may be regarded as an epic in prose.

Herodotus lost no chance to compare the freedom of the Greeks with what he considered the slavishness of Orientals. The reason for tiny Greece's remarkable victory over the Persian empire he assigned to the superiority of a free society over despotism. As we pick up the narrative, the Persian king Xerxes has just crossed the Hellespont into Thrace and is in the process of reviewing his troops. The conversation with Demaratus, the former king of Sparta, certainly never occurred; but it illustrates the Greeks' conception of themselves and of the reasons for their success against Persia.

HERODOTUS: FROM THE HISTORIES

Having sailed from one end to the other of the line of anchored ships, Xerxes[1] went ashore again and sent for Demar-

From *The Histories*, trans. by Aubrey de Sélincourt, Baltimore: Penguin Books, 1954, pp. 447-9, 487-9. Reprinted by permission of Penguin Books.

1. Ruled from 485 to 465 B.C.

atus,[2] the son of Ariston, who was accompanying him in the march to Greece. "Demaratus," he said, "it would give me pleasure at this point to put to you a few questions. You are a Greek, and a native, moreover, of by no means the meanest or weakest city in that country—as I learn not only from yourself but from the other Greeks I have spoken with. Tell me, then—will the Greeks dare to lift a hand against me? My own belief is that all the Greeks and all the other western peoples gathered together would be insufficient to withstand the attack of my army—and still more so if they are not united. But it is your opinion upon this subject that I should like to hear."

"My lord," Demaratus replied, "is it a true answer you would like, or merely an agreeable one?"

"Tell me the truth," said the king; "and I promise that you will not suffer by it." Encouraged by this Demaratus continued: "My lord, you bid me speak nothing but the truth, to say nothing which might later be proved a lie. Very well then; this is my answer: poverty is my country's inheritance from of old, but valour she won for herself by wisdom and the strength of law. By her valour Greece now keeps both poverty and bondage at bay.

"I think highly of all Greeks of Dorian[3] descent, but what I am about to say will apply not to all Dorians, but to the Spartans only. First then, they will not under any circumstances accept terms from you which would mean slavery for Greece; secondly, they will fight you even if the rest of Greece submits. Moreover, there is no use in asking if their numbers are adequate to enable them to do this; suppose a thousand of them take the field—then that thousand will fight you; and so will any number, greater than this or less."

Xerxes laughed. "My dear Demaratus," he exclaimed, "what an extraordinary thing to say! Do you really suppose a thousand men would fight an army like mine? Now tell me, would *you*, who were once, as you say, king of these people, be willing

2. Demaratus had ruled Sparta from 510 to 491 B.C. In the latter year he was deposed and went into exile in Persia.

3. The Dorians immigrated to Greece from the northern Balkans sometime about 1100 B.C. They were the ancestors of the Spartans and many other Greeks.

at this moment to fight ten men single-handed? I hardly think so; yet, if things in Sparta are really as you have described them, then, according to your laws, you as king ought to take on a double share—so that if every Spartan is a match for ten men of mine, I should expect you to be a match for twenty. Only in that way can you prove the truth of your claim. But if you Greeks, who think so much of yourselves, are all of the size and quality of those I have spoken with when they have visited my court—and of yourself, Demaratus—there is some danger of your words being nothing but an empty boast. But let me put my point as reasonably as I can—how is it possible that a thousand men, or ten thousand, or fifty thousand, should stand up to an army as big as mine, especially if they were not under a single master, but all perfectly free to do as they pleased? Suppose them to have five thousand men: in that case we should be more than a thousand to one! If, like ours, their troops were subject to the control of a single man, then possibly for fear of him, in spite of the disparity in numbers, they might show some sort of factitious courage, or let themselves be whipped into battle; but, as every man is free to follow his fancy, it is not conceivable that they should do either. Indeed, my own opinion is that even on equal terms the Greeks could hardly face the Persians alone. We, too, have this thing that you were speaking of—I do not say it is common, but it does exist; for instance, amongst the Persians in my bodyguard there are men who would willingly fight with three Greeks together. But you know nothing of such things, or you could not talk such nonsense."

"My lord," Demaratus answered, "I knew before I began that if I spoke the truth you would not like it. But, as you demanded the plain truth and nothing less, I told you how things are with the Spartans. Yet you are well aware that I now feel but little affection for my countrymen, who robbed me of my hereditary power and privileges and made me a fugitive without a home—whereas your father welcomed me at his court and gave me the means of livelihood and somewhere to live. Surely it is unreasonable to reject kindness; any sensible man will cherish it. Personally I do not claim to be able to fight ten men—or two; indeed I should prefer not even to fight with one. But should it be necessary—should there be some great cause to urge me on—then nothing would give me more pleasure than to stand up to one of those men of yours who claim to be a match for three Greeks. So it is with the Spartans; fighting singly, they are as good as any, but fighting together they are the best soldiers in the world. They are free—yes—but not entirely free; for they have a master, and that master is Law, which they fear much more than your subjects fear you. Whatever this master commands, they do; and his command never varies: it is never to retreat in battle, however great the odds, but always to stand firm, and to conquer or die. If, my lord, you think that what I have said is nonsense—very well; I am willing henceforward to hold my tongue. This time I spoke because you forced me to speak. In any case, I pray that all may turn out as you desire."

Xerxes was not at all angry with Demaratus' answer. He turned it off with a laugh and good-humouredly let him go.

. . . .

[In the intervening pages, Herodotus has described the passage of Xerxes' army southward to a point just north of Thermopylae. The incident recounted here occurred shortly before the famous battle in which three hundred Spartans opposed an overwhelming Persian force.]

During the conference[4] Xerxes sent a man on horseback to ascertain the strength of the Greek force and to observe what the troops were doing. He had heard before he left Thessaly[5] that a small force was concentrated here, led by the Lacedaemonians[6] under Leonidas[7] of the house of Heracles.[8] The Per-

4. A meeting Xerxes held with his staff.

5. Region of northeastern Greece.

6. Or Spartans. In Greek mythology, Lacedaemon was a son of the god Zeus; the goddess Sparta was his wife. The two names were used interchangeably in referring to the city named after them.

7. Leonidas was king of Sparta (491-480 B.C.). He died at the battle of Thermopylae.

8. The god Heracles (in Latin: Hercules) was supposed to be the ancestor of various peoples known for their strength. He was the special patron of the Dorians as against other Greeks.

sian rider approached the camp and took a thorough survey of all he could see—which was not, however, the whole Greek army; for the men on the further side of the wall which, after its reconstruction, was now guarded, were out of sight. He did, none the less, carefully observe the troops who were stationed on the outside of the wall. At that moment these happened to be the Spartans, and some of them were stripped for exercise, while others were combing their hair. The Persian spy watched them in astonishment; nevertheless he made sure of their numbers, and of everything else he needed to know, as accurately as he could, and then rode quietly off. No one attempted to catch him, or took the least notice of him.

Back in his own camp he told Xerxes what he had seen. Xerxes was bewildered; the truth, namely that the Spartans were preparing themselves to kill and to be killed according to their strength, was beyond his comprehension, and what they were doing seemed to him merely absurd. Accordingly he sent for Demaratus, the son of Ariston, who had come with the army, and questioned him about the spy's report, in the hope of finding out what the unaccountable behaviour of the Spartans might mean. "Once before," Demaratus said, " when we began our march against Greece, you heard me speak of these men. I told you then how I saw this enterprise would turn out, and you laughed at me. I strive for nothing, my lord, more earnestly than to observe the truth in your presence; so hear me once more. These men have come to fight us for possession of the pass, and for that struggle they are preparing. It is the common practice of the Spartans to pay careful attention to their hair when they are about to risk their lives. But I assure you that if you can defeat these men and the rest of the Spartans who are still at home, there is no other people in the world who will dare to stand firm or lift a hand against you. You have now to deal with the finest kingdom in Greece, and with the bravest men."

Xerxes, unable to believe what Demaratus said, asked further how it was possible that so small a force could fight with his army. "My lord," Demaratus replied, "treat me as a liar, if what I have foretold does not take place." But still Xerxes was unconvinced.

For four days Xerxes waited, in constant expectation that the Greeks would make good their escape; then, on the fifth, when still they had made no move and their continued presence seemed mere impudent and reckless folly, he was seized with rage and sent forward the Medes and Cissians[9] with orders to take them alive and bring them into his presence. The Medes charged, and in the struggle which ensued many fell; but others took their places, and in spite of terrible losses refused to be beaten off. They made it plain enough to anyone, and not least to the king himself, that he had in his army many men, indeed, but few soldiers. All day the battle continued; the Medes, after their rough handling, were at length withdrawn and their place was taken by Hydarnes[10] and his picked Persian[11] troops—the King's Immortals—who advanced to the attack in full confidence of bringing the business to a quick and easy end. But, once engaged, they were no more successful than the Medes had been; all went as before, the two armies fighting in a confined space, the Persians using shorter spears than the Greeks and having no advantage from their numbers.

On the Spartan side it was a memorable fight; they were men who understood war pitted against an inexperienced enemy, and amongst the feints they employed was to turn their backs in a body and pretend to be retreating in confusion, whereupon the enemy would come on with a great clatter and roar, supposing the battle won; but the Spartans, just as the Persians were on them, would wheel and face them and inflict in the new struggle innumerable casualties. The Spartans had their losses too, but not many. At last the Persians, finding that their assaults upon the pass, whether by divisions or by any other way they could think of, were all useless, broke off the engagement and withdrew. Xerxes was watching the battle from where he sat; and it is said that in the course of the attacks three times, in terror for his army, he leapt to his feet.

9. Media was a region of northwestern Iran; the Medes were one of the dominant peoples in the Persian empire. The Cissians were a wild people from a district in Susiana (southwestern Iran).

10. Persian satrap of a province on the Asiatic seaboard.

11. "Persian" in the narrower sense refers to the inhabitants of the province of Persia (Pars) in southwestern Iran.

Next day the fighting began again, but with no better success for the Persians, who renewed their onslaught in the hope that the Greeks, being so few in number, might be badly enough disabled by wounds to prevent further resistance. But the Greeks never slackened; their troops were ordered in divisions corresponding to the states from which they came, and each division took its turn in the line except the Phocian,[12] which had been posted to guard the track over the mountains. So when the Persians found that things were no better for them than on the previous day, they once more withdrew.

How to deal with the situation Xerxes had no idea; but while he was still wondering what his next move should be, a man from Malis[13] got himself admitted to his presence. This was Ephialtes, the son of Eurydemus, and he had come, in hope of a rich reward, to tell the king about the track which led over the hills to Thermopylae—and the information he gave was to prove the death of the Greeks who held the pass.

12. Phocis was a district in southern Greece northwest of Boeotia.
13. An area just north of Thermopylae.

Introduction to Thucydides

Athens, the valiant little city-state which had successfully resisted the gigantic Persian empire, soon became an imperial power herself. In his history of the Peloponnesian War (431-404 B.C.), Greece's greatest historian relates the story of Athens' rise to empire and eventual downfall.

Thucydides was born into a leading family at Athens, probably about 460 B.C., for we know that he was a fairly young man in 431 B.C. when the war began. In 424 B.C. the Athenians elected him one of their generals and assigned him to protect the gold mines of Thrace. There he proved unable to prevent the capture of Amphipolis by the Spartan general Brasidas, for which the Athenians sent him into exile for the duration of the war. No doubt oppressed by this failure, and excluded from any active role in political or military affairs, Thucydides lived thenceforth in obscurity, gathering material for his great work. Although he returned to Athens at the conclusion of peace in 404 B.C., he lived only a few years more. His history remains unfinished, breaking off abruptly in the twenty-first year of the war.

A generation younger than Herodotus, Thucydides possessed a logical and analytic mind sharpened by contact with Sophist argumentation. His chosen theme, however, was rigorously circumscribed. The history and customs of foreign peoples did not concern him. His gaze was directed exclusively upon Greece, and more particularly upon Athens. While admitting his ignorance of more ancient civilizations, he nonetheless regarded the Peloponnesian War as "the greatest movement yet known to history."* His own century he likewise ranked above all others, asserting that prior to his own time "there was nothing on a great scale, either in war or in other matters."* He upheld a strict standard of factual accuracy and expressly rejected the legendary and the fabulous. By his own account, he took great pains to discover the true course of events, relying partly on his own observations, partly on the reports of eyewitnesses or participants in the war, and then attempted to extract the truth from divergent accounts. In reproducing the speeches of various leaders, he claimed only to give the gist of what was said, not a word-for-word transcription.

His grasp of the underlying forces of history was subtler and more profound than that of Herodotus. Thucydides believed that the ultimate causes of events lie in human nature, which is fundamentally unchanging. Events bring out particular aspects of this nature—ambition, pride, greed, fear—which in turn give rise to future events. There is no place in his history for the whims of individuals or the decrees of an unknowable Fate. The future must resemble the past because it is built upon the same human basis. It is this concept which gives Thucydides' work its expressed purpose: "to provide an exact knowledge of the past as an aid to the interpretation of the future."†

This conception—which involves a necessary progression from one event to the next—gives Thucydides' account of the war its dramatic form. The story unfolds like a tragedy of Aeschylus or Sophocles; the hero is Athens. Thucydides relates the course of events in a tone of personal detachment which nonetheless allows

* Chapter I, page 3.
† Chapter I, page 14.

the reader to identify with the protagonist's tragic fate. Athens, once the defender of Greek freedom, begins the conflict as the overlord of formerly independent Greek states. Her oppressive measures are the cause of much misery in the subject cities. Finally, like the heroes of the tragic drama, Athens overreaches herself. Her attempt to conquer Syracuse in distant Sicily ends in disaster and leads to her ultimate defeat in the war.

THUCYDIDES: FROM THE PELOPONNESIAN WAR

From Supremacy to Empire

The way in which Athens came to be placed in the circumstances under which her power grew was this. After the Medes[1] had returned from Europe, defeated by sea and land by the Hellenes,[2] and after those of them who had fled with their ships to Mycale[3] had been destroyed, Leotychides, King of the Lacedæmonians, the commander of the Hellenes at Mycale, departed home with the allies from Peloponnese. But the Athenians and the allies from Ionia and Hellespont,[4] who had now revolted from the king, remained and laid siege to Sestos,[5] which was still held by the Medes. After wintering before it, they became masters of the place on its evacuation by the barbarians; and after this they sailed away from Hellespont to their respective cities. Meanwhile the Athenian people, after the departure of the barbarian from their country, at once proceeded to carry over their children and wives, and such property as they had left, from the places where they had deposited them, and prepared to rebuild their city and their walls. For only isolated

From Thucydides, *The History of the Peloponnesian War*, trans. by Richard Crawley, London: Longmans, Green & Co., 1874, pp. 57-63, 74, 119-28, 219-27.

1. "Medes" here refers to the forces of the entire Persian empire.
2. Hellen was a mythical figure who was supposedly the ancestor of all the Greek tribes, or "Hellenes."
3. A promontory on the western coast of Asia Minor, opposite the island of Samos.
4. Ancient name for the Dardanelles, the narrow strait joining the Aegean Sea with the Sea of Marmora.
5. The place on the northern shore of the Hellespont where Xerxes crossed over into Greece on his bridge of boats.

portions of the circumference had been left standing, and most of the houses were in ruins; though a few remained, in which the Persian grandees had taken up their quarters.

Perceiving what they were going to do, the Lacedæmonians sent an embassy to Athens. They would have themselves preferred to see neither her nor any other city in possession of a wall; though here they acted principally at the instigation of their allies, who were alarmed at the strength of her newly acquired navy, and the valour which she had displayed in the war with the Medes. They begged her not only to abstain from building walls for herself, but also to join them in throwing down the walls that still held together of the ultra-Peloponnesian cities. The real meaning of their advice, the suspicion that it contained against the Athenians, was not proclaimed; it was urged that so the barbarian, in the event of a third invasion, would not have any strong place, such as he now had in Thebes,[6] for his base of operations; and that Peloponnese would suffice for all as a base both for retreat and offence. After the Lacedæmonians had thus spoken, they were, on the advice of Themistocles,[7] immediately dismissed by the Athenians, with the answer that ambassadors should be sent to Sparta to discuss the question. Themistocles told the Athenians to send him off with all speed to Lacedæmon, but not to despatch his colleagues as soon as they had selected them, but to wait until they had raised their wall to the height from which defence was possible. Meanwhile the whole population in the city was to labour at the wall, the Athenians, their wives and their children, sparing no edifice, private or public, which might be of any use to the work, but throwing all down. After giving these instructions, and adding that he would be responsible for all other matters there, he departed. Arrived at Lacedæmon he did not seek an audience with the authorities, but tried to gain time and made excuses. When any of the government asked him why he did not appear in the assembly, he would say that he was waiting for his col-

6. Thebes, the capital of Boeotia (northwest of Attica), had sympathized with the Persian invaders.

7. The commander of the Athenian forces at the victory of Salamis in 480 B.C., and leader of the democratic party at Athens.

leagues, who had been detained in Athens by some engagement; however, that he expected their speedy arrival, and wondered that they were not yet there. At first the Lacedæmonians trusted the words of Themistocles, through their friendship for him; but when others arrived, all distinctly declaring that the work was going on and already attaining some elevation, they did not know how to disbelieve it. Aware of this, he told them that rumours are deceptive, and should not be trusted; they should send some reputable persons from Sparta to inspect, whose report might be trusted. They despatched them accordingly. Concerning these Themistocles secretly sent word to the Athenians to detain them as far as possible without putting them under open constraint, and not to let them go until they had themselves returned. For his colleagues had now joined him, Abronichus, son of Lysicles, and Aristides, son of Lysimachus, with the news that the wall was sufficiently advanced; and he feared that when the Lacedæmonians heard the facts, they might refuse to let them go. So the Athenians detained the envoys according to his message, and Themistocles had an audience with the Lacedæmonians, and at last openly told them that Athens was now fortified sufficiently to protect its inhabitants; that any embassy which the Lacedæmonians or their allies might wish to send to them, should in future proceed on the assumption that the people to whom they were going was able to distinguish both its own and the general interests. That when the Athenians thought fit to abandon their city and to embark in their ships, they ventured on that perilous step without consulting them; and that on the other hand, wherever they had deliberated with the Lacedæmonians, they had proved themselves to be in judgment second to none. That they now thought it fit that their city should have a wall, and that this would be more for the advantage of both the citizens of Athens and the Hellenic confederacy; for without equal military strength it was impossible to contribute equal or fair counsel to the common interest. It followed, he observed, either that all the members of the confederacy should be without walls, or that the present step should be considered a right one.

The Lacedæmonians did not betray any open signs of anger against the Athenians at what they heard. The embassy, it seems, was prompted not by a desire to obstruct, but to guide the counsels of their government: besides, Spartan feeling was at that time very friendly towards Athens on account of the patriotism which she had displayed in the struggle with the Mede. Still the defeat of their wishes could not but cause them secret annoyance. The envoys of each state departed home without complaint.

. . . .

Meanwhile Pausanias,[8] son of Cleombrotus, was sent out from Lacedæmon as commander-in-chief of the Hellenes, with twenty ships from Peloponnese. With him sailed the Athenians with thirty ships, and a number of the other allies. They made an expedition against Cyprus and subdued most of the island, and afterwards against Byzantium, which was in the hands of the Medes, and compelled it to surrender. This event took place while the Spartans were still supreme. But the violence of Pausanias had already begun to be disagreeable to the Hellenes, particularly to the Ionians and the newly liberated populations. These resorted to the Athenians and requested them as their kinsmen to become their leaders, and to stop any attempt at violence on the part of Pausanias. The Athenians accepted their overtures, and determined to put down any attempt of the kind and to settle everything else as their interests might seem to demand. In the meantime the Lacedæmonians recalled Pausanias for an investigation of the reports which had reached them. Manifold and grave accusations had been brought against him by Hellenes arriving in Sparta; and, to all appearance, there had been in him more of the mimicry of a despot than of the attitude of a general. As it happened, his recall came just at the time when the hatred which he had inspired had induced the allies to desert him, the soldiers from Peloponnese excepted, and to range themselves by the side of the Athenians. On his arrival at Lacedæmon, he was censured for his private acts of oppression, but was acquitted on the heaviest counts and pronounced not guilty; it must be known that the charge of Medism formed one of the principal, and to all appearance one of the best-founded articles against him. The Lacedæmonians did

8. King of Sparta and leader of the Greeks at the victory of Plataea in 479 B.C.

not, however, restore him to his command, but sent out Dorkis and certain others with a small force; who found the allies no longer inclined to concede to them the supremacy. Perceiving this they departed, and the Lacedæmonians did not send out any to succeed them. They feared for those who went out a deterioration similar to that observable in Pausanias; besides, they desired to be rid of the Median war, and were satisfied of the competency of the Athenians for the position, and of their friendship at the time towards themselves.

The Athenians having thus succeeded to the supremacy by the voluntary act of the allies through their hatred of Pausanias, fixed which cities were to contribute money against the barbarian, which ships; their professed object being to retaliate for their sufferings by ravaging the king's country. Now was the time that the office of "Treasurers for Hellas" was first instituted by the Athenians. These officers received the tribute, as the money contributed was called. The tribute was first fixed at four hundred and sixty talents.[9] The common treasury was at Delos,[10] and the congresses were held in the temple. Their supremacy commenced with independent allies who acted on the resolutions of a common congress. It was marked by the following undertakings in war and in administration during the interval between the Median and the present war, against the barbarian, against their own rebel allies, and against the Peloponnesian powers which would come in contact with them on various occasions. . . .

First the Athenians besieged and captured Eion[11] on the Strymon[12] from the Medes, and made slaves of the inhabitants, being under the command of Cimon,[13] son of Miltiades.[14] Next

9. The talent was a unit of weight, the equivalent of 60 minas. Its value varied from city to city.

10. A small Aegean island approximately halfway between European and Asiatic Greece.

11. City on the coast of Macedonia (northeastern Greece).

12. River flowing almost directly southward from Bulgaria into Macedonia and the Aegean Sea.

13. An Athenian statesman and general, afterwards commander of the Greek fleet that defeated the Persians off the coast of southern Asia Minor in 468 B.C.

14. The victorious Athenian general at the battle of Marathon (490 B.C.).

they enslaved Scyros[15] the island in the Ægean, containing a Dolopian[16] population, and colonised it themselves. This was followed by a war against Carystus,[17] in which the rest of Eubœa remained neutral, and which was ended by surrender on conditions. After this Naxos[18] left the confederacy, and a war ensued, and she had to return after a siege; this was the first instance of the engagement being broken by the subjugation of an allied city, a precedent which was followed by that of the rest in the order which circumstances prescribed. Of all the causes of defection, that connected with arrears of tribute and vessels, and with failure of service, was the chief; for the Athenians were very severe and exacting, and made themselves offensive by applying the screw of necessity to men who were not used to and in fact not disposed for any continuous labour. In some other respects the Athenians were not the old popular rulers they had been at first; and if they had more than their fair share of service, it was correspondingly easy for them to reduce any that tried to leave the confederacy. For this the allies had themselves to blame; the wish to get off service making most of them arrange to pay their share of the expense in money instead of in ships, and so to avoid having to leave their homes. Thus while Athens was increasing her navy with the funds which they contributed, a revolt always found them without resources of experience for war.

. . . .

After this, though not many years later, we at length come to . . . the events that served as a pretext for the present war. All these actions of the Hellenes against each other and the barbarian occurred in the fifty years' interval between the retreat of Xerxes and the beginning of the present war. During this interval the Athenians succeeded in placing their empire on a firmer basis, and advanced their own home power to a very great height. The Lacedaemonians, though fully aware of it, opposed it only for a little while, but remained inactive during most of the period,

15. East and north of Euboea.
16. From the region southwest of Thessaly.
17. City at the southern tip of the island of Euboea.
18. An island of the Aegean Sea about midway between European Greece and Asia.

being of old slow to go to war except under the pressure of necessity, and in the present instance being hampered by wars at home; until the growth of the Athenian power could be no longer ignored, and their own confederacy became the object of its encroachments. They then felt that they could endure it no longer, but that the time had come for them to throw themselves heart and soul upon the hostile power, and break it, if they could, by commencing the present war. . . .

Funeral Oration of Pericles

[Pericles was officially one of ten elected military commanders, or *strategoi,* at Athens. But through his lengthy tenure of office (467-428 B.C., with brief intermissions) and the force of his personality, he became the dominant force in the government.

His famous Funeral Oration was given in the winter following the outbreak of the war. It is a moving statement of faith in the Athenian form of government, as well as an analysis of democracy's strengths and weaknesses. The oration is clearly not unbiased, for the speaker was touched by his own patriotism; but it is nonetheless the finest exposition of the democratic ideal in classical literature.]

In the same winter the Athenians gave a funeral at the public cost to those who had first fallen in this war. It was a custom of their ancestors. . . . Pericles, son of Xanthippus, was chosen to pronounce their eulogium. When the proper time arrived, he advanced from the sepulchre to an elevated platform in order to be heard by as many of the crowd as possible, and spoke as follows:

"Most of my predecessors in this place have commended him who made this speech part of the law, telling us that it is well that it should be delivered at the burial of those who fall in battle. For myself, I should have thought that the worth which had displayed itself in deeds, would be sufficiently rewarded by honours also shown by deeds; such as you now see in this funeral prepared at the people's cost. And I could have wished that the reputations of many brave men were not to be imperilled in the mouth of a single individual, to stand or fall according as he spoke well or ill. For it is hard to speak properly upon a subject where it is even difficult to convince your hearers that you are speaking the truth. On the one hand, the friend who is familiar with every fact of the story, may think that some point has not been set forth with that fulness which he wishes and knows it to deserve; on the other, he who is a stranger to the matter may be led by envy to suspect exaggeration if he hears anything above his own nature. For men can endure to hear others praised only so long as they can severally persuade themselves of their own ability to equal the actions recounted: when this point is passed, envy comes in and with it incredulity. However, since our ancestors have stamped this custom with their approval, it becomes my duty to obey the law and to try to satisfy your several wishes and opinions as best I may.

"I shall begin with our ancestors: it is both just and proper that they should have the honour of the first mention on an occasion like the present. They dwelt in the country without break in the succession from generation to generation, and handed it down free to the present time by their valour. And if our more remote ancestors deserve praise, much more do our own fathers, who added to their inheritance the empire which we now possess, and spared no pains to be able to leave their acquisitions to us of the present generation. Lastly, there are few parts of our dominions that have not been augmented by those of us here, who are still more or less in the vigour of life; while the mother country has been furnished by us with everything that can enable her to depend on her own resources whether for war or for peace. That part of our history which tells of the military achievements which gave us our several possessions, or of the ready valour with which either we or our fathers stemmed the tide of Hellenic or foreign aggression, is a theme too familiar to my hearers for me to dilate on, and I shall therefore pass it by. But what was the road by which we reached our position, what the form of government under which our greatness grew, what the national habits out of which it sprang; these are questions which I may try to solve before I proceed to my panegyric upon these men; since I think this to be a subject upon which on the present occasion a speaker may properly dwell, and to which the whole assemblage, whether citizens or foreigners, may listen with advantage.

"Our constitution does not copy the laws of neighbouring

states; we are rather a pattern to others than imitators ourselves. Its administration favours the many instead of the few; this is why it is called a democracy. If we look to the laws, they afford equal justice to all in their private differences; if to social standing, advancement in public life falls to reputation for capacity, class considerations not being allowed to interfere with merit; nor again does poverty bar the way, if a man is able to serve the state, he is not hindered by the obscurity of his condition. The freedom which we enjoy in our government extends also to our ordinary life. There, far from exercising a jealous surveillance over each other, we do not feel called upon to be angry with our neighbour for doing what he likes, or even to indulge in those injurious looks which cannot fail to be offensive, although they inflict no positive penalty. But all this ease in our private relations does not make us lawless as citizens. Against this fear is our chief safeguard, teaching us to obey the magistrates and the laws, particularly such as regard the protection of the injured, whether they are actually on the statute book, or belong to that code which, although unwritten, yet cannot be broken without acknowledged disgrace.

"Further, we provide plenty of means for the mind to refresh itself from business. We celebrate games and sacrifices all the year round, and the elegance of our private establishments forms a daily source of pleasure and helps to banish the spleen; while the magnitude of our city draws the produce of the world into our harbour, so that to the Athenian the fruits of other countries are as familiar a luxury as those of his own.

"If we turn to our military policy, there also we differ from our antagonists. We throw open our city to the world, and never by alien acts exclude foreigners from any opportunity of learning or observing, although the eyes of an enemy may occasionally profit by our liberality; trusting less in system and policy than to the native spirit of our citizens; while in education, where our rivals from their very cradles by a painful discipline seek after manliness, at Athens we live exactly as we please, and yet are just as ready to encounter every legitimate danger. In proof of this it may be noticed that the Lacedæmonians do not invade our country alone, but bring with them all their confederates; while we Athenians advance unsupported into the territory of a neighbour, and fighting upon a foreign soil usually vanquish with ease men who are defending their homes. Our united force was never yet encountered by any enemy, because we have at once to attend to our marine and to despatch our citizens by land upon a hundred different services; so that, wherever they engage with some such fraction of our strength, a success against a detachment is magnified into a victory over the nation, and a defeat into a reverse suffered at the hands of our entire people. And yet if with habits not of labour but of ease, and courage not of art but of nature, we are still willing to encounter danger, we have the double advantage of escaping the experience of hardships in anticipation and of facing them in the hour of need as fearlessly as those who are never free from them.

"Nor are these the only points in which our city is worthy of admiration. We cultivate refinement without extravagance and knowledge without effeminacy; wealth we employ more for use than for show, and place the real disgrace of poverty not in owning to the fact but in declining the struggle against it. Our public men have, besides politics, their private affairs to attend to, and our ordinary citizens, though occupied with the pursuits of industry, are still fair judges of public matters; for, unlike any other nation, regarding him who takes no part in these duties not as unambitious but as useless, we Athenians are able to judge at all events if we cannot originate, and instead of looking on discussion as a stumbling-block in the way of action, we think it an indispensable preliminary to any wise action at all. Again, in our enterprises we present the singular spectacle of daring and deliberation, each carried to its highest point, and both united in the same persons; although usually decision is the fruit of ignorance, hesitation of reflexion. But the palm of courage will surely be adjudged most justly to those, who best know the difference between hardship and pleasure and yet are never tempted to shrink from danger. In generosity we are equally singular, acquiring our friends by conferring not by receiving favours. Yet, of course, the doer of the favour is the firmer friend of the two, in order by continued kindness to keep the recipient in his debt; while the debtor feels less keenly from the very consciousness that the return he makes will be a payment, not a free gift. And it is only the Athenians who, fearless of consequences, confer their benefits not from calculations of expediency, but in the confidence of liberality.

"In short, I say that as a city we are the school of Hellas; while I doubt if the world can produce a man, who where he has only himself to depend upon, is equal to so many emergencies, and graced by so happy a versatility as the Athenian. And that this is no mere boast thrown out for the occasion, but plain matter of fact, the power of the state acquired by these habits proves. For Athens alone of her contemporaries is found when tested to be greater than her reputation, and alone gives no occasion to her assailants to blush at the antagonist by whom they have been worsted, or to her subjects to question her title by merit to rule. Rather, the admiration of the present and succeeding ages will be ours, since we have not left our power without witness, but have shown it by mighty proofs; and far from needing a Homer for our panegyrist, or other of his craft whose verses might charm for the moment only for the impression which they gave to melt at the touch of fact, we have forced every sea and land to be the highway of our daring, and everywhere, whether for evil or for good, have left imperishable monuments behind us. Such is the Athens for which these men, in the assertion of their resolve not to lose her, nobly fought and died; and well may every one of their survivors be ready to suffer in her cause.

"Indeed if I have dwelt at some length upon the character of our country, it has been to show that our stake in the struggle is not the same as theirs who have no such blessings to lose, and also that the panegyric of the men over whom I am now speaking might be by definite proofs established. That panegyric is now in a great measure complete; for the Athens that I have celebrated is only what the heroism of these and their like have made her, men whose fame, unlike that of most Hellenes, will be found to be only commensurate with their deserts. And if a test of worth be wanted, it is to be found in their closing scene, and this not only in the cases in which it set the final seal upon their merit, but also in those in which it gave the first intimation of their having any. For there is justice in the claim that steadfastness in his country's battles should be as a cloak to cover a man's other imperfections; since the good action has blotted out the bad, and his merit as a citizen more than outweighed his demerits as an individual. But none of these allowed either wealth with its prospect of future enjoyment to unnerve his spirit, or poverty with its hope of a day of freedom and riches to tempt him to shrink from danger. No, holding that vengeance upon their enemies was more to be desired than any personal blessings, and reckoning this to be the most glorious of hazards, they joyfully determined to accept the risk, to make sure of their vengeance and to let their wishes wait; and while committing to hope the uncertainty of final success, in the business before them they thought fit to act boldly and trust in themselves. Thus choosing to die resisting, rather than to live submitting, they fled only from dishonour, but met danger face to face, and after one brief moment, while at the summit of their fortune, escaped, not from their fear, but from their glory.

"So died these men as became Athenians. You, their survivors, must determine to have as unaltering a resolution in the field, though you may pray that it may have a happier issue. And not contented with ideas derived only from words of the advantages which are bound up with the defence of your country, though these would furnish a valuable text to a speaker even before an audience so alive to them as the present, you must yourselves realise the power of Athens, and feed your eyes upon her from day to day, till love of her fills your hearts; and then when all her greatness shall break upon you, you must reflect that it was by courage, sense of duty, and a keen feeling of honour in action that men were enabled to win all this, and that no personal failure in an enterprise could make them consent to deprive their country of their valour, but they laid it at her feet as the most glorious contribution that they could offer. For this offering of their lives made in common by them all they each of them individually received that renown which never grows old, and for a sepulchre, not so much that in which their bones have been deposited, but that noblest of shrines wherein their glory is laid up to be eternally remembered upon every occasion on which deed or story shall fall for its commemoration. For heroes have the whole earth for their tomb; and in lands far from their own, where the column with its epitaph declares it, there is enshrined in every breast a record unwritten with no tablet to preserve it, except that of the heart. These take as your model, and judging happiness to be the fruit of freedom and freedom of valour, never decline the dangers of war. For it is not the miserable that would most justly be unsparing of their lives; these have nothing to hope for: it is rather they to whom continued life may bring reverses as yet unknown, and to whom a fall, if it came, would be most tremendous in its consequences. And surely, to a man of spirit, the degradation of cowardice must be immeasurably more grievous than the unfelt death which strikes him in the midst of his strength and patriotism!

"Comfort, therefore, not condolence, is what I have to offer to the parents of the dead who may be here. Numberless are the chances to which, as they know, the life of man is subject; but fortunate indeed are they who draw for their lot a death so glorious as that which has caused your mourning, and to whom life has been so exactly measured as to terminate in the happiness in which it has been passed. Still I know that this is a hard saying, especially when those are in question of whom you will constantly be reminded by seeing in the homes of others blessings of which once you also boasted: for grief is felt not so much for the want of what we have never known, as for the loss of that to which we have been long accustomed. Yet you who are still of an age to beget children must bear up in the hope of having others in their stead; not only will they help you to forget those whom you have lost, but will be to the state at once a reinforcement and a security; for never can a fair or just policy be expected of the citizen who does not, like his fellows, bring to the decision the interests and apprehensions of a father. While those of you who have passed your prime must congratulate yourselves with the thought that the best part of your life was fortunate, and that the brief span that remains will be cheered by the fame of the departed. For it is only the love of honour that never grows old; and honour it is, not gain, as some would have it, that rejoices the heart of age and helplessness.

"Turning to the sons or brothers of the dead, I see an arduous struggle before you. When a man is gone, all are wont to praise him, and should your merit be ever so transcendent, you will still find it difficult not merely to overtake, but even to approach their renown. The living have envy to contend with, while those who are no longer in our path are honoured with a goodwill into which rivalry does not enter. On the other hand, if I must say anything on the subject of female excellence to those of you who will now be in widowhood, it will be all comprised in this brief exhortation. Great will be your glory in not falling short of your natural character; and greatest will be hers who is least talked of among the men whether for good or for bad.

"My task is now finished. I have performed it to the best of my ability, and in words, at least, the requirements of the law are now satisfied. If deeds be in question, those who are here interred have received part of their honours already, and for the rest, their children will be brought up till manhood at the public expense: the state thus offers a valuable prize, as the garland of victory in this race of valour, for the reward both of those who have fallen and their survivors. And where the rewards for merit are greatest, there are found the best citizens.

"And now that you have brought to a close your lamentations for your relatives, you may depart."

. . . .

The Corcyræan Revolution

[Corcyra (the modern Corfu) was an important commercial city, a strategically important way station between Greece proper and the Greek colonies in southern Italy and Sicily. The events described here occurred in the fourth year of the war (427 B.C.) Thucydides' analysis of the disintegration of polis solidarity and the excesses of party spirit among the Corcyreans distills into small compass the effect of the war upon all Greek cities to some degree. The tightly-knit polis society could never be restored after the warring parties had treated one another in so brutal a fashion.]

The Corcyræan revolution began with the return of the prisoners taken in the sea-fights off Epidamnus.[19] These the Corin-

19. Later the Roman Dyrrhachium, Durazzo (Dürres) in present-day Albania. This was the usual landing place for persons crossing into Greece from Brundisium (modern Brindisi) in Italy.

thians had released, nominally upon the security of eight hundred talents given by their *Proxeni*,[20] but in reality upon their engagement to bring over Corcyra to Corinth. These men proceeded to canvass each of the citizens, and to intrigue with the view of detaching the city from Athens. Upon the arrival of an Athenian and a Corinthian vessel, with envoys on board, a conference was held in which the Corcyræans voted to remain allies of the Athenians according to their agreement, but to be friends of the Peloponnesians as they had been formerly. Meanwhile, the returned prisoners brought Peithias, a volunteer *Proxenus* of the Athenians and leader of the commons, to trial, upon the charge of enslaving Corcyra to Athens. He, being acquitted, retorted by accusing five of the richest of their number of cutting stakes in the ground sacred to Zeus and Alcinous,[21] the legal penalty being a stater for each stake. Upon their conviction, the amount of the penalty being very large, they seated themselves as suppliants in the temples, to be allowed to pay it by instalments; but Peithias, who was one of the senate, prevailed upon that body to enforce the law; upon which the accused, rendered desperate by the law, and also learning that Peithias had the intention, while still a member of the senate, to persuade the people to conclude a defensive and offensive alliance with Athens, banded together armed with daggers, and suddenly bursting into the senate killed Peithias and sixty others, senators and private persons; some few only of the party of Peithias taking refuge in the Athenian galley, which had not yet departed.

After this outrage, the conspirators summoned the Corcyræans to an assembly, and said that this would turn out for the best, and would save them from being enslaved by Athens: for the future, they moved to receive neither party unless they came peacefully in a single ship, treating any larger number as enemies. This motion made, they compelled it to be adopted, and instantly sent off envoys to Athens to justify what had been done and to dissuade the refugees there from any hostile proceedings which might lead to a reaction.

20. Consular representatives of a foreign state who looked after the interests of its citizens.

21. In Homer's *Odyssey*, Alcinous was the godly ruler of a mythical people inhabiting the island of Corfu.

Upon the arrival of the embassy the Athenians arrested the envoys and all who listened to them, as revolutionists, and lodged them in Ægina.[22] Meanwhile a Corinthian galley arriving in the island with Lacedæmonian envoys, the dominant Corcyræan party attacked the commons and defeated them in battle. Night coming on, the commons took refuge in the Acropolis and the higher parts of the city, and concentrated themselves there, having also possession of the Hyllaic harbour; their adversaries occupying the market-place where most of them lived, and the harbour adjoining, looking towards the mainland.

The next day passed in skirmishes of little importance, each party sending into the country to offer freedom to the slaves and to invite them to join them. The mass of the slaves answered the appeal of the commons; their antagonists being reinforced by eight hundred mercenaries from the continent.

After a day's interval hostilities recommenced, victory remaining with the commons, who had the advantage in numbers and position, the women also valiantly assisting them, pelting with tiles from the houses, and supporting the mêlée with a fortitude beyond their sex. Towards dusk, the oligarchs in full rout, fearing that the victorious commons might assault and carry the arsenal and put them to the sword, fired the houses round the market-place and the lodging-houses, in order to bar their advance; sparing neither their own, nor those of their neighbours; by which much stuff of the merchants was consumed and the city risked total destruction, if a wind had come to help the flame by blowing on it. Hostilities now ceasing, both sides kept quiet, passing the night on guard, while the Corinthian ship stole out to sea upon the victory of the commons, and most of the mercenaries passed over secretly to the continent.

The next day the Athenian general, Nicostratus, son of Diitrephes, came up from Naupactus[23] with twelve ships and five hundred Messenian[24] heavy infantry. He at once endeavoured to bring about a settlement, and persuaded the two parties to agree

22. Aegina was a stony island off the southern coast of Attica, also a city on that island.

23. Naupactus (modern Lepanto) was a harbor at the western end of the Gulf of Corinth; it served as the base of Athenian operations against western Greece.

24. Messenia was a district in the southwestern Peloponnesus.

together to bring to trial ten of the ringleaders, who presently fled, while the rest were to live in peace, making terms with each other, and entering into a defensive and offensive alliance with the Athenians. This arranged, he was about to sail away, when the leaders of the commons induced him to leave them five of his ships to make their adversaries less disposed to move, while they manned and sent with him an equal number of their own. He had no sooner consented, than they began to enroll their enemies for the ships; and these fearing that they might be sent off to Athens, seated themselves as suppliants in the temple of the Dioscuri.[25] An attempt on the part of Nicostratus to reassure them and to persuade them to rise proving unsuccessful, the commons armed upon this pretext, alleging the refusal of their adversaries to sail with them as a proof of the hollowness of their intentions, and took their arms out of their houses, and would have dispatched some whom they fell in with, if Nicostratus had not prevented it. The rest of the party seeing what was going on, seated themselves as suppliants in the temple of Hera,[26] being not less than four hundred in number; until the commons, fearing that they might adopt some desperate resolution, induced them to rise, and conveyed them over to the island in front of the temple, where provisions were sent across to them.

At this stage in the revolution, on the fourth or fifth day after the removal of the men to the island, the Peloponnesian ships arrived from Cyllene[27] where they had been stationed since their return from Ionia, fifty-three in number, still under the command of Alcidas, but with Brasidas[28] also on board as his adviser; and dropping anchor at Sybota, a harbour on the mainland,[29] at daybreak made sail for Corcyra.

The Corcyræans in great confusion and alarm at the state of

25. Castor and Pollux, the twin sons of Zeus, were regarded as the ideal types of bravery and military prowess.
26. The queen of heaven, sister and wife of Zeus.
27. A seaport town of Elis in the northwestern Peloponnesus.
28. Brasidas was the most distinguished of the Spartan generals in the first part of the war. He was slain in 422 B.C. after successfully resisting an Athenian attempt to recapture Amphipolis.
29. Opposite Corcyra.

things in the city and at the approach of the invader, at once proceeded to equip sixty vessels, which they sent out, as fast as they were manned, against the enemy, in spite of the Athenians recommending them to let them sail out first, and to follow themselves afterwards with all their ships together. Upon their vessels coming up to the enemy in this straggling fashion, two immediately deserted; in others the crews were fighting among themselves, and there was no order in anything that was done; so that the Peloponnesians seeing their confusion, placed twenty ships to oppose the Corcyræans, and ranged the rest against the twelve Athenian ships, amongst which were the two vessels *Salaminia* and *Paralus*.

While the Corcyræans, attacking without judgment and in small detachments, were already crippled by their own misconduct, the Athenians, afraid of the numbers of the enemy and of being surrounded, did not venture to attack the main body or even the centre of the division opposed to them, but fell upon its wing and sank one vessel; after which the Peloponnesians formed in a circle, and the Athenians rowed round them and tried to throw them into disorder. Perceiving this, the division opposed to the Corcyræans fearing a repetition of the disaster of Naupactus, came to support their friends, and the whole fleet now bore down, united, upon the Athenians, who retired before it, backing water, retiring as leisurely as possible in order to give the Corcyræans time to escape, while the enemy was thus kept occupied. Such was the character of this sea-fight, which lasted until sunset.

The Corcyræans now feared that the enemy would follow up their victory and sail against the town and rescue the men in the island, or strike some other blow equally decisive, and accordingly carried the men over again to the temple of Hera, and kept guard over the city. The Peloponnesians, however, although victorious in the sea-fight, did not venture to attack the town, but took the thirteen Corcyræan vessels which they had captured, and with them sailed back to the continent from whence they had put out. The next day equally they refrained from attacking the city, although the disorder and panic were at their height, and though Brasidas, it is said, urged Alcidas, his superior officer, to do so, but they landed upon the promontory of Leukimme[30] and laid waste the country.

Meanwhile the commons in Corcyra, being still in great fear of the fleet attacking them, came to a parley with the suppliants and their friends, in order to save the town; and prevailed upon some of them to go on board the ships, of which they still manned thirty, against the expected attack. But the Peloponnesians after ravaging the country until midday sailed away, and towards nightfall were informed by beacon signals of the approach of sixty Athenian vessels from Leucas,[31] under the command of Eurymedon, son of Thucles; which had been sent off by the Athenians upon the news of the revolution and of the fleet with Alcidas being about to sail for Corcyra.

The Peloponnesians accordingly at once set off in haste by night for home, coasting along shore; and hauling their ships across the Isthmus of Leucas, in order not to be seen doubling it, so departed. The Corcyræans, made aware of the approach of the Athenian fleet and of the departure of the enemy, brought the Messenians from outside the walls into the town, and ordered the fleet which they had manned to sail round into the Hyllaic harbour; and while it was so doing, slew such of their enemies as they laid hands on, dispatching afterwards as they landed them, those whom they had persuaded to go on board the ships. Next they went to the sanctuary of Hera and persuaded about fifty men to take their trial, and condemned them all to death. The mass of the suppliants who had refused to do so, on seeing what was taking place, slew each other there in the consecrated ground; while some hanged themselves upon the trees, and others destroyed themselves as they were severally able. During seven days that Eurymedon stayed with his sixty ships, the Corcyræans were engaged in butchering those of their fellow-citizens whom they regarded as their enemies: and although the crime imputed was that of attempting to put down the democracy, some were slain also for private hatred, others by their debtors because of the monies owed to them.

30. On the island of Corcyra (opposite Sybota).

31. A promontory on the west coast of Acarnania (western Greece). It has since become an island.

Death thus raged in every shape; and, as usually happens at such times, there was no length to which violence did not go; sons were killed by their fathers, and suppliants dragged from the altar or slain upon it; while some were even walled up in the temple of Dionysus and died there.

So bloody was the march of the revolution, and the impression which it made was the greater as it was one of the first to occur. Later on, one may say, the whole Hellenic world was convulsed; struggles being everywhere made by the popular chiefs to bring in the Athenians, and by the oligarchs to introduce the Lacedæmonians. In peace there would have been neither the pretext nor the wish to make such an invitation; but in war, with an alliance always at the command of either faction for the hurt of their adversaries and their own corresponding advantage, opportunities for bringing in the foreigner were never wanting to the revolutionary parties. The sufferings which revolution entailed upon the cities were many and terrible, such as have occurred and always will occur, as long as the nature of mankind remains the same; though in a severer or milder form, and varying in their symptoms, according to the variety of the particular cases. In peace and prosperity states and individuals have better sentiments, because they do not find themselves suddenly confronted with imperious necessities; but war takes away the easy supply of daily wants, and so proves a rough master, that brings most men's characters to a level with their fortunes. Revolution thus ran its course from city to city, and the places which it arrived at last, from having heard what had been done before, carried to a still greater excess the refinement of their inventions, as manifested in the cunning of their enterprises and the atrocity of their reprisals. Words had to change their ordinary meaning and to take that which was now given them. Reckless audacity came to be considered the courage of a loyal ally; prudent hesitation, specious cowardice; moderation was held to be a cloak for unmanliness; ability to see all sides of a question inaptness to act on any. Frantic violence became the attribute of manliness; cautious plotting, a justifiable means of self-defence. The advocate of extreme measures was always trustworthy; his opponent a man to be suspected. To succeed in a plot was to have a shrewd head, to divine a plot a still shrewder; but to try to provide against having to do either was to break up your party and to be afraid of your adversaries. In fine, to forestall an intending criminal, or to suggest the idea of a crime where it was wanting, was equally commended, until even blood became a weaker tie than party, from the superior readiness of those united by the latter to dare everything without reserve; for such associations had not in view the blessings derivable from established institutions but were formed by ambition for their overthrow; and the confidence of their members in each other rested less on any religious sanction than upon complicity in crime. The fair proposals of an adversary were met with jealous precautions by the stronger of the two, and not with a generous confidence. Revenge also was held of more account than self-preservation. Oaths of reconciliation, being only proffered on either side to meet an immediate difficulty, only held good so long as no other weapon was at hand; but when opportunity offered, he who first ventured to seize it and to take his enemy off his guard, thought this perfidious vengeance sweeter than an open one, since, considerations of safety apart, success by treachery won him the palm of superior intelligence. Indeed it is generally the case that men are readier to call rogues clever than simpletons honest, and are as ashamed of being the second as they are proud of being the first. The cause of all these evils was the lust for power arising from greed and ambition; and from these passions proceeded the violence of parties once engaged in contention. The leaders in the cities, each provided with the fairest professions, on the one side with the cry of political equality of the people, on the other of a moderate aristocracy, sought prizes for themselves in those public interests which they pretended to cherish, and, recoiling from no means in their struggles for ascendancy, engaged in the direct excesses; in their acts of vengeance they went to even greater lengths, not stopping at what justice or the good of the state demanded, but making the party caprice of the moment their only standard, and invoking with equal readiness the condemnation of an unjust verdict or the authority of the strong arm to glut the animosities of the hour. Thus religion was in honour with neither party; but the use of fair phrases to arrive at guilty ends was in high reputation. Meanwhile the moderate part of the citizens perished between the two, either for not joining in the quarrel, or because envy would not suffer them to escape.

Thus every form of iniquity took root in the Hellenic countries by reason of the troubles. The ancient simplicity into which honour so largely entered was laughed down and disappeared; and society became divided into camps in which no man trusted his fellow. To put an end to this, there was neither promise to be depended upon, nor oath that could command respect; but all parties dwelling rather in their calculation upon the hopelessness of a permanent state of things, were more intent upon self-defence than capable of confidence. In this contest the blunter wits were most successful. Apprehensive of their own deficiencies and of the cleverness of their antagonists, they feared to be worsted in debate and to be surprised by the combinations of their more versatile opponents, and so at once boldly had recourse to action: while their adversaries, arrogantly thinking that they should know in time, and that it was unnecessary to secure by action what policy afforded, often fell victims to their want of precaution.

Meanwhile Corcyra gave the first example of most of the crimes alluded to; of the reprisals exacted by the governed who had never experienced equitable treatment or indeed aught but insolence from their rulers—when their hour came; of the iniquitous resolves of those who desired to get rid of their accustomed poverty, and ardently coveted their neighbour's goods; and lastly, of the savage and pitiless excesses into which men who had begun the struggle not in a class but in a party spirit, were hurried by their ungovernable passions. In the confusion into which life was now thrown in the cities, human nature, always rebelling against the law and now its master, gladly showed itself ungoverned in passion, above respect for justice, and the enemy of all superiority; since revenge would not have been set above religion, and gain above justice, had it not been for the fatal power of envy. Indeed men too often take upon themselves in the prosecution of their revenge to set the example of doing away with those general laws to which all alike can look for salvation in adversity, instead of allowing them to subsist against the day of danger when their aid may be required.

Introduction to Plato

Plato was born at Athens about 427 B.C., the year after the death of Pericles. His family had long been accustomed to play a prominent part in civil affairs and traced its descent from the early kings of the city. Plato himself tells us that he originally intended to enter public life, which according to Greek notions was the most fitting activity for an able man. But his young manhood coincided with the slow collapse of Athens in the Peloponnesian War. The conduct of the oligarchs—his relatives—in their brief tenure of power in 404-403 B.C. revolted him; the restored democrats did even worse when in 399 B.C. they put to death his beloved friend Socrates. Disillusioned with both political factions, Plato abandoned the idea of a political career and turned to philosophy.

Undoubtedly the great formative influence on his thought was Socrates. The older philosopher was a longtime family friend; and as a young man Plato came under his spell. He was present at Socrates' trial and conviction; illness kept him from the death scene. Probably he left Athens for a time after Socrates' death, possibly fearing for his own safety; perhaps he traveled to Africa and Egypt, as later biographers assert, though this is uncertain. But it is likely that at this time he composed the series of short dramatic dialogues which are a lasting ornament to Greek literature as well as philosophy. In them Socrates appears as protagonist, examining ideas in conversations with fellow-citizens, though one wonders to what extent the words put into Socrates' mouth actually belong to Plato. The dialogues were probably intended as popularizations for the educated public; there is nothing technical or esoteric about them. They deal with ethics and metaphysics, politics and law, often jumbled together; they show considerable dramatic power, but are loosely constructed and wander from subject to subject with little continuity.

Little is known of Plato's life before about age forty, when he founded the Academy. The Academy was originally a society of scholars devoted to the pursuit of knowledge, but it evolved into something very like our modern universities. The traveling lecturer so common in the fifth century B.C. now began to be replaced by institutions of learning with a permanent location and a fixed program of studies. Mathematics was the backbone of the Academic curriculum; this included geometry and astronomy and was closely linked to philosophy, for in Plato's mind numbers, forms, and relations were Ideas, or universal archetypes. Plato himself gave lectures on philosophy, though except for a few notes in Aristotle no record of their contents has survived. Apparently some twenty years of Plato's life were occupied with the organization and administration of the Academy, which produced outstanding scientists and administrators throughout the late classical and Hellenistic period.

In 367 and again in 361 B.C., Plato interrupted his work at the Academy to become tutor to a king—Dionysius II, the young tyrant of Sicily. The invitation was extended by Dionysius' uncle, Dion, a lover of philosophy and an admirer of Plato. We do not know whether Plato seriously hoped to make of Dionysius—already thirty years old and corrupted by the luxury and license of Syracuse—the "philosopher-king" whom he designated as the ideal ruler. Perhaps he had never lost his early inclination to become a legislator and governor of men. In any event, the Syracusan experiment proved a dismal failure. It is not recorded that Dionysius' policies were in any way modified by the presence of his illustrious tutor; and Plato eventually returned to Athens. It was probably then that he wrote those works so distinct in style from the Socratic dialogues: the *Timaeus*—his only treatise on cosmology and natural science—and the *Laws*, which contain his maturest thoughts on ethics, education, and justice.

Philosophy to Plato was the knowledge of Ideas, or generalized concepts, of which all visible objects are merely pale copies. Ideas are not present in the sense-world; nonetheless they are more real than sense-objects, because they are eternal and unchanging. The highest Idea is the Idea of the Good, or God. Knowledge is virtue, and the love of wisdom is the highest love.

Anticipating later Christianity, Plato regarded the human body as evil, but its soul as divine. Perhaps this dichotomy was suggested to him by the Orphic and Pythagorean mysteries which existed in his day as a sort of religious underworld, and with which he undoubtedly was familiar. He presumes (through the mouth of Socrates) that each soul exists eternally, that from time to time it assumes a bodily shell, and that after the death of a particular body it is re-incarnated in favorable or unfavorable circumstances according to whether its character in life has been good or evil. Ethics, therefore, is the cultivation of the soul.

Always the aristocrat, Plato had no use for democratic government. He knew too much of the inner workings of politics, and lacked faith in the common man. In the *Laws*, written in his old age, he produced an outline of an ideal state regulated by the principles of philosophy. Partly modeled on Sparta, Plato's state was managed by an intellectual elite which controlled all aspects of daily life and carefully eliminated opposition. The rule of Reason was to be imposed by force.

Plato is typically Greek in the clarity of his thought and in his belief that order and Reason rule the universe. Beauty he defined as symmetry; ethics is the "ordering" of the soul. His influence in antiquity can scarcely be overrated. He is the only major classical author whose works have survived in entirety; presumably they were copied and re-copied too many times ever to have been lost. Plato's other-worldliness made him congenial to the religious mind; his philosophy is the principal Greek component in the Hellenistic religious synthesis represented by such authors as Philo and Plotinus. His influence upon Christianity was likewise considerable, if indirect. He adumbrated most of the problems with which philosophy has since concerned itself, so that no subsequent thinkers in the Western world have been able to ignore him.

Introduction to Plato's Apology

Plato's *Apology* narrates the trial and conviction of Socrates in the year 399 B.C. Presumably it is a faithful account of those events; not only was Plato an eyewitness, but the work was probably circulated within a few years of Socrates' death, when persons familiar with the circumstances could easily have noticed any inaccuracies.

The formal indictment against Socrates charged him with being an "evildoer," a "curious person" who investigated (forbidden) supernatural matters, and a "corrupter of young men" who taught them "to make the worse appear the better cause." Probably the actual bases for the charge were the philosopher's attitude of skeptical reserve toward the democracy and his associations with persons of known anti-democratic views like the traitor Alcibiades. The charge of irreligion perhaps meant that Socrates did not conform to the state cult (not that he did not believe in the gods), perhaps also that he had revealed some of the sacred mysteries of the Orphics and Pythagoreans with whom he was known to associate. But the trial proceedings take on a note of irony through the inability of the prosecutor to say what he really means by the charges. Most of Socrates' alleged offences must have occurred under the so-called "old democracy" prior to 404 B.C.; but by its own Act of Oblivion, the restored democracy had forbidden the questioning of citizens about acts committed under the former regime. To admit the real nature of the accusations against Socrates would have thrown the case out of court.

The instigator of the trial was Anytus, a respected leader of the restored democracy, who appears to have been an able man. Evidently he had personal motives for complaint: his own son had become a drunkard and ne'er-do-well after a period of keeping company with Socrates. But it is unlikely that Anytus and his colleagues intended to put Socrates to death. More probably, they wished merely to frighten him away from Athens and put an end to an influence they considered undesirable. Plato takes care to point out that at several points in the affair Socrates might easily have saved himself. He could have left Athens before the trial, as accused persons often did; or he might have obtained a favorable verdict by a few concessions to popular sentiment or by proposing a substantial fine. Finally, he could have escaped from prison.

Socrates based his defense less upon the specific charges against him than upon a justification of his entire life. His career had consisted of the pursuit of wisdom—the examination of himself and his countrymen—because he regarded the unexamined life as not worth living. In prodding his hearers to analyze their own firmest assumptions, he considered himself a benefactor, not an injurer of the state. To propose a serious punishment for himself would have been to admit guilt. In accepting the ultimate penalty, Socrates bore witness to his conviction that the evil to be avoided was not death, but the betrayal of one's conscience.

PLATO: FROM THE APOLOGY

And now, Athenians, I am not going to argue for my own
sake, as you may think, but for yours, that you may not sin
against God[1] by condemning me, who am his gift to you. For 30e
if you kill me you will not easily find a successor to me, who,
if I may use such a ludicrous figure of speech, am a sort of gad-
fly, given to the state by God; and the state is a great and noble
steed who is tardy in his motions owing to his very size, and
requires to be stirred into life. I am that gadfly which God has
attached to the state, and all day long and in all places am al-
ways fastening upon you, arousing and persuading and re- 31a
proaching you. You will not easily find another like me, and
therefore I would advise you to spare me. I dare say that you
may feel out of temper (like a person who is suddenly awak-
ened from sleep), and you think that you might easily strike
me dead as Anytus[2] advises, and then you would sleep on for the
remainder of your lives, unless God in his care of you sent you
another gadfly. When I say that I am given to you by God, the
proof of my mission is this:—if I had been like other men, I b
should not have neglected all my own concerns or patiently
seen the neglect of them during all these years, and have been
doing yours, coming to you individually like a father or elder
brother, exhorting you to regard virtue; such conduct, I say,
would be unlike human nature. If I gained anything, or if my
exhortations were paid, there would be some sense in my doing
so; but now, as you see for yourselves, not even the unfailing
impudence of my accusers dares to say that I have ever exacted
or sought pay of anyone; of that they can produce no witness. c
And I have a sufficient witness to the truth of what I say—my
poverty.

Someone may wonder why I go about in private giving advice and busying myself with the concerns of others, but do not

From *The Dialogues of Plato*, trans. by Benjamin Jowett, 4th ed., Oxford: At the Clarendon Press, 1953, I, 355-63. Reprinted by permission of the Clarendon Press.

1. "God" in the general sense, not "the gods" or a specific deity.
2. Anytus, Meletus, and Lycon were the three accusers of Socrates.

venture to come forward in public and advise the state.[3] I will tell you why. You have heard me speak at sundry times and in divers places of a superhuman oracle or sign which comes to me, and is the divinity which Meletus[4] ridicules in the indict- d
ment. This sign, which is a kind of voice, first began to come to me when I was a child; from time to time it forbids me to do something which I am going to do, but never commands anything. This is what deters me from being a politician. And rightly, as I think. For I am certain, O men of Athens, that if I had engaged in politics, I should have perished long ago, and done no good either to you or to myself. And do not be offended e
at my telling you the truth: for the truth is, that no man who sets himself firmly against you or any other multitude, honestly striving to keep the state from many lawless and unrighteous deeds, will save his life; he who will fight for the right, if he 32a
would live even for a brief space, must have a private station and not a public one.

I can give you convincing evidence of what I say, not words only, but what you value far more—actions. Let me relate to you a passage of my own life which will prove to you that to no man should I ever wrongly yield from fear of death, and that I should in fact be willing to perish for not yielding. I will tell you a tale of the courts, not very interesting perhaps, but nevertheless true. The only office of state which I ever held, O men of Athens, was that of senator:[5] the tribe Antiochis, which is b
my tribe, had the presidency at the trial of the generals who had not taken up the bodies of the slain after the battle of Arginusae;[6] and you proposed to try them in a body, contrary to law, as you all thought afterwards; but at the time I was the

3. It is implied that there is something suspicious about a man putting his talents at the service of private individuals, but refusing to serve the state.

4. The actual prosecutor.

5. Member of the Council that prepared the agenda for the assembly of citizens.

6. This was Athens' last victory over Sparta, fought in 406 B.C. off the Arginusae Islands (southeast of Lesbos). Because the crews of twenty-five Athenian ships sunk by the enemy had been allowed to drown in a storm, the Assembly condemned the eight victorious generals to death. It was feared that the souls of the dead seamen, deprived of a proper burial, would wander about the earth and disturb the living.

only one of the Prytanes[7] who was opposed to the illegality, and
I gave my vote against you; and when the orators threatened
to impeach and arrest me, and you called and shouted, I made
up my mind that I would run the risk, having law and justice
with me, rather than take part in your injustice because I feared c
imprisonment and death. This happened in the days of the de-
mocracy. But when the oligarchy of the Thirty was in power,[8]
they sent for me and four others into the rotunda, and bade us
bring Leon the Salaminian from Salamis, as they wanted to put
him to death. This was a specimen of the sort of commands
which they were always giving with the view of implicating as
many as possible in their crimes; and then I showed again, not d
in word only but in deed, that, if I may be allowed to use such
an expression, I care not a straw for death, and that my great
and only care is lest I should do an unrighteous or unholy
thing. For the strong arm of that oppressive power did not
frighten me into doing wrong; and when we came out of the ro-
tunda the other four went to Salamis and fetched Leon, but I
went quietly home. For which I might have lost my life, had
not the power of the Thirty shortly afterwards come to an end.
And many will witness to my words. e

Now do you really imagine that I could have survived all
these years, if I had led a public life, supposing that like a good
man I had always maintained the right and had made justice,
as I ought, the first thing? No indeed, men of Athens, neither
I nor any other man. But I have been always the same in all my 33a
actions, public as well as private, and never have I yielded any
base compliance to those who are slanderously termed my dis-
ciples, or to any other. Not that I have ever had any regular dis-
ciples. But if anyone likes to come and hear me while I am
pursuing my mission, whether he be young or old, he is not
excluded. Nor do I converse only with those who pay; but any-

7. The Prytanes were members of a subcommittee of the governing Council. They remained constantly in session in order to be always available to deal with urgent official business.

8. The government of the Thirty was established in 404 B.C. under Spartan patronage after the final Athenian defeat in the Peloponnesian War. By their harsh confiscations and punishments they managed to alienate so much support that the democracy was restored one year later.

one, whether he be rich or poor, may ask and answer me and b
listen to my words; and whether he turns out to be a bad man
or a good one, neither result can be justly imputed to me;
for I never taught nor professed to teach anything. And if any-
one says that he has ever learned or heard anything from me in
private which all the world has not heard, let me tell you that
he is lying.

But I shall be asked, Why do people delight in continually
conversing with you? I have told you already, Athenians, the c
whole truth about this matter: they like to hear the cross-ex-
amination of the pretenders to wisdom; there is amusement in
it. Now this duty of cross-examining other men has been im-
posed upon me by God; and has been signified to me by oracles,
dreams, and in every way in which the will of divine power
was ever intimated to anyone. This is true, O Athenians; or, if
not true, can easily be disproved. If I really am or have been
corrupting the youth, those of them who are now grown up d
and have become sensible that I gave them bad advice in the
days of their youth should of course come forward as accusers,
and take their revenge; or if they do not like to come them-
selves, some of their relatives, fathers, brothers, or other kins-
men, should think of the evil their families have suffered at my
hands. Now is their time. Many of them I see in the court.
There is Crito,[9] who is of the same age and of the same deme
with myself, and there is Critobulus his son, whom I also see. e
Then again there is Lysanias of Sphettus, who is the father of
Aeschines—he is present; and also there is Antiphon of Ceph-
isus, who is the father of Epigenes; and there are the brothers
of several who have associated with me. There is Nicostratus
the son of Theodotides, and the brother of Theodotus (now
Theodotus himself is dead, and therefore he, at any rate, will
not seek to stop him); and there is Paralus the son of Demodo-
cus, who had a brother Theages; and Adeimantus the son of 34a
Ariston, whose brother Plato[10] is present; and Aeantodorus, who
is the brother of Apollodorus, whom I also see. I might mention a

9. The rich friend of Socrates who was his interlocutor in the dialogue called "Crito."

10. This is one of Plato's few references to himself in any of his writings.

great many others, some of whom Meletus should have pro-
duced as witnesses in the course of his speech; and let him still
produce them, if he has forgotten—I will make way for him.
And let him say, if he has any testimony of the sort which he
can produce. Nay, Athenians, the very opposite is the truth.
For all these are ready to witness on behalf of the corrupter, of
the injurer of their kindred, as Meletus and Anytus call me;
not the corrupted youth only—there might have been a motive b
for that—but their uncorrupted elder relatives. Why should
they too support me with their testimony? Why, indeed, ex-
cept for the sake of truth and justice, and because they know
that I am speaking the truth, and that Meletus is a liar.

Well, Athenians, this and the like of this is all the defence
which I have to offer. Yet a word more. Perhaps there may be
someone who is offended at me, when he calls to mind how he c
himself on a similar, or even a less serious occasion, prayed and
entreated the judges with many tears, and how he produced his
children in court to excite compassion, together with a host of
relations and friends;[11] whereas I, who am probably in danger
of my life, will do none of these things. The contrast may occur
to his mind, and he may be set against me, and vote in anger
because he is displeased at me on this account. Now if there be
such a person among you,—mind, I do not say that there is,— d
to him I may fairly reply: My friend, I am a man, and like
other men, a creature of flesh and blood, and not "of wood or
stone," as Homer says; and I have a family, yes, and sons, O
Athenians, three in number, one almost a man, and two others
who are still young; and yet I will not bring any of them hither
in order to petition you for an acquittal. And why not? Not
from any self-assertion or want of respect for you. Whether I e
am or am not afraid of death is another question, of which I
will not now speak. But when I think of my own good name,
and yours, and that of the whole state, I feel that such conduct
would be discreditable. One who has reached my years, and
has the name I have, ought not to demean himself. Whether
this opinion of me be deserved or not, at any rate the world has
decided that Socrates is in some way superior to other men. 35a

11. This was customary procedure to excite the sympathy of the court.

And if those among you who are said to be superior in wisdom
or courage, or any other virtue, demean themselves in this way,
how shameful is their conduct! I have seen men of reputation
behaving in the strangest manner while they were being tried:
they seemed to fancy that they were going to suffer something
dreadful if they had to die, and that they would live for ever if
you spared them; and I think that such are a dishonour to the
state, and that any stranger coming in would have said of them
that the most eminent men of Athens, to whom the Athenians b
themselves give office and honour, are no better than women.
And I say that these things ought not to be done to you by those
who have a reputation in any walk of life; and if they are done,
you ought not to permit them; you ought rather to show that
you are far more disposed to condemn the man who gets up a
doleful scene and makes the city ridiculous, than him who holds
his peace.

But, setting aside the question of honour, there seems to be
something wrong in asking a favour of a judge, and thus pro- c
curing an acquittal, instead of informing and convincing him.
For his duty is not to make a present of justice, but to give judge-
ment; and he has sworn that he will judge according to the
laws, and not according to his own good pleasure; and we ought
not to encourage you, nor should you allow yourselves to be
encouraged, in this habit of perjury—there can be no piety in
that. Do not then require me to do what I consider dishon-
ourable and impious and wrong, especially now, when I am d
being tried for impiety on the indictment of Meletus. For if,
O men of Athens, by force of persuasion and entreaty I could
overpower your oaths, then I should be teaching you to believe
that there are no gods, and in defending should simply convict
myself of the charge of not believing in them.[12] But that is not
so—far otherwise. For I do believe that there are gods, and in
a sense higher than that in which any of my accusers believe
in them. And to you and to God I commit my cause, to be
determined as is best for you and me.

There are many reasons why I am not grieved, O men of
Athens, at the vote of condemnation. I expected it, and am only 36a

12. Because oaths were sworn by the gods.

surprised that the votes are so nearly equal; for I had thought
that the majority against me would have been far larger; but
now, had thirty votes gone over to the other side, I should have
been acquitted.[13] And I may say, I think, that I have escaped
Meletus. I may say more; for without the assistance of Anytus
and Lycon,[14] anyone may see that he would not have had a fifth
part of the votes, as the law requires, in which case he would
have incurred a fine of a thousand drachmas. b

And so he proposes death as the penalty. And what shall I
propose on my part, O men of Athens? Clearly that which is
my due. And what is my due? What ought I to have done to
me, or to pay—a man who has never had the wit to keep quiet
during his whole life; but has been careless of what the many
care for—wealth, and family interests, and military offices, and
speaking in the assembly, and magistracies, and plots, and
parties. Reflecting that I was really too honest a man to be a c
politician and live, I did not go where I could do no good to
you or to myself; but where I could do privately the greatest
good (as I affirm it to be) to everyone of you, thither I went,
and sought to persuade every man among you that he must
look to himself, and seek virtue and wisdom before he looks to
his private interests, and look to the state before he looks to the
interests of the state; and that this should be the order which he
observes in all his actions. What shall be done to such an one? d
Doubtless some good thing, O men of Athens, if he has his
reward; and the good should be of a kind suitable to him.
What would be a reward suitable to a poor man who is your
benefactor, and who desires leisure that he may instruct you?
There can be no reward so fitting as maintenance in the Pryta-
neum,[15] O men of Athens, a reward which he deserves far more
than the citizen who has won the prize at Olympia in the horse

13. In other words, if Socrates had managed his case differently, he might have been acquitted.

14. One of Socrates' three accusers.

15. The right to reside in the Prytaneum (town hall) was a high civic honor granted to a very few Athenian citizens. A subcommittee of the governing council of the city was required to stay in or near the Prytaneum at all times during its term of office, in order to be instantly available for pressing business.

or chariot race,[16] whether the chariots were drawn by two
horses or by many. For I am in want, and he has enough; and e
he only gives you the appearance of happiness, and I give you
the reality. And if I am to estimate the penalty fairly, I should 37a
say that maintenance in the Prytaneum is the just return.

Perhaps you think that I am braving you in what I am say-
ing now, as in what I said before about the tears and prayers.
But this is not so. I speak rather because I am convinced that
I never intentionally wronged anyone, although I cannot
convince you—the time has been too short; if there were a law
at Athens, as there is in other cities, that a capital cause should
not be decided in one day, then I believe that I should have b
convinced you. But I cannot in a moment refute great slanders;
and, as I am convinced that I never wronged another, I will
assuredly not wrong myself. I will not say of myself that I
deserve any evil, nor propose any penalty. Why should I? Be-
cause I am afraid of the penalty of death which Meletus pro-
poses? When I do not know whether death is a good or an evil,
why should I propose a penalty which would certainly be an
evil? Shall I say imprisonment? And why should I live in
prison, and be the slave of the magistrates of the year—of the c
Eleven? Or shall the penalty be a fine, and imprisonment until
the fine is paid? There is the same objection. I should have to
lie in prison, for money I have none, and cannot pay. And if I
say exile (and this may possibly be the penalty which you will
affix), I must indeed be blinded by the love of life, if I am so
irrational as to expect that when you, who are my own citizens,
cannot endure my discourses and arguments, and have found d
them so grievous and odious that you will have no more of
them, others are likely to endure them. No indeed, men of
Athens, that is not very likely. And what a life should I lead,
at my age, wandering from city to city, ever changing my place
of exile, and always being driven out! For I am quite sure that
wherever I go, there, as here, the young men will flock to listen
to me; and if I drive them away, their elders will drive me out

16. The Panhellenic games were held every fourth year at the town of Olympia in the Peloponnesus. The first of these contests was organized in 776 B.C., which is the oldest exact date in Greek history.

at their request; and if I let them come, their fathers and friends e
will drive me out for their sakes.

Someone will say: Yes, Socrates, but cannot you hold your
tongue, and then you may go into a foreign city, and no one
will interfere with you? Now I have great difficulty in making
you understand my answer to this. For if I tell you that to do
as you say would be a disobedience to God, and therefore that
I cannot hold my tongue, you will not believe that I am serious; 38a
and if I say again that daily to discourse about virtue, and of
those other things about which you hear me examining myself
and others, is the greatest good of man, and that the unex-
amined life is no life for a human being, you are still less likely
to believe me. Yet I say what is true, although a thing of which
it is hard for me to persuade you. Also, I have never been ac-
customed to think that I deserve to suffer any harm. Had I
money I might have estimated the offence at what I was able b
to pay, and not have been much the worse. But I have none,
and therefore I must ask you to proportion the fine to my
means. Well, perhaps I could afford a mina,[17] and therefore I
propose that penalty: Plato, Crito, Critobulus, and Apollodorus,
my friends here, bid me say thirty minas,[18] and they will be
the sureties. Let thirty minas be the penalty; for which sum
they will be ample security to you.

17. This penalty is so light that the court is certain to reject it.

18. In view of the serious economic crisis which followed the Athenian defeat in 404 B.C., Socrates' friends could probably have raised such a sum only with considerable difficulty.

Introduction to Plato's Crito

The conversation reported in this dialogue took place between Socrates and his friend Crito in the prison where Socrates was awaiting execution. Crito strongly urges him to escape and go into exile; no one will blame him; for his trial was clearly illegal and his condemnation unjust. If Socrates insists upon dying, public opinion will believe that his friends refused to raise the money to bribe his jailors; his enemies can only be gratified thereby. It is wrong for him to desert friends and family; he can live well in exile. Socrates, however, seeks to justify the apparently paradoxical view that he is duty-bound to respect the court's verdict.

PLATO: FROM THE CRITO

Socrates. From these premisses I proceed to argue the question
whether it is or is not right for me to try and escape without the
consent of the Athenians: and if it is clearly right, then I will c
make the attempt; but if not, I will abstain. The other considerations which you mention, of money and loss of character and the duty of educating one's children, are, I fear, only the doctrines of the multitude, who would restore people to life, if they were able, as thoughtlessly as they put them to death—and with as little reason. But now, since the argument has carried us thus far, the only question which remains to be considered is, whether we shall do rightly, I by escaping and you by help-
ing me. and by paying the agents of my escape in money and d
thanks; or whether in reality we shall not do rightly; and if the latter, then death or any other calamity which may ensue on my remaining quietly here must not be allowed to enter into the calculation.

Crito. I think that you are right, Socrates; how then shall we proceed?

Soc. Let us consider the matter together, and do you either
refute me if you can, and I will be convinced; or else cease, my e
dear friend, from repeating to me that I ought to escape against the wishes of the Athenians: for I am very eager that what I do should be done with your approval. And now please to con-
sider my first position, and try how you can best answer me. 49a

Cr. I will.

From *The Dialogues of Plato*, trans. by Benjamin Jowett, 4th ed., Oxford: At the Clarendon Press, 1953, I, 377-84. Reprinted by permission of the Clarendon Press.

Soc. Are we to say that we are never intentionally to do wrong, or that in one way we ought and in another way we ought not to do wrong, or is doing wrong always evil and dishonourable, as has already been often acknowledged by us? Are all the admissions we have made within these last few days to be thrown over? And have we, at our age, been earnestly discoursing with one another all our life long only to discover that we are no better than children? Or, in spite of the opinion b
of the many, and in spite of all consequences whether for the better or the worse, shall we insist on the truth of what was then said, that injustice is always an evil and dishonour to him who acts unjustly? Shall we say so or not?

Cr. Yes.

Soc. Then we must do no wrong?

Cr. Certainly not.

Soc. Nor when injured injure in return, as the many imagine; for we must injure no one at all?

Cr. Clearly not. c

Soc. Again Crito, may we do evil?

Cr. Surely not, Socrates.

Soc. And what of doing evil in return for evil, which is the morality of the many—is that just or not?

Cr. Not just.

Soc. For doing evil to another is the same as injuring him?

Cr. Very true.

Soc. Then we ought not to retaliate or render evil for evil to anyone, whatever evil we may have suffered from him. But I would have you consider, Crito, whether you really mean d
what you are saying. For this opinion has never been held, and never will be held, by any considerable number of persons; and those who are agreed and those who are not agreed upon this point have no common ground, and can only despise one another when they see how widely they differ. Tell me, then, whether you agree with and assent to my first principle, that neither injury nor retaliation nor warding off evil by evil is ever right. And shall that be the premiss of our argument? Or do you decline and dissent from this? For so I have ever thought, e
and continue to think; but, if you are of another opinion, let

me hear what you have to say. If, however, you remain of the same mind as formerly, I will proceed to the next step.

Cr. You may proceed, for I have not changed my mind.

Soc. Then I will go on to the next point, which may be put in the form of a question:—Ought a man to do what he admits to be right, or ought he to betray the right?

Cr. He ought to do what he thinks right.

Soc. But if this is true, what is the application? In leaving
the prison against the will of the Athenians, do I wrong any? 50a
or rather do I not wrong those whom I ought least to wrong?
Do I not desert the principles which were acknowledged by us
to be just—what do you say?

Cr. I cannot answer your question, Socrates; for I do not understand it.

Soc. Then consider the matter in this way:—Imagine that
I am about to run away (you may call the proceeding by any
name which you like), and the laws and the state appear to me
and interrogate me:[1] "Tell us, Socrates," they say; "what are
you about? are you not going by an act of yours to bring us to b
ruin—the laws, and the whole state, as far as in you lies? Do
you imagine that a state can subsist and not be overthrown, in
which the decisions of law have no power, but are set aside
and trampled upon by individuals?" What will be our answer,
Crito, to these and the like words? Anyone, and especially a
rhetorician, will have a good deal to say against the subversion
of the law which requires a sentence to be carried out. Shall we
reply, "Yes; but the state has injured us and given an unjust c
sentence." Suppose we say that?

Cr. Very good, Socrates.

Soc. "And was that our agreement with you?" the law would
answer; "or were you to abide by the sentence of the state?"
And if we were to express our astonishment at their words, the
law would probably add: "Answer, Socrates, instead of opening
your eyes—you are in the habit of asking and answering ques-
tions. Tell us,—What complaint have you to make against us
which justifies you in attempting to ruin us and the state? In d

1. The laws personified; or law as a Platonic Idea.

the first place did we not bring you into existence? Your father
married your mother by our aid and begat you. Say whether
you have any objection to urge against those of us who regu-
late marriage?" None, I should reply. "Or against those of us
who after birth regulate the nurture and education of children,
in which you also were trained? Were not the laws, which
have the charge of education, right in commanding your father
to train you in music and gymnastic?" Right, I should reply. e
"Well then, since you were brought into the world and nur-
tured and educated by us, can you deny in the first place that
you are our child and slave, as your fathers were before you?
And if this is true you cannot suppose that you are on equal
terms with us in matters of right and wrong, or think that you
have a right to do to us what we are doing to you. Would you
have any right to strike or revile or do any other evil to your
father or your master, if you had one, because you have been
struck or reviled by him, or received some other evil at his 51a
hands?—you would not say this? And because we think right
to destroy you, do you think that you have any right to destroy
us in return, and your country as far as in you lies? Will you,
O professor of true virtue, pretend that you are justified in this?
Has a philosopher like you failed to discover that our country
is more precious and higher and holier far than mother or
father or any ancestor, and more to be regarded in the eyes of
the gods and of men of understanding? also to be soothed, and b
gently and reverently entreated when angry, even more than a
father, and either to be persuaded, or if not persuaded, to be
obeyed? And when we are punished by her, whether with im-
prisonment or stripes, the punishment is to be endured in si-
lence; and if she lead us to wounds or death in battle, thither we
follow as is right; neither may anyone yield or retreat or leave
his rank, but whether in battle or in a court of law, or in any
other place, he must do what his city and his country order c
him; or he must change their view of what is just: and if he
may do no violence to his father or mother, much less may he
do violence to his country." What answer shall we make to this,
Crito? Do the laws speak truly, or do they not?

Cr. I think that they do.

Soc. Then the laws will say: "Consider, Socrates, if we are speaking truly that in your present attempt you are going to do us a wrong. For, having brought you into the world, and nurtured and educated you, and given you and every other citizen
a share in every good which we had to give, we further pro- d
claim to any Athenian by the liberty which we allow him, that if he does not like us, the laws, when he has become of age and has seen the ways of the city, and made our acquaintance, he may go where he pleases and take his goods with him. None of us laws will forbid him or interfere with anyone who does not like us and the city, and who wants to emigrate to a colony or to any other city; he may go where he likes, with his property.
But he who has experience of the manner in which we order e
justice and administer the state, and still remains, has by so doing entered into an implied contract that he will do as we command him. And he who disobeys us is, as we maintain, thrice wrong; first, because in disobeying us he is disobeying his parents; secondly, because we are the authors of his education; thirdly, because having made an agreement with us that he will duly obey our commands, he neither obeys them nor convinces us that our commands are unjust; although we do not roughly
require unquestioning obedience, but give him the alternative 52a
of obeying or convincing us;—that is what we offer, and he does neither.

"These are the sort of accusations to which, as we were saying, you, Socrates, will be exposed if you accomplish your intentions; you, above all other Athenians." Suppose now I ask, why I rather than anybody else? no doubt they will justly retort upon me that I above all other Athenians have acknowledged
the agreement. "There is clear proof," they will say, "Socrates, b
that we and the city were not displeasing to you. Of all Athenians you have been the most constant resident in the city, which, as you never leave, you may be supposed to love. For you never went out of the city either to see the games, except once when you went to the Isthmus,[2] or to any other place unless when you were on military service; nor did you travel as

2. The Isthmus of Corinth, the narrow strip of land separating central Greece from the Peloponnesus.

other men do. Nor had you any curiosity to know other states
or their laws: your affections did not go beyond us and our
state; we were your special favourites, and you acquiesced in c
our government of you; and here in this city you begat your
children, which is a proof of your satisfaction. Moreover, you
might in the course of the trial, if you had liked, have fixed the
penalty at banishment; you might then have done with the
state's assent what you are now setting out to do without it.
But you pretended that you preferred death to exile,[3] and that
you were not unwilling to die. And now you have forgotten
these fine sentiments, and pay no respect to us the laws, of
whom you are the destroyer; and are doing what only a mis- d
erable slave would do, running away and turning your back
upon the compacts and agreements of your citizenship which
you made with us. And first of all answer this very question:
Are we right in saying that you agreed to live under our gov-
ernment in deed, and not in word only? Is that true or not?"
How shall we answer, Crito? Must we not assent?

Cr. We cannot help it, Socrates.

Soc. Then will they not say: "You, Socrates, are breaking
the covenants and agreements which you made with us at your e
leisure, not under any compulsion or deception or in enforced
haste, but after you have had seventy years to think of them,
during which time you were at liberty to leave the city, if we
were not to your mind or if our covenants appeared to you to
be unfair. You had your choice, and might have gone either to
Lacedaemon or Crete, both which states are often praised by
you for their good government, or to some other Hellenic or
foreign state. Whereas you, above all other Athenians, seemed 53a
to be so fond of the state, and obviously therefore of us her laws
(for who would care about a state without its laws?), that you
never stirred out of her; the halt, the blind, the maimed were
not more stationary in her than you were. And now you refuse
to abide by your agreements. Not so, Socrates, if you will take
our advice; do not make yourself ridiculous by leaving the city.

"For just consider, if you transgress and err in this sort of
way, what good will you do either to yourself or to your

3. As recounted in the *Apology*, 37d.

friends? That your friends will be in danger of being driven b
into exile and deprived of citizenship, or of losing their prop-
erty, is tolerably certain; and you yourself, if you fly to one of
the neighbouring cities, as, for example, Thebes or Megara,
both of which are well governed, will come to them as an
enemy of their government and all patriotic citizens will look
askance at you as a subverter of the laws, and you will confirm
in the minds of the judges the justice of their own condemna-
tion of you. For he who is a corrupter of the laws is more than c
likely to be a corrupter of the young and foolish portion of man-
kind. Will you then flee from well-ordered cities and virtuous
men? and is existence worth having on these terms? Or will
you go to them without shame, and talk to them, saying—what
will you say to them? What you say here about virtue and
justice and institutions and laws being the best things among
men? Would that be decent of Socrates? Surely not. But if you d
go away from well-governed states to Crito's friends in Thes-
saly, where there is great disorder and licence, they will be
charmed to hear the tale of your escape from prison, set off with
ludicrous particulars of the manner in which you were wrapped
in a goatskin or some other disguise, and metamorphosed as the
manner is of runaways; but will there be no one to remind you
that in your old age, when little time was left to you, you were
not ashamed to violate the most sacred laws from a greedy de- e
sire of life? Perhaps not, if you keep them in a good temper;
but if they are out of temper you will hear many degrading
things. You will live, but how?—fawning upon all men, and
the servant of all men; and doing what?—faring sumptuously
in Thessaly, having gone abroad in order that you may get a
dinner. And where will be your fine sentiments about justice
and virtue? Say that you wish to live for the sake of your chil- 54a
dren—you want to bring them up and educate them—will you
take them into Thessaly and deprive them of Athenian citizen-
ship? Is this the benefit which you will confer upon them? Or
are you under the impression that they will be better cared for
and educated here if you are still alive, although absent from
them; for your friends will take care of them? Do you fancy
that if you have left Athens for Thessaly they will take care of
them, but if you have left it for the other world that they will

not take care of them? Nay; but if they who call themselves friends are good for anything, they will—to be sure they will. b

"Listen, then, Socrates, to us who have brought you up. Think not of life and children first, and of justice afterwards, but of justice first, that you may so vindicate yourself before the princes of the world below. For neither will you nor any that belong to you be happier or holier or juster in this life, or happier in another, if you do as Crito bids. Now you depart, if it must be so, in innocence, a sufferer and not a doer of evil; a victim, not of the laws but of men.[4] But if you leave the city, c
basely returning evil for evil and injury for injury, breaking the covenants and agreements which you have made with us, and wronging those whom you ought least of all to wrong, that is to say, yourself, your friends, your country, and us, we shall be angry with you while you live, and our brethren, the laws in the world below, will give you no friendly welcome; for they will know that you have done your best to destroy us. Listen, then, to us and not to Crito." d

This, dear Crito, is the voice which I seem to hear murmuring in my ears, like the sound of the flute in the ears of the mystic; that voice, I say, is humming in my ears, and prevents me from hearing any other. Be assured, then, that anything more which you may say to shake this my faith will be said in vain. Yet speak, if you have anything to say.

Cr. I have nothing to say.

Soc. It is enough then, Crito. Let us fulfil the will of God, e
and follow whither He leads.

4. Socrates' argument presupposes that if a man is legally but unjustly convicted, the fault lies not with the laws but with the men who misuse them.

Introduction to Plato's Phaedo

In the *Phaedo*, by common consent one of his greatest dialogues, Plato treats of the nature and destiny of the human soul. The literary form is, once again, a conversation between Socrates and his friends, ostensibly as repeated by an onlooker, Phaedo of Elis, to a group of friends in the Peloponnesian town of Phlius. At least one of Phaedo's listeners, Echecrates, we know from independent sources as a Pythagorean; perhaps they all were, and Phaedo told his story in the local Pythagorean meeting house. A cardinal doctrine of the Pythagoreans was the immortality of the soul and its transmigration after the death of the body into another human or animal form; thus Phaedo's hearers would have been particularly interested in Socrates' views on this subject. But there is no reason to doubt that the dialogue represents a real conversation of Socrates and presents the substance of his views. Plato is careful to give the names of those present, many of whom we know from other sources to have been alive at that time; and any misrepresentations would have been easily detected by his readers.

During the last day of Socrates' life, the discussion turns naturally to the fate of the soul after death. Socrates declares, first of all, that death does not frighten him. He is going to a better place —perhaps to dwell among men wiser and better than himself, perhaps among the gods themselves. And what is death, except the separation of the soul from the body? The body is a hindrance to the attainment of knowledge and virtue; in life, the philosopher strives constantly to free his soul from communion with the body. Therefore in effect the philosopher's very life is the pursuit of death.

The basis of all Socrates' arguments is that the soul is divine—meaning that it is also immortal. Only this assumption can justify a life dedicated to wisdom and virtue; for the body disintegrates at death, but the soul takes its character with it into the afterlife. As for the opinion that after the death of a person his soul wanders about and eventually enters another body—this is exceedingly probable, though one cannot be entirely certain. Many arguments speak in favor of the transmigration of souls. All things are generated out of their opposites; thus the living are generated from the dead and the dead from the living. Our souls before the birth of the body must have existed in another world, because Nature is a cyclic process of eternal return; otherwise all things would eventually come to the same identical state. According to the doctrine of reminiscence, our knowledge of such absolutes as beauty or justice must be recalled from a previous life; for certainly there are no absolutes in the sense-world for us to perceive.

Socrates' partners in this discussion, Simmias and Cebes, accept all these arguments. Still, they fear that after a certain number of transmigrations the soul might be blown away and scattered. To this objection Socrates now addresses himself.

PLATO: FROM THE PHAEDO

Well then, added Socrates, let us suppose that there are two sorts of existences—one seen, the other unseen.

Let us suppose them.

The seen is the changing, and the unseen is the unchanging?

That may be also supposed.

And, further, of ourselves is not one part body, another part b
soul?

To be sure.

And to which class is the body more alike and akin?

Clearly to the seen—no one can doubt that.

And is the soul seen or not seen?

Not by man, Socrates.

And what we mean by "seen" and "not seen" is that which is or is not visible to the eye of man?

Yes, to the eye of man.

And is the soul seen or not seen?

Not seen.

Unseen then?

Yes.

Then the soul is more like to the unseen, and the body to the seen?

That follows necessarily, Socrates. c

And were we not saying some time ago that the soul when using the body as an instrument of perception, that is to say, when using the sense of sight or hearing or some other sense (for the meaning of perceiving through the body is perceiving through the senses)—were we not saying that the soul too is then dragged by the body into the region of the changeable, and wanders and is confused; the world spins round her, and she is like a drunkard, when she touches change?

From *The Dialogues of Plato*, trans. by Benjamin Jowett, 4th ed., Oxford: At the Clarendon Press, 1953, I, 433-9, 474-7. Reprinted by permission of the Clarendon Press.

Very true.

But when returning into herself she reflects, then she passes d
into the other world, the region of purity, and eternity, and im-
mortality, and unchangeableness, which are her kindred, and
with them she ever lives, when she is by herself and is not let
or hindered; then she ceases from her wandering, and being in
contact with things unchanging is unchanging in relation to
them. And this state of the soul is called wisdom?

That is well and truly said, Socrates, he replied.

And to which class is the soul more nearly alike and akin, as
far as may be inferred from this argument, as well as from the e
preceding one?

I think, Socrates, that, in the opinion of everyone who follows the argument, the soul will be infinitely more like the unchangeable—even the most stupid person will not deny that.

And the body is more like the changing?

Yes.

Yet once more consider the matter in another light: When the soul and the body are united, then nature orders the soul to rule and govern, and the body to obey and serve. Now which of these two functions is like to the divine? and which to the mortal? Does not the divine appear to you to be that which is formed to govern and command, and the mortal to be that which is by its nature subject and servant?

True.

And which does the soul resemble?

The soul resembles the divine, and the body the mortal—there can be no doubt of that, Socrates.

Then reflect, Cebes: of all which has been said is not this the
conclusion?—that the soul is in the very likeness of the divine, b
and immortal, and rational, and uniform, and indissoluble, and
unchangeable; and that the body is in the very likeness of the
human, and mortal, and irrational, and multiform, and dis-
soluble, and changeable. Can we, my dear Cebes, find any pos-
sible ground for rejecting this conclusion?

We cannot.

But if it be true, then is not the body liable to speedy dissolution? and is not the soul almost or altogether indissoluble?

Certainly. c

And do you further observe, that after a man is dead, the
body, or visible part of him, which is lying in the visible world,
and is called a corpse, and would naturally be dissolved and de-
composed and dissipated, is not dissolved or decomposed at once,
but may remain for some time, nay even for a long time, if the
constitution be sound at the time of death, and the season of the
year favourable? For the body when shrunk and embalmed, as
the manner is in Egypt, may remain almost entire for a pro-
digious time; and even in decay, there are still some portions, d
such as the bones and ligaments, which are practically inde-
structible:—Do you agree?

Yes.

And is it likely that the soul, which is invisible, in passing to
the place of the true Hades, which like her is invisible, and
pure, and noble, and on her way to the good and wise God,
whither, if God will, my soul is also soon to go,—that the soul,
I repeat, if this be her nature, is blown away and destroyed im-
mediately on quitting the body, as the many say? That can
never be, my dear Simmias and Cebes. The truth rather is that e
the soul which is pure at departing and draws after her no
bodily taint, having never voluntarily during life had con-
nexion with the body, which she is ever avoiding, herself gath-
ered into herself, and making such abstraction her perpetual
study—all this means that she has been a true disciple of philos-
ophy; and therefore has in fact been always practising how to
die without complaint. For is not such a life the practice of
death? 81a

Certainly.

That soul, I say, herself invisible, departs to the invisible world—to the divine and immortal and rational: thither arriving, she is secure of bliss and is released from the error and folly of men, their fears and wild passions and all other human ills, and for ever dwells, as they say of the initiated, in company with the gods. Is not this true, Cebes?

Yes, said Cebes, beyond a doubt.

But the soul which has been polluted, and is impure at the b
time of her departure, and is the companion and servant of the
body always, and is in love with and bewitched by the body
and by the desires and pleasures of the body, until she is led to

believe that the truth only exists in a bodily form, which a man may touch and see, and drink and eat, and use for the purposes of his lusts,—the soul, I mean, accustomed to hate and fear and avoid that which to the bodily eye is dark and invisible, but is the object of mind and can be attained by philosophy;— do you suppose that such a soul will depart pure and unalloyed? c

Impossible, he replied.

She is intermixed with the corporeal, which the continual association and constant care of the body have wrought into her nature.

Very true.

And this corporeal element, my friend, is burdensome and weighty and earthy, and is visible; a soul thus hampered is depressed and dragged down again into the visible world, because she is afraid of the invisible and of the other world—prowling
about tombs and sepulchres, near which, as they tell us, are d
seen certain ghostly apparitions of souls, spectres emanating from souls which have not departed pure, but still retain something of the visible element: which is why they can be seen.

That is very likely, Socrates.

Yes, that is very likely, Cebes; and these must be the souls, not of the good, but of the evil, which are compelled to wander about such places in payment of the penalty of their former evil way of life; and they continue to wander until through the
craving after their constant associate, the corporeal, they are e
imprisoned finally in another body. And they may be supposed to find their prisons in natures of the same character as they have cultivated in their former lives.

What natures do you mean, Socrates?

What I mean is that men who have followed after gluttony, and wantonness, and drunkenness, and have had no thought of avoiding them, would pass into asses and animals of that sort.
What do you think? 82a

I think such an opinion to be exceedingly probable.

And those who have chosen the portion of injustice, and tyranny, and violence, will pass into wolves, or into hawks and kites;—whither else can we suppose them to go?

Yes, said Cebes; into such creatures, beyond question.

And there is no difficulty, he said, in assigning to each class of them places answering to their several natures and propensities?

There is not, he said.

Even among these, some are happier than others; and the happiest both in themselves and in the place to which they go are those who have practised the virtues of the populace, the social virtues which are called by them temperance and justice, b
and are acquired by habit and practice without philosophy and mind.

Why are they the happiest?

Because they may be expected to pass into some gentle and social kind which is like their own, such as bees or wasps or ants, or back again into the form of man, and worthy men may be supposed to spring from them.

Very likely.

But to the company of the gods no one who has not studied philosophy and who is not entirely pure at the time of his depar- c
ture is admitted, save only the lover of knowledge. And this is the reason, Simmias and Cebes, why the true votaries of philosophy abstain from all fleshly lusts, and hold out against them and refuse to give themselves up to them,—not because they fear poverty or the ruin of their families, like the lovers of money, and the world in general; nor like the lovers of power and honour, because they dread the dishonour or disgrace of evil deeds.

No, Socrates, that would not become them, said Cebes.

No indeed, he replied; and therefore they who have any care d
of their own souls, and do not merely live for the body and its fashioning, say farewell to all this; they will not walk in the ways of the blind: and when philosophy offers them purification and release from evil, they feel that they ought not to resist her influence, and whither she leads they turn and follow.

What do you mean, Socrates?

I will tell you, he said. The lovers of knowledge are conscious that the soul was simply fastened and glued to the body—until e
philosophy[1] took her in hand, she could only view real existence

1. Philosophy personified.

through the bars of a prison, not in and through herself, and she
was wallowing in the mire of every sort of ignorance. This was
her original state; and then, as I was saying, and as the lovers
of knowledge are well aware, philosophy saw the ingenuity of
her prison—a prison built by lust so that a captive might be 83a
the principal accomplice in his own captivity—and took her
in hand, and gently comforted her and sought to release her,
pointing out that the eye and the ear and the other senses are
full of deception, and persuading her to retire from them, and
abstain from all but the necessary use of them, and be gathered
up and collected into herself, bidding her trust only in herself
and her own pure apprehension of pure existence, and to mis- b
trust whatever comes to her through other channels and is subject to variation; for such things are sensible and visible, but
what she sees in her own nature is of the mind and invisible.
And the soul of the true philosopher thinks that she ought not
to resist this deliverance, and therefore abstains from pleasures
and desires and pains, as far as she is able; reflecting that when
a man has great joys or fears or desires, he suffers from them
not merely the sort of evil which might be anticipated—as for
example, the loss of his health or property which he has sacri- c
ficed to his lusts—but an evil greater far, which is the greatest
and worst of all evils, and one of which he never thinks.

What is it, Socrates? said Cebes.

The evil is that when the feeling of pleasure or pain is most intense, every soul of man imagines the objects of this intense feeling to be then plainest and truest, though they are not so. And the things of sight are the chief of these objects, are they not?

Yes.

And is not this the state in which the soul becomes most
firmly gripped by the body? d

How so?

Why, because each pleasure and pain is a sort of nail which nails and rivets the soul to the body, until she becomes like the body, and believes that to be true which the body affirms to be true; and from agreeing with the body and having the same delights she is obliged to have the same habits and haunts, and

is not likely ever to be pure at her departure to the world below, but is always infected by the body; and so she sinks into an-
other body and there germinates and grows, and has therefore e
no part in the communion of the divine and pure and simple.

Most true, Socrates, answered Cebes.

And this, Cebes, is the reason why the true lovers of knowledge are temperate and brave; and not for the reason which the world gives.

Certainly not. 84a

Certainly not! The soul of a philosopher will reason in quite another way; she will not ask philosophy to release her in order that in the very process of release she may deliver herself up again to the thraldom of pleasures and pains, doing a work only to be undone again, weaving and in turn unweaving her Penelope's web.[2] But she will calm passion, and follow reason, and dwell always with her, contemplating the true and the divine and that which is beyond appearance and opinion, and
thence deriving nourishment. Thus she seeks to live while she b
lives, and after death she hopes to go to her own kindred and to that which is like her, and to be freed from human ills. Thus nurtured, Simmias and Cebes, a soul will never fear that at her departure from the body she will be scattered and blown away by the winds and be nowhere and nothing.

. . . .

A man of sense ought not to assert that the description which d
I have given of the soul and her mansions is exactly true. But I do say that, inasmuch as the soul is shown to be immortal, he may venture to think, not improperly or unworthily, that something of the kind is true. The venture is a glorious one, and he ought to comfort himself with words of power like these, which is the reason why I lengthen out the tale. Wherefore,
I say, let a man be of good cheer about his soul, who having e
cast away the pleasures and ornaments of the body as alien to him and working harm rather than good, has sought after the

2. In Homer's *Odyssey*, Penelope was the wife of Ulysses, who after twenty years' absence was presumed dead. She promised to accept one of her suitors when the web she was weaving would be finished; but each night she unravelled what she had woven during the day.

pleasures of knowledge; and has arrayed the soul, not in some
foreign attire, but in her own proper jewels, temperance, and
justice, and courage, and nobility, and truth—in these adorned 115a
she is ready to go on her journey to the world below. You, Simmias and Cebes, and you others, will depart at some time or other. Me already, as a tragic poet would say, the voice of fate calls. Soon I must drink the poison; and I think that I had better repair to the bath first, in order that the women may not have the trouble of washing my body after I am dead.

When he had done speaking, Crito said: And have you any b
commands for us, Socrates—anything to say about your children, or any other matter in which we can serve you?

Nothing particular, Crito, he replied: only, as I have always told you, take care of yourselves; that is a service which you may be ever rendering to me and mine and to yourselves, whether you promise to do so or not. But if you have no thought for yourselves, and care not to walk in the path of life which I have shown you, not now for the first time, then however much and however earnestly you may promise at the moment, it will
be of no avail. c

We will do our best, said Crito: And in what way shall we bury you?

In any way that you like; but you must first get hold of me, and take care that I do not run away from you. Then he turned to us, and added with a smile:—I cannot make Crito believe that I am the same Socrates who have been talking and conducting the argument; he fancies that I am the other Socrates
whom he will soon see, a dead body—and indeed he asks, How d
shall he bury me? And though I have spoken many words in the endeavour to show that when I have drunk the poison I shall leave you and go to the joys of the blessed,—these words of mine, with which I was comforting you and myself, have had, as I perceive, no effect upon Crito. And therefore I want you to be surety for me to him now, as at the trial he was surety to the judges for me: but let the promise be of another sort; for he was surety for me to the judges that I would remain, and you must be my surety to him that I shall not remain, but go away and depart; and then he will suffer less at my death, and

not be grieved when he sees my body being burned or buried. e
I would not have him sorrow at my hard lot, or say at the bur-
ial, Thus we lay out Socrates, or, Thus we follow him to the
grave or bury him; for be well assured, my dear Crito, that false
words are not only evil in themselves, but they infect the soul
with evil. Be of good cheer then and say that you are burying
my body only, and do with that whatever is usual, and what
you think best. 116a

When he had spoken these words, he arose and went into a
chamber to bathe; Crito followed him and told us to wait. So
we remained behind, talking and thinking of the subject of
discourse, and also of the greatness of our loss; he was like a
father of whom we were being bereaved, and we were about
to pass the rest of our lives as orphans. When he had taken the
bath his children were brought to him—(he had two young b
sons and an elder one); and the women of his family also
came, and he talked to them and gave them a few directions in
the presence of Crito; then he dismissed them and returned
to us.

Now the hour of sunset was near, for a good deal of time had
passed while he was within. When he came out, he sat down
with us again after his bath, but not much was said. Soon the
jailer, who was the servant of the Eleven, entered and stood by
him, saying:—To you, Socrates, whom after your time here I c
know to be the noblest and gentlest and best of all who ever
came to this place, I will not impute the angry feelings of other
men, who rage and swear at me, when, in obedience to the
authorities, I bid them drink the poison—indeed, I am sure that
you are not angry with me; for others, as you are aware, and
not I, are to blame. And so fare you well, and try to bear lightly
what must needs be—you know my errand. Then bursting into d
tears he turned and started on his way out.

Socrates looked up at him and said: I return your good wishes, and will do as you bid. Then turning to us, he said, How charming the man is: since I have been in prison he has always been coming to see me, and at times he would talk to me, and was as good to me as could be, and now see how generously he sorrows on my account. We must do as he says,

Crito; and therefore let the cup be brought, if the poison is prepared: if not, let the attendant prepare some.

But, said Crito, the sun is still upon the hill-tops, and is not e
yet set. I know that many a one takes the draught quite a long
time after the announcement has been made to him, when he
has eaten and drunk to his satisfaction and enjoyed the society
of his chosen friends; do not hurry—there is time enough.

Socrates said: Yes, Crito, and therein they of whom you speak
act logically, for they think that they will be gainers by the
delay; but I likewise act logically in not following their ex-
ample, for I do not think that I should gain anything by drink-
ing the poison a little later; I should only be ridiculous in my 117a
own eyes for sparing and saving a life which is already down to
its dregs. Please then to do as I say, and not to refuse me.

Crito made a sign to the servant, who was standing by; and
he went out, and having been absent for some time, returned
with the jailer carrying the cup of poison. Socrates said: You,
my good friend, who are experienced in these matters, shall
give me directions how I am to proceed. The man answered:
You have only to walk about until your legs are heavy, and
then to lie down, and the poison will act. At the same time he b
handed the cup to Socrates, who in the easiest and gentlest
manner, without the least fear or change of colour or feature,
and looking at the man sideways with that droll glance of his,
took the cup and said: What do you say about making a liba-
tion out of this cup to any god? May I, or not? The man an-
swered: We only prepare, Socrates, just so much as we deem
enough. I understand, he said: but a prayer to the gods I may c
and must offer, that they will prosper my journey from this to
the other world—even so—and so be it according to my prayer.
Then he held his breath and drank off the poison quite readily
and cheerfully. And hitherto most of us had been fairly able to
control our sorrow; but now when we saw him drinking, and
saw too that he had finished the draught, we could no longer
forbear, and in spite of myself my own tears were flowing fast;
so that I covered my face and wept, not indeed for him, but at
the thought of my own calamity in having to part from such a
friend. Nor was I the first; for Crito, when he found himself d

unable to restrain his tears, had got up, and I followed; and at that moment, Apollodorus, who had been weeping all the time, burst out in a loud and passionate cry which broke us all down. Socrates alone retained his calmness: What is this strange outcry? he said. I sent away the women mainly in order that they might not misbehave in this fashion, for I have been told that a man should die in peace. Be quiet then, and bear yourselves e with fortitude. When we heard his words we were ashamed, and refrained our tears; and he walked about until, as he said, his legs began to fail, and then he lay on his back, according to the directions, and the man who gave him the poison now and then looked at his feet and legs; and after a while he pressed his foot hard, and asked him if he could feel; and he said, No; and then his leg, and so upwards and upwards, and showed us that he was becoming cold and stiff. And he felt them himself, and said: When the poison reaches the heart, that will be the end. He was beginning to grow cold about the groin, when he uncovered his face, for he had covered himself up, and said —they were his last words—he said: Crito, I owe a cock to Aesculapius;[3] will you remember to pay the debt? The debt shall be paid, said Crito; is there anything else? There was no answer to this question; but in a minute or two a movement was heard, and the attendant uncovered him; his eyes were set, and Crito closed his eyes and mouth.

Such was the end, Echecrates, of our friend; concerning whom we may truly say that of all the men of his time whom we have known, he was the wisest and justest and best.

3. Aesculapius was the god of medicine, who cured the sick and restored the dead to life. Apparently Socrates had once promised him a cock as a propitiary offering.

II

Eastern Hellenism

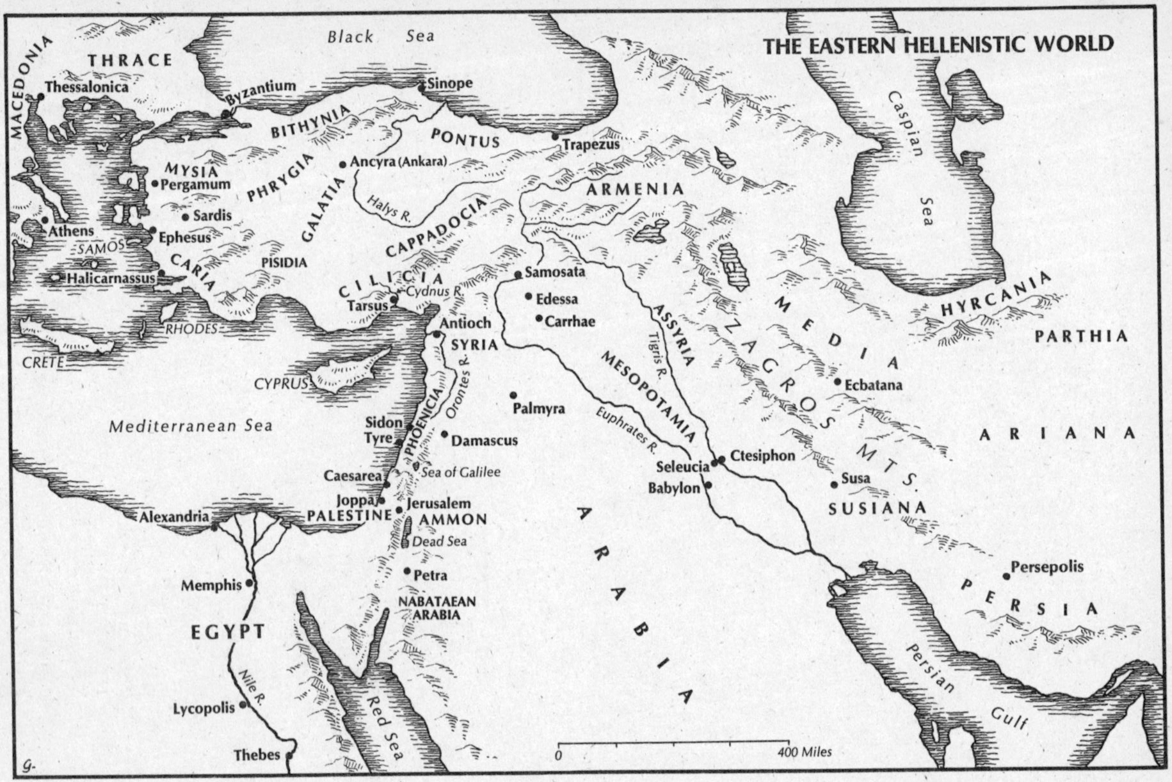
THE EASTERN HELLENISTIC WORLD
MACEDONIA
THRACE
Thessalonica
Black Sea
Byzantium
Sinope
BITHYNIA
PONTUS
Trapezus
Caspian Sea
MYSIA
Pergamum
PHRYGIA
Ancyra (Ankara)
GALATIA
Halys R.
ARMENIA
Sardis
Athens
Ephesus
SAMOS
CARIA
Halicarnassus
PISIDIA
CAPPADOCIA
CILICIA
Cydnus R.
Tarsus
Samosata
Edessa
Carrhae
RHODES
CRETE
Antioch
SYRIA
CYPRUS
Orontes R.
PHOENICIA
Sidon
Tyre
Damascus
Palmyra
Mediterranean Sea
Caesarea
Sea of Galilee
Joppa
Jerusalem
PALESTINE
AMMON
Dead Sea
Alexandria
Petra
NABATAEAN ARABIA
Memphis
EGYPT
Nile R.
Lycopolis
Thebes
Red Sea
ARABIA
ASSYRIA
Tigris R.
MESOPOTAMIA
Euphrates R.
Seleucia
Ctesiphon
Babylon
ZAGROS MTS.
MEDIA
Ecbatana
HYRCANIA
PARTHIA
ARIANA
Susa
SUSIANA
Persepolis
PERSIA
Persian Gulf
0
400 Miles

Introduction to the Rosetta Decree

The Rosetta stone, like the Behistun inscription of Darius, was one of those crucial discoveries of archaeology which at one stroke enormously advanced the study of an ancient tongue and thereby revealed to the world a hitherto unknown dimension of human history. For two thousand years previously, the existence of a major civilization in Egypt in the third and second millennia B.C. had been scarcely suspected. Pre-Hellenistic Egypt, like Mesopotamia, was known only as it appeared in the days of its decline to Greek travelers like Herodotus or Xenophon, or through an occasional mention in the Bible. The decipherment of the Rosetta stone, by enabling scholars to read the hieroglyphic script which abounded on Egyptian temples and monuments, made Egypt the first of the pre-Greek civilizations to be discovered in modern times, and opened up a whole new view of the antiquity of civilization itself.

The stone itself—a large slab of black basalt—is dated 196 B.C. and contains a decree of the Greek king Ptolemy V (reigned 204-181 B.C.). Like similar stelae of the same period, it was probably intended as a commemorative monument to be placed on a low pedestal in a temple. The top third of the slab records the decree in the formal hieroglyphic script of ancient Egypt; the middle third gives it in demotic, the popular Egyptian speech of the time; the bottom third has it in Greek. The position of the demotic text on approximately the "eye-line" of the viewer suggests that this was the original version, from which the others are translations. This supposition is borne out by internal considerations. The demotic text gives fuller details than the others and reads more naturally. The hieroglyphic version was probably included in order to suggest continuity from the revered ancient Pharaohs down to the current one. It is unlikely that in Ptolemaic times more than a very few priests could read hieroglyphic; indeed, the errors in the text suggest that the writer himself was not too familiar with the script.

The decipherment of Egyptian hieroglyphics was an indirect result of Napoleon's invasion of Egypt. The Rosetta stone was discovered in 1799 by French troops at the town of Rosetta near one of the mouths of the Nile. An archaeologist accompanying the army, J. F. Champollion, spent twenty years trying to unravel the inscription. Champollion had already succeeded in identifying eleven hieroglyphic symbols on an obelisk bearing a Greek title—the first proof that the ancient Egyptians had had an alphabet. Applying this knowledge to the hieroglyphic text of the Rosetta stone and comparing it with the demotic and Greek, he finally managed to read the entire inscription.

The Rosetta decree demonstrates clearly to what extent the Ptolemies had become Egyptianized, at least for public purposes. Ptolemy V's coronation ceremonies followed the traditional Egyptian ritual. Though his dynasty was Macedonian by origin, Ptolemy termed himself the "chosen of Ptah" and was careful to legitimate his rule by proving that the blood of Amen-Ra flowed in his veins. In accordance with the policy of the earlier Ptolemies, he identified Greek gods with their closest Egyptian counterparts.

But this policy of accommodation was unable to reconcile many of the native Egyptians to foreign rule. Members of the priesthood—their power lessened under the Macedonian regime—no doubt fostered hatred against the Ptolemies. Resentment of the foreigner combined with economic grievances to produce a major revolt in 216 B.C. On the Rosetta stone Ptolemy V recounted his measures aimed at winning over the rebels and claimed credit for great public benefactions. Nonetheless, another widespread revolt broke out in 189 B.C. near the end of his reign.

THE ROSETTA DECREE

1 In the ninth year (the fourth day of the month Xandikos,[1] which correspondeth to the eighteenth day of the month Meshir of the Egyptians) of the young King, who hath risen as King in the place of his father, the lord of the uraei[2] Crowns of the South and the North, whose might is great, who hath estab-

Trans. by E. A. Wallis Budge in his *The Rosetta Stone*, Vol. 18 of *Books on Egypt and Chaldaea*, London: Kegan Paul, Trench, Truebner & Co., 1904, pp. 45-56. Reprinted by permission of Routledge & Kegan Paul, Ltd.

1. The Macedonian name for April.
2. The uraeus-serpent was a symbol of Egyptian royalty.

lished Egypt and hath made it prosperous, whose heart is disposed benevolently towards the gods, who hath gained the mastery over his enemies, who hath made better (or, happier) the lives of men, the lord of the years of the periods (or, cycles) of thirty years, who is like unto Ptah the Great,[3] the King who is like unto Ra,[4]

2 the king of the Upper Country and of the Lower Country,[5] the son of the Father-loving Gods,[6] whom Ptah hath chosen, and to whom Ra hath given the victory, the living image of Amen,[7] the son of the Sun, Ptolemy, the ever-living, beloved of Ptah, the God who maketh himself manifest, whose good deeds are beautiful, the son of Ptolemy and Arsinoë, the Father-loving Gods: when Aetus, the son of Aetus, was a priest of Alexander,[8] and of the Saviour-Gods,[9] and

3 of the Brother-Gods,[10] and of the Beneficent-Gods,[11] and of the Father-loving Gods, and of the King Ptolemy, the god, who maketh himself manifest, whose good deeds are beautiful; and when Pyrrha, the daughter of Philinus, was the bearer of the gift of victory of Berenice, the Beneficent,[12] and when Areia, the daughter of Diogenes, was the bearer

4 of the basket of Arsinoë, the Brother-loving,[13] and when Irene, the daughter of Ptolemy, was the priestess of Arsinoë, the Father-loving;[14] on this day a Decree:—The priests who declare

3. Ptah, the craftsman-god, is replaced in the Greek version by Hephaestus.
4. Ra (Re) is called Helios in the Greek version; both were sun-gods.
5. I.e., Upper and Lower Egypt.
6. In Greek, "father-loving" becomes *Philopator*, which was the eponym of the king's father, Ptolemy IV Philopator.
7. Amen (Amun), the chief of the gods, becomes Zeus in the Greek text. But it was Ptah rather than Amen who gave Ptolemy his throne.
8. Alexander the Great was worshipped as a god.
9. In Greek: *Soter*. The founder of the Ptolemaic dynasty called himself Ptolemy I Soter.
10. In Greek: *Adelphi*. The second king of the dynasty called himself Ptolemy II Philadelphus.
11. In Greek: *Euergetes*, referring to Ptolemy III Euergetes.
12. Berenice was the queen of Ptolemy III. She was supposed to have presented a lock of her hair to the gods in thanks for one of her husband's successes. The constellation Berenice's Hair was named after her.
13. Arsinoe was the wife of Ptolemy II. The basket contained the fruits of the earth; a priestess of the goddess Demeter bore it on her head.
14. This Arsinoe was the wife of Ptolemy IV and mother of Ptolemy V.

oracles, and the servants of the gods, and the priests who enter into the sanctuary to array the gods in their apparel, and the scribes of the holy books, and the scribes of the Two Houses of Life, and the other priests who had come from the temples of Egypt

5 (to Memphis), to the festival of the reception of the exalted rank by king Ptolemy, the ever-living, the beloved of Ptah, the God who maketh himself manifest,[15] whose deeds are beautiful[16] (and) are from the hand of his father, who have gathered themselves together to Memphis, spake, saying,

"Inasmuch as it hath happened that King Ptolemy, the ever-living, the God who maketh himself manifest, whose deeds are beautiful, the son of King Ptolemy

6 "and the Queen Arsinoë, the Father-loving Gods, hath conferred many benefits upon the Temples of Egypt, and upon all those who were under his royal dominion, being a God, the son of a God and Goddess, the image of Horus,[17] the son of Isis[18] (and) of Osiris,[19] who avenged (or, saved) his father Osiris; and inasmuch as his heart is benevolently disposed towards the Gods, and he hath given much money (and) much corn to the Temples of Egypt,

7 "and he hath expended large sums in order to establish the peace of Egypt, and to place the temples in prosperous circumstances, and all those who depend upon him, and all those who are under his dominion; and of the taxes and the dues to the government which exist in Egypt, one part he hath diminished, (and) one part he hath entirely abolished, so that he might make the troops and all the other folk contented during the time of his

15. Or: "who cometh forth"; in Greek, *Epiphanes,* which was the eponym of Ptolemy V. The word was generally applied to the rising of a star.
16. Or: "lord of beauties," in Greek, *Eucharistos,* an allusion to the king's representing the sun.
17. Horus, the victorious god of light, who overcame darkness, winter, and drought, was identified with Apollo by the Greeks.
18. Isis was a goddess of the underworld, representing the feminine, productive principle.
19. Osiris was a male fertility deity who in Egyptian mythology was murdered by his brother Set (Tryphon). The Greek identified Osiris with Dionysus.

8 "rule; and he hath given up the debts which the inhabitants of Egypt, and those who were under his royal dominion, owed to the king, and which formed a very large amount (of money); and he hath set free from prison those who had been condemned to be there under judgments which had been given a long time ago; and the revenues of the gods, and the money and the grain which the people were obliged to contribute

9 "to the Temples as the Syntaxis (i.e., the yearly covenanted contribution), and also the share of the vineyards and the orchards which belonged to the gods, and everything else which (the temples) had been ordered to possess under his father, (he hath commanded) to remain as they had been formerly; and in the matter of the priests he hath ordered that men shall pay no higher tax to become priests than they did up to the first year of his father's reign;

10 "and he hath released those who hold offices in the temples from making the journey which they had been wont to make annually (pilgrimage?) to the House of Alexander;[20] and he hath ordered that sailors shall not be pressed (into naval service); and he hath remitted two-thirds of the (number of) pieces of byssus[21] cloth which the temples were obliged to pay to the palace; and everything which had been neglected for a very long time he hath brought back into the state in which it was formerly;

11 "and he hath taken great care that every honour which it was customary to pay to the gods, and every ceremony which it was customary to perform for them, shall be carried out in the proper manner; and he hath administered justice to all people, even as doth Thoth, the twice-great;[22] and he hath ordered in respect of those of the troops who come back, and the other people also, who during the strife of the revolution[23] which took place had been ill-disposed (towards the government),

20. I.e., the Egyptian priests shall not be required to pay homage to Alexander.

21. Byssus was a linen cloth made of fine yellow flax and used as a mummy wrapping.

22. "Twice-great" and "thrice-great" were common epithets of the god Thoth. Like his Greek counterpart, Hermes, he was the scribe of the gods.

23. Reference to the revolt of 216 B.C.

12 "that when they return to their homes and lands they shall have the power to remain in possession of their property; and he hath taken great care to send troops, both cavalry (and) ships against those who came to fight against Egypt by sea and by land, and hath in consequence expended a very large amount of money and grain, in order that the temples and the inhabitants of Egypt might remain in peace; and, for example, he marched against the town of Shekan (Lycopolis),[24] which was in the possession of the

13 "enemy,[25] and was provided with catapults and was made ready for war with weapons of every kind; and he surrounded the said town with walls and a rampart against the enemy who were therein, for they had caused very great injury to Egypt, and they had forsaken the way of the command of the king, and also the ordinances

14 "of the gods; and he caused the canals which supplied the said town with water to be blocked, which none of the kings who were his predecessors were ever able to do, and spent a large amount of money on the carrying out of the work; and he ordered soldiers, both infantry and cavalry, (to go) to the mouths of the said canals in order to watch and to guard them against the extraordinary rise of the waters (of the Nile) which took place in the eighth year (of his reign)

15 "in the aforementioned canals, which watered the fields and were unusually deep; and in a very short time the King captured the town with a strong hand,[26] and smote the enemy who were therein, and annihilated them like Ra, and (like) Horus, the son of Isis, who did the same thing to their enemies in the aforesaid place;

16 "and the gods permitted him to slay the enemy, (that is,) the troops who had gathered themselves together, and who had been the first to stir up revolution in the borders (of the land),

24. A city of central Egypt (now Asyut).

25. The enemy is not named; but the reference below to having "forsaken the way of the command of the king" seems to connect the enemy with the revolt of 216 B.C.

26. The king caused the mouths of the canals supplying the city with water to be blocked up and guarded with troops. Despite an unusually heavy flood the dams held and the people of Lycopolis were forced to surrender when their water supply ran out.

and who had committed sacrilegious acts towards the temples, having forsaken the way of the King and his father, in Memphis at the festival of his reception of the exalted sovereignty (of the country) from the hand of his father; and he caused them to suffer death upon wood (i.e., he crucified them); and moreover he hath remitted the remainder of the debts

17 "which the temples owed to the King for the period up to the ninth year [of his reign], which amounted to a very large sum both in money and in grain, and also the price of the cloths of byssus which the temples owed in respect of those which they ought to have delivered to the royal house, and also the tax which they ought to have contributed for dividing the cloth into pieces during the afore-named period;[27] and he hath remitted also the [tax of one] *artaba* which had been formerly demanded from the corn-lands of estates of the temples, and the Keramion[28] which ought

18 "to have been contributed [to the royal house] from the vineyards of the temples; and he hath conferred many benefits upon Apis and Mnevis,[29] and the other sacred animals of Egypt, far more than any of his ancestors; and he hath observed their commands at all times, and he hath spent in a lavish and splendid manner whatsoever sums were needed for burying them in a suitable manner, and he hath provided whatsoever they received

19 "for their temples; and he hath maintained in a proper manner the former customary festivals and burnt-offerings, as well as the other ceremonial observances which the temples were in duty bound to perform, and [all] the other ceremonial observances of Egypt, as was right; and he hath given gold, and silver, and grain in great abundance, and many other things to the House of Apis,[30] and he hath caused new buildings of most beautiful work to be built for it;

27. Evidently the charges for measuring and examining the byssus cloths brought to the treasury were usually paid by the priests.

28. A tax of a jar of wine.

29. Apis and Mnevis, usually mentioned together, were the black bulls in which the gods Osiris and Ra were supposedly incarnated. They symbolized generative power and continued life.

30. Probably a temple housing an actual bull regarded as the incarnate Osiris.

20 "and he hath built new Temples, and shrines, and altars for the gods, and hath caused many other things to be done in a fitting manner, for he possessed the heart of a God which was benevolently disposed towards the Gods, and was careful to inquire concerning the ceremonial observances of the temple in order that he might cause them to be renewed during his reign in the manner which was suitable; and in return for these things may the gods give him victory, and power, and might, and life,

21 "strength, and health, and all other good things, and may they grant that sovereignty and dominion may remain with him and with his children for ever with happy results."

And the priests of all the temples of Egypt have passed a Decree to increase the ceremonial observances of honour which are paid in the temples to King Ptolemy the ever-living, the God who maketh himself manifest, whose deeds are beautiful,

22 and those which are paid to the Father-loving Gods who begot him, and those which are paid to the Beneficent Gods, who begot his begetters, and those which are paid to the Brother-Gods, who begot the begetters of his begetters, and the Saviour-God who begot the fathers of his father, and they (i.e., the priests) have therefore decided to set up a statue of King Ptolemy, the everliving, the God who maketh himself manifest, whose deeds are beautiful,

23 which shall be called "Ptolemy, the Saviour of Egypt," side by side with a statue of the Lord of the gods (?),[31] who giveth him the weapon of victory,[32] in every temple, and in the most prominent place thereof, and they shall fashion the statue after the manner of the Egyptians; and the priests shall worship the statues in all the temples three times each day;

24 and they shall set before them the things which are usually offered up (?), and they shall perform for them all the other ceremonies which it is proper to perform for the other gods, and make processions and observe name-days in their honour; and they shall cause a divine image of King Ptolemy, the god who

31. Probably the dominant god of the temple.

32. In Egyptian art a god is frequently portrayed as presenting the weapon of victory (*khepesh*) to the king.

maketh himself manifest, whose deeds are beautiful, the son of King Ptolemy and of Queen Arsinoë, the Father-loving Gods, to appear with the golden shrines [which are] in all temples;

25 and they shall establish them in the sanctuaries, together with the other golden shrines; and on the days of the great festivals upon which they cause the gods to appear,[33] they shall cause to appear also the shrines of the God who maketh himself manifest, whose deeds are beautiful, together with them; and in order that the shrine [of the King] may be distinguished both at the present time, and in future days, they shall set upon the shrine ten royal double crowns made of gold, and upon each of the double crowns there shall be placed a serpent,

26 such as it is right and proper to make for the gold double crown, instead of the serpent which is found on the other shrines,[34] in such a manner that the Sekhent crown occupieth the middle place[35]—for it hath happened that the King appeared in this crown at Memphis when he performed the ceremonies which it was right and proper for him to perform on his receiving his exalted rank [of king][36]—and upon the upper surface of the four-cornered portion which is round about the double crown,

27 and in front of the aforesaid double crown, they shall place a papyrus and a plant of the south;[37] and they shall set them in such a way that a vulture upon a *neb*, [38] beneath which a plant of the South shall be found,[39] shall be affixed to the right-hand upper corner of the golden shrine, and a serpent, under which is

33. I.e., when the images of the gods go forth in procession.
34. The double crown was to be adorned with the serpent which symbolized royalty, not merely with the serpent used for the ornamentation of shrines.
35. The Sekhent crown was composed of the white crown of the South, symbolizing the desert, and the red crown of the North, symbolizing the dark-colored mud of the Delta. It was the mark of sovereignty over the Two Lands of Egypt.
36. I.e., at his official coronation.
37. The papyrus plant was a symbol of the South, the lotus plant of the North.
38. A hieroglyphic sign in the shape of a half-moon with the flat side upward.
39. The hieroglyphic which results from the combination of these signs means "lord of the shrine of the goddess of Nekhebet." Nekhebet was an ancient ecclesiastical city.

a *neb* placed upon a papyrus plant[40] shall be affixed to the left-hand side [at the upper corner], and the interpretation of these things is, "The King who illumineth Upper and Lower Egypt";[41] —and inasmuch as the thirtieth day of the month Mesore, whereon

28 the Birthday of the King is celebrated, which hath already been ordered to be observed as a day of festival, and as a day for a procession, in the temples, as well as the seventeenth day of the month Paape, whereon the King performed the ceremonies connected with his reception of the exalted rank of King [which days] have been the source of the benefits wherein all men have participated, that is to say, the birth of the everliving King, and the reception [by him] of [his] exalted rank: these days, that is, the seventeenth and the thirtieth, shall be kept as days of festival in every temple in Egypt, and every month,

29 on these days, burnt offerings and libations shall be made, and everything else which it is right and customary to perform on other days of festivals shall be duly performed. [And the priests also decreed] that the things which are brought [to the temples] as offerings shall be given unto the persons who minister in the temples; and festivals and processions shall be established in the temples and in all Egypt in honour of King Ptolemy, the ever-living, the God who maketh himself manifest, whose deeds are beautiful, every year, from the first day of the month of Thoth even to the fifth day of the same, and on these days the people shall wear garlands,

30 and burnt offerings and drink offerings shall be offered up thereon, and everything which it is customary to perform on these days shall be performed; and the priests in all the temples of Egypt, in addition to the titles which they already hold, shall have the title, "Priests of the God who maketh himself manifest, whose deeds are beautiful," and this title shall be endorsed on all deeds and documents which are laid up [in the temples], and the title of every priest of the God who maketh himself manifest, whose deeds are beautiful, shall be engraved upon his ring;

40. The hieroglyphic now means "lord of the shrine of the goddess of Uatchet." Uatchet (Per-Uatchet) was another ecclesiastical center.

41. I.e., the sun-god.

31 and the people of the country, and the soldiers who wish to make to appear the aforesaid golden shrine of the God who maketh himself manifest, whose deeds are beautiful, shall be permitted (?) to have it with them in their habitations, and they shall celebrate each year the festivals which are described above, and they shall make the [prescribed] processions; and in order that it may be made known why the Egyptians pay honour—as is most right and proper to do—to the God who maketh himself manifest, whose deeds are beautiful,
32 [the priests have decreed] that this Decree shall be inscribed upon a stele of hard stone in the writing of the divine words,[42] and in the writing of the books,[43] and in the writings of the Greeks, and that [a similar stele] shall be set up in the temples of the first, and second, and third order, side by side with the statue of the God Ptolemy, the everliving.

42. I.e., in the ancient hieroglyphic script.
43. I.e., in the demotic.

Introduction to II Maccabees

The books of I and II Maccabees belong in the ranks of both historical and religious literature. They are among those fifteen disputed books (apocryphal to Protestants, canonical for Roman Catholics) which are included in the Greek Septuagint but excluded from the Hebrew version of the Old Testament. As religious documents, they record the perpetual struggle of the Jews to guard their ancient law and traditions against the encroachments of an alien faith—in this case, the language and culture of the Greeks. As history, they constitute a principal source for the experiences of the Jewish nation in the second century B.C.

The two books of Maccabees offer parallel accounts of the Jewish revolt from 180 B.C. through the great victory of Judas Maccabeus over the Seleucid armies in 161 B.C. The first book of Maccabees carries the story further, through the death of Judas and the continuation of the revolt under his brothers. First Maccabees was written about 104 B.C.; Second Maccabees is a first-century B.C. abridgement of a longer work, now lost, which was composed about the same time. In both books the theological interpretation of history—which attributes events to the personal intervention of God—is paramount. As a historical source I Maccabees is undoubtedly more reliable, soberer in tone, less tendentious. But II Maccabees gives a more vivid sense of the resentment and outrage felt by pious Jews at the attempt of Greek rulers to Hellenize their ancient faith.

Palestine in the Maccabean period enjoyed the advantages and disadvantages of a geographical position between two powerful neighbors, Syria and Egypt, each of which sought to bring the Jewish states within its own sphere of influence. Both powers were then ruled by Macedonian dynasties—the Seleucids and the Ptolemies—and actively promoted the spread of the Greek language and style of life within their territories. This Hellenization policy was intended to give cultural unity to the diverse peoples of their respective empires. But to pious Jews, any compromise with a foreign religion represented a betrayal of their ancient traditions.

In 198 B.C. Palestine came under Seleucid hegemony, and a policy of promoting Greek culture was instituted. But the Seleucid king Antiochus IV (reigned 175-164 B.C.), not content with making Hellenization attractive to his Jewish subjects, sought to enforce it upon them. He outlawed certain practices central to the Jewish religion, such as circumcision, and forced Jews to defile themselves in their own eyes by building shrines to pagan gods and sacrificing animals they considered unclean. Antiochus' decrees threatened the very existence of Judaism, and left to its adherents no choice between religious betrayal and political revolt. Their first uprising was led by a priest of the Hasmonean family, Mattathias. Under Mattathias' sons Judas, Jonathan, and Simon (called "Maccabeus," or "hammer") it became a prolonged rebellion which linked the causes of Jewish political independence and religious integrity.

In 142 B.C., after a long struggle which took advantage of quarrels among Egypt, Syria, Rome, and Parthia, Simon Maccabeus established himself as king of an independent Judean state. The little kingdom soon expanded to include all of Palestine and Transjordania. Though originating in the battle for Jewish religious freedom, it now enforced Judaism at sword's point. But the Hasmonean dynasty soon lost much of its religious zeal, and, paradoxically, yielded increasingly to Hellenistic influences. The end of

Jewish political independence was a direct result of family discord. In 63 B.C. one party in a dynastic struggle invited the Roman general Pompey to intervene in its favor. When the disappointed party refused to yield, Pompey captured Jerusalem and subordinated the Jewish kingdom to the Roman province of Syria. Thus the political side of the Maccabean revolt ultimately ended in failure; but in its religious aspect it served to harden Jewish resistance to cultural and religious assimilation.

FROM THE SECOND BOOK OF MACCABEES

Chapter 4

7 When Seleucus[1] died and Antiochus who was called Epiph-
anes[2] succeeded to the kingdom, Jason[3] the brother of Onias[4]
obtained the high priesthood by corruption, 8 promising
the king at an interview three hundred and sixty talents[5] of
silver and, from another source of revenue, eighty talents.
9 In addition to this he promised to pay one hundred and
fifty more if permission were given to establish by his authority
a gymnasium and a body of youth for it, and to enrol the men
of Jerusalem as citizens of Antioch.[6] 10 When the king as-
sented and Jason came to office, he at once shifted his country-
men over to the Greek way of life. 11 He set aside the

1. Seleucus IV Philopator, reigned 187-175 B.C.
2. The king whose Hellenizing policy provoked the Maccabean revolt. "Epiphanes" means "god manifest."
3. Jason is the Greek form of the Hebrew "Joshua."
4. Onias III, high priest prior to the accession of Antiochus IV Epiphanes, was known for his piety and strict observance of the religious law. He had collaborated with the pro-Egyptian party among the Jews.
5. The talent was a Roman and Attic unit of money equal to 6000 denarii or drachmas.
6. Thereby Jerusalem would gain various commercial advantages, including the right to coin money.

existing royal concessions to the Jews,[7] secured through John
the father of Eupolemus, who went on the mission to establish
friendship and alliance with the Romans;[8] and he destroyed the
lawful[9] ways of living and introduced new customs contrary to
the law. 12 For with alacrity he founded a gymnasium
right under the citadel, and he induced the noblest of the young
men to wear the Greek hat.[10] 13 There was such an ex-
treme of Hellenization and increase in the adoption of foreign
ways because of the surpassing wickedness of Jason, who was
ungodly and no high priest,[11] 14 that the priests were no
longer intent upon their service at the altar. Despising the
sanctuary and neglecting the sacrifices, they hastened to take
part in the unlawful proceedings in the wrestling arena after
the call to the discus, 15 disdaining the honors prized by
their fathers and putting the highest value upon Greek forms of
prestige. 16 For this reason heavy disaster overtook them,
and those whose ways of living they admired and wished to
imitate completely became their enemies and punished them.
17 For it is no light thing to show irreverence to the divine
laws—a fact which later events will make clear.
18 When the quadrennial games[12] were being held at Tyre[13]
and the king was present, 19 the vile Jason sent envoys,
chosen as being Antiochian citizens from Jerusalem, to carry
three hundred silver drachmas[14] for the sacrifice to Hercules.[15]
Those who carried the money, however, thought best not to use
it for sacrifice, because that was inappropriate, but to expend it

7. The book of II Maccabees 3:3-4 states that in the time of Antiochus' predecessor Seleucus "the kings themselves honored the place [Jerusalem] and glorified the temple with the finest presents, so that even Seleucus, the king of Asia, defrayed from his own revenues all the expenses connected with the service of the sacrifices."

8. This passage indicates that, to some degree at least, the Jews had succeeded in playing off Rome against Syria.

9. I.e., lawful according to the Jewish religion.

10. The hat was worn as a badge of religion or nationality.

11. Because he had violated the religious law and attained his office through bribery.

12. Athletic contests in the Greek style.

13. A major port of southern Phoenicia (Lebanon).

14. The drachma was a Greek coin approximately equal to the Roman denarius. One hundred drachmas made a mina; 6000 equaled a talent.

15. Greek god identified with the Tyrian god Melkart.

for another purpose. 20 So this money was intended by the
sender for the sacrifice to Hercules, but by the decision of its
carriers it was applied to the construction of triremes.[16]
21 When Apollonius[17] the son of Menestheus was sent to
Egypt for the coronation of Philometor[18] as king, Antiochus
learned that Philometor had become hostile to his government,
and he took measures for his own security. Therefore upon ar-
riving at Joppa[19] he proceeded to Jerusalem. 22 He was
welcomed magnificently by Jason and the city, and ushered in
with a blaze of torches and with shouts. Then he marched into
Phoenicia.
23 After a period of three years Jason sent Menelaus, the
brother of the previously mentioned Simon,[20] to carry the
money to the king and to complete the records of essential busi-
ness. 24 But he, when presented to the king, extolled him
with an air of authority, and secured the high priesthood for
himself, outbidding Jason by three hundred talents of silver.
25 After receiving the king's orders he returned, possessing
no qualification for the high priesthood, but having the hot
temper of a cruel tyrant and the rage of a savage wild beast.
26 So Jason, who after supplanting his own brother was sup-
planted by another man, was driven as a fugitive into the land
of Ammon.[21] 27 And Menelaus held the office,[22] but he did
not pay regularly any of the money promised to the king.
28 When Sostratus the captain of the citadel kept requesting
payment, for the collection of the revenue was his responsi-
bility, the two of them were summoned by the king on account
of this issue. 29 Menelaus left his own brother Lysimachus
as deputy in the high priesthood, while Sostratus left Crates,
the commander of the Cyprian troops.[23]

16. The standard war vessel in ancient times.
17. Governor of southern Syria and Phoenicia under the Seleucids.
18. Ptolemy VI Philometor, crowned about 172 B.C.
19. Now Jaffa: a port on the central Mediterranean coast of Palestine.
20. This Simon was a member of a pro-Syrian family who in the time of Seleucus IV had conspired against the pious high priest Onias III (see II Maccabees 3:4-12).
21. The region around present-day Amman, Transjordan.
22. Until 162 B.C., when he was executed.
23. The Cyprians were mercenaries.

30 While such was the state of affairs, it happened that the
people of Tarsus and of Mallus[24] revolted because their cities
had been given as a present to Antiochis, the king's concubine.[25]
31 So the king went hastily to settle the trouble, leaving An-
dronicus, a man of high rank, to act as his deputy. 32 But
Menelaus, thinking he had obtained a suitable opportunity, stole
some of the gold vessels of the temple and gave them to An-
dronicus;[26] other vessels, as it happened, he had sold to Tyre
and the neighboring cities. 33 When Onias[27] became fully
aware of these acts he publicly exposed them, having first with-
drawn to a place of sanctuary at Daphne near Antioch.[28]
34 Therefore Menelaus, taking Andronicus aside, urged him
to kill Onias. Andronicus came to Onias, and resorting to treach-
ery offered him sworn pledges and gave him his right hand,
and in spite of his suspicion persuaded Onias to come out from
the place of sanctuary; then, with no regard for justice, he im-
mediately put him out of the way. 35 For this reason not
only Jews, but many also of other nations, were grieved and
displeased at the unjust murder of the man.[29] 36 When the
king returned from the region of Cilicia,[30] the Jews in the city
appealed to him with regard to the unreasonable murder of
Onias, and the Greeks shared their hatred of the crime.
37 Therefore Antiochus was grieved at heart and filled with
pity, and wept because of the moderation and good conduct of
the deceased; 38 and inflamed with anger, he immediately
stripped off the purple robe from Andronicus,[31] tore off his gar-
ments, and led him about the whole city to that very place
where he had committed the outrage against Onias, and there

24. Tarsus and Mallus were cities in Cilicia (southern Asia Minor).

25. I.e., the revenues of these cities were assigned to support the concubine. The king was extravagant (see I Macc. 3:30) and constantly in search of new sources of revenue.

26. Either as tribute or as bribery.

27. The former high priest (see note 4 above).

28. This was a temple to Apollo and Artemis, where Onias should have been safe; the place was supposedly protected by the gods.

29. Unjust because Onias had been lured under false pretenses from a place of sanctuary.

30. Province of southern Asia Minor northwest of Syria.

31. I.e., degraded him before execution.

he dispatched the bloodthirsty fellow. The Lord thus repaid him
with the punishment he deserved.

. . . .

Chapter 5

1 About this time Antiochus made his second invasion of
Egypt.[32] 2 And it happened that over all the city,[33] for al-
most forty days, there appeared golden-clad horsemen charging
through the air, in companies fully armed with lances and
drawn swords— 3 troops of horsemen drawn up, attacks
and counterattacks made on this side and on that, brandishing
of shields, massing of spears, hurling of missiles, the flash of
golden trappings, and armor of all sorts. 4 Therefore all
men prayed that the apparition might prove to have been a
good omen.
5 When a false rumor arose that Antiochus was dead, Jason
took no less than a thousand men and suddenly made an assault
upon the city.[34] When the troops upon the wall had been forced
back and at last the city was being taken, Menelaus took refuge
in the citadel. 6 But Jason kept relentlessly slaughtering
his fellow citizens, not realizing that success at the cost of one's
kindred is the greatest misfortune, but imagining that he was
setting up trophies of victory over enemies and not over fellow
countrymen. 7 He did not gain control of the government,
however; and in the end got only disgrace from his conspiracy,
and fled again into the country of the Ammonites. 8 Finally
he met a miserable end. Accused before Aretas the ruler of the
Arabs,[35] fleeing from city to city, pursued by all men, hated as
a rebel against the laws, and abhorred as the executioner of his
country and his fellow citizens, he was cast ashore in Egypt;
9 and he who had driven many from their own country into
exile died in exile, having embarked to go to the Lacedaemo-

32. In 169 B.C. In 171 B.C. the Seleucid armies had entered Palestine, though they did not reach Egypt; perhaps the writer regarded this as the first invasion.

33. Jerusalem.

34. Jason, the former high priest, evidently hoped to recover his old position with Egyptian aid.

35. Ruler of Nabatean Arabia, the area immediately to the southeast of Palestine; its capital was Petra.

nians in hope of finding protection because of their kinship.[36]
10 He who had cast out many to lie unburied[37] had no one to
mourn for him; he had no funeral of any sort and no place
in the tomb of his fathers.
11 When news of what had happened reached the king, he
took it to mean that Judea was in revolt. So, raging inwardly,
he left Egypt[38] and took the city[39] by storm. 12 And he
commanded his soldiers to cut down relentlessly every one they
met and to slay those who went into the houses. 13 Then
there was killing of young and old, destruction of boys, women,
and children, and slaughter of virgins and infants. 14 Within
the total of three days eighty thousand were destroyed, forty
thousand in hand-to-hand fighting; and as many were sold into
slavery as were slain.
15 Not content with this, Antiochus dared to enter the most
holy temple in all the world, guided by Menelaus, who had
become a traitor both to the laws and to his country. 16 He
took the holy vessels with his polluted hands, and swept away
with profane hands the votive offerings which other kings had
made to enhance the glory and honor of the place. 17 Anti-
ochus was elated in spirit, and did not perceive that the Lord
was angered for a little while because of the sins of those who
dwelt in the city, and that therefore he was disregarding the
holy place. 18 But if it had not happened that they were
involved in many sins, this man would have been scourged and
turned back from his rash act as soon as he came forward, just
as Heliodorus[40] was, whom Seleucus the king sent to inspect the
treasury. 19 But the Lord did not choose the nation for the
sake of the holy place, but the place for the sake of the nation.
20 Therefore the place itself shared in the misfortunes that

36. The Jews maintained friendly relations with the Spartans, who in an earlier letter had claimed to be descendants of Abraham.

37. Like other ancient peoples, the Jews regarded corpses with horror; to leave a body unburied was a terrible outrage.

38. Antiochus had been forced out of Egypt by the Roman envoy, who threatened war with Rome if he annexed that country. The report of this incident in I Maccabees 1:16-28 does not connect the return of Antiochus with Jason's revolt.

39. Jerusalem.

40. According to II Maccabees 3:7-40, Heliodorus received a vision from God which made him refrain from taking the temple funds.

befell the nation and afterward participated in its benefits; and
what was forsaken in the wrath of the Almighty was restored
again in all its glory when the great Lord became reconciled.
21 So Antiochus carried off eighteen hundred talents from the
temple, and hurried away to Antioch, thinking in his arro-
gance that he could sail on the land and walk on the sea, be-
cause his mind was elated.[41] 22 And he left governors to
afflict the people: at Jerusalem, Philip, by birth a Phrygian[42]
and in character more barbarous than the man who appointed
him; 23 and at Gerizim,[43] Andronicus; and besides these
Menelaus, who lorded it over his fellow citizens worse than the
others did. In his malice toward the Jewish citizens, 24 An-
tiochus sent Apollonius, the captain of the Mysians,[44] with an
army of twenty-two thousand, and commanded him to slay all
the grown men and to sell the women and boys as slaves.
25 When this man arrived in Jerusalem, he pretended to be
peaceably disposed and waited until the holy sabbath day;
then, finding the Jews not at work, he ordered his men to
parade under arms.[45] 26 He put to the sword all those who
came out to see them, then rushed into the city with his armed
men and killed great numbers of people.
27 But Judas Maccabeus, with about nine others, got away to
the wilderness, and kept himself and his companions alive in
the mountains as wild animals do; they continued to live on
what grew wild, so that they might not share in the defile-
ment.[46]

Chapter 6

1 Not long after this, the king sent an Athenian senator to
compel the Jews to forsake the laws of their fathers and cease

41. Antiochus' arrogance was that of a "god manifest" (Epiphanes).
42. Phrygia lay in north central Asia Minor.
43. A place in Samaria (the region of Palestine northwest of the Dead Sea). See note 50, below.
44. Mysia was an area in the extreme northwest corner of Asia Minor.
45. At this time pious Jews did not fight on the Sabbath. The prohibition ceased to be observed after the incident in which Seleucid troops slaughtered a group of Jewish rebels who refused to resist an attack on the Sabbath.
46. Defilement: the anti-Jewish decrees of Antiochus. Ths account in II Maccabees neglects to mention Judas' father Mattathias, the original leader of the revolt.

to live by the laws of God,[47] 2 and also to pollute the
temple[48] in Jerusalem and call it the temple of Olympian Zeus,[49]
and to call the one in Gerizim the temple of Zeus the Friend of
Strangers,[50] as did the people who dwelt in that place.
3 Harsh and utterly grievous was the onslaught of evil.
4 For the temple was filled with debauchery and reveling by
the Gentiles, who dallied with harlots and had intercourse with
women within the sacred precincts,[51] and besides brought in
things for sacrifice that were unfit.[52] 5 The altar was cov-
ered with abominable offerings which were forbidden by the
laws. 6 A man could neither keep the sabbath, nor observe
the feasts of his fathers, nor so much as confess himself to be a
Jew.[53]
7 On the monthly celebration of the king's birthday, the Jews
were taken, under bitter constraint, to partake of the sacrifices;
and when the feast of Dionysus[54] came, they were compelled to
walk in the procession in honor of Dionysus, wearing wreaths
of ivy.[55] 8 At the suggestion of Ptolemy[56] a decree was is-
sued to the neighboring Greek cities, that they should adopt the
same policy toward the Jews[57] and make them partake of the
sacrifices, 9 and should slay those who did not choose to

47. The account here is chronologically confused: Antiochus' Hellenizing measures preceded the inception of the revolt.

48. Antiochus' officials erected an altar to Zeus, possibly also a statue of him, in the temple.

49. In accordance with the common practice in Hellenistic times of identifying foreign deities with Greek gods bearing similar characteristics, Yahweh was called "Zeus."

50. Gerizim was the sacred mountain of the Samarians. The inhabitants of Samaria were of mixed Jewish and Assyrian origin (dating from the time of Shalmaneser V's deportations in the eighth century B.C.). Not being of pure Jewish stock, they regarded themselves as "strangers" among the Jews.

51. Temple prostitution was a feature of various Syrian fertility cults.

52. I.e., swine and certain other animals regarded as unclean.

53. I.e., one loyal to the Jewish religion.

54. Dionysus was the god of wine and the grape harvest.

55. Ivy was a symbol of Dionysus.

56. This Ptolemy was a former Egyptian governor of Cyprus who had deserted to Antiochus Epiphanes. He served as governor of southern Syria and Phoenicia under the Seleucids at the time of Judas Maccabeus' first campaign.

57. I.e., the Jews outside Judea.

change over to Greek customs. One could see, therefore, the
misery that had come upon them. 10 For example, two
women were brought in for having circumcised their children.
These women they publicly paraded about the city, with their
babies hung at their breasts, then hurled them down headlong
from the wall. 11 Others who had assembled in the caves
near by, to observe the seventh day secretly, were betrayed to
Philip[58] and were all burned together, because their piety kept
them from defending themselves, in view of their regard for
that most holy day.
12 Now I urge those who read this book not to be depressed
by such calamities, but to recognize that these punishments
were designed not to destroy but to discipline our people.
13 In fact, not to let the impious alone for long, but to punish
them immediately, is a sign of great kindness. 14 For in the
case of the other nations the Lord waits patiently to punish
them until they have reached the full measure of their sins;
but he does not deal in this way with us, 15 in order that
he may not take vengeance on us afterward when our sins have
reached their height. 16 Therefore he never withdraws his
mercy from us. Though he disciplines us with calamities, he
does not forsake his own people. 17 Let what we have said
serve as a reminder; we must go on briefly with the story.
18 Eleazar, one of the scribes[59] in high position, a man now
advanced in age and of noble presence, was being forced to
open his mouth to eat swine's flesh. 19 But he, welcoming
death with honor rather than life with pollution, went up to
the rack of his own accord, spitting out the flesh, 20 as men
ought to go who have the courage to refuse things that it is not
right to taste, even for the natural love of life.
21 Those who were in charge of that unlawful sacrifice took
the man aside, because of their long acquaintance with him,
and privately urged him to bring meat of his own providing,
proper for him to use, and pretend that he was eating the flesh
of the sacrificial meal which had been commanded by the king,

58. The governor of Jerusalem under Antiochus.

59. Scribes were men learned in the Mosaic law, though not necessarily priests.

22 so that by doing this he might be saved from death, and be treated kindly on account of his old friendship with them.
23 But making a high resolve, worthy of his years and the dignity of his old age and the gray hairs which he had reached with distinction and his excellent life even from childhood, and moreover according to the holy God-given law, he declared himself quickly, telling them to send him to Hades.
24 "Such pretense is not worthy of our time of life," he said, "lest many of the young should suppose that Eleazar in his
ninetieth year has gone over to an alien religion, 25 and
through my pretense, for the sake of living a brief moment longer, they should be led astray because of me, while I defile
and disgrace my old age. 26 For even if for the present I
should avoid the punishment of men, yet whether I live or die
I shall not escape the hands of the Almighty. 27 Therefore,
by manfully giving up my life now, I will show myself worthy
of my old age 28 and leave to the young a noble example
of how to die a good death willingly and nobly for the revered and holy laws."
When he had said this, he went at once to the rack. 29 And
those who a little before had acted toward him with good will now changed to ill will, because the words he had uttered were
in their opinion sheer madness. 30 When he was about to
die under the blows, he groaned aloud and said: "It is clear to the Lord in his holy knowledge that, though I might have been saved from death, I am enduring terrible sufferings in my body under this beating, but in my soul I am glad to suffer these things because I fear[60] him."
31 So in this way he died, leaving in his death an example of nobility and a memorial of courage, not only to the young but to the great body of his nation.

. . . .

Chapter 8

1 But Judas, who was also called Maccabeus, and his companions secretly entered the villages and summoned their kinsmen and enlisted those who had continued in the Jewish faith,

60. I.e., revere.

and so they gathered about six thousand men. 2 They be-
sought the Lord to look upon the people who were oppressed by
all, and to have pity on the temple which had been profaned
by ungodly men, 3 and to have mercy on the city which
was being destroyed and about to be leveled to the ground, and
to hearken to the blood that cried out to him, 4 and to re-
member also the lawless destruction of the innocent babies and
the blasphemies committed against his name, and to show his
hatred of evil.
5 As soon as Maccabeus got his army organized, the Gentiles
could not withstand him, for the wrath of the Lord had turned
to mercy.[61] 6 Coming without warning, he would set fire
to towns and villages. He captured strategic positions and put
to flight not a few of the enemy. 7 He found the nights
most advantageous for such attacks. And talk of his valor spread
everywhere.
8 When Philip[58] saw that the man was gaining ground little
by little, and that he was pushing ahead with more frequent
successes, he wrote to Ptolemy,[56] the governor of Coelesyria and
Phoenicia, for aid to the king's government. 9 And Ptolemy
promptly appointed Nicanor the son of Patroclus, one of the
king's chief friends, and sent him, in command of no fewer
than twenty thousand Gentiles of all nations, to wipe out the
whole race of Judea. He associated with him Gorgias, a general
and a man of experience in military service.[62] 10 Nicanor
determined to make up for the king the tribute due to the
Romans,[63] two thousand talents, by selling the captured Jews
into slavery.[64] 11 And he immediately sent to the cities on
the seacoast, inviting them to buy Jewish slaves and promising
to hand over ninety slaves for a talent, not expecting the judg-
ment from the Almighty that was about to overtake him.
12 Word came to Judas concerning Nicanor's invasion; and

61. Compare 5:17 above.
62. The account in I Maccabees names Gorgias, not Nicanor, as Judas' principal opponent.
63. The Seleucids had been paying tribute to Rome ever since the battle of Magnesia (189 B.C.), when Scipio Africanus defeated Antiochus III.
64. According to II Maccabees 8:34 and I Maccabees 3:41, slave traders joined Nicanor's expedition.

when he told his companions of the arrival of the army,
13 those who were cowardly and distrustful of God's justice
ran off and got away.[65] 14 Others sold all their remaining
property,[66] and at the same time besought the Lord to rescue
those who had been sold by the ungodly Nicanor before he ever
met them, 15 if not for their own sake, yet for the sake of
the covenants made with their fathers,[67] and because he had
called them by his holy and glorious name.[68] 16 But Mac-
cabeus gathered his men together, to the number of six thou-
sand, and exhorted them not to be frightened by the enemy and
not to fear the great multitude of Gentiles who were wickedly
coming against them, but to fight nobly, 17 keeping before
their eyes the lawless outrage which the Gentiles had com-
mitted against the holy place,[69] and the torture of the derided
city, and besides, the overthrow of their ancestral way of life.
18 "For they trust to arms and acts of daring," he said, "but
we trust in the Almighty God, who is able with a single nod to
strike down those who are coming against us and even the
whole world."

19 Moreover he told them of the times when help came to
their ancestors; both the time of Sennacherib, when one hun-
dred and eighty-five thousand perished,[70] 20 and the time
of the battle with the Galatians that took place in Babylonia,
when eight thousand in all went into the affair, with four
thousand Macedonians;[71] and when the Macedonians were hard
pressed, the eight thousand, by the help that came to them from
heaven, destroyed one hundred and twenty thousand and took
much booty.

65. I Maccabees 3:56 tells this differently: "And he [Judas] said to those who were building houses, or were betrothed, or were planting vineyards, or were fainthearted, that each should return to his home, according to the law."
66. In order to escape and join Judas' army.
67. The covenants which the Lord made with Moses and the patriarchs.
68. I.e., the Lord had called them His people.
69. Described above in 5:15-16.
70. As recorded in II Kings 19:35.
71. Men of Galatia (a region in central Asia Minor) often served as mercenaries. Evidently in this instance Jewish forces had aided Antiochus III and the Macedonians.

21 With these words he filled them with good courage and
made them ready to die for their laws and their country; then
he divided his army into four parts. 22 He appointed his
brothers also, Simon and Joseph[72] and Jonathan, each to com-
mand a division, putting fifteen hundred men under each.
23 Besides, he appointed Eleazar[73] to read aloud from the holy
book, and gave the watchword, "God's help"; then, leading the
first division himself, he joined battle with Nicanor.
24 With the Almighty as their ally, they slew more than
nine thousand of the enemy, and wounded and disabled most
of Nicanor's army, and forced them all to flee. 25 They
captured the money of those who had come to buy them as
slaves. After pursuing them for some distance, they were
obliged to return because the hour was late. 26 For it was
the day before the sabbath, and for that reason they did not
continue their pursuit. 27 And when they had collected
the arms of the enemy and stripped them of their spoils, they
kept the sabbath, giving great praise and thanks to the Lord,
who had preserved them for that day and allotted it to them as
the beginning of mercy. 28 After the sabbath they gave
some of the spoils to those who had been tortured and to the
widows and orphans, and distributed the rest among themselves
and their children. 29 When they had done this, they made
common supplication and besought the merciful Lord to be
wholly reconciled with his servants.
30 In encounters with the forces of Timothy and Bacchides[74]
they killed more than twenty thousand of them and got posses-
sion of some exceedingly high strongholds, and they divided
very much plunder, giving to those who had been tortured and
to the orphans and widows, and also to the aged, shares equal
to their own. 31 Collecting the arms of the enemy, they
stored them all carefully in strategic places, and carried the
rest of the spoils to Jerusalem. 32 They killed the com-
mander of Timothy's forces, a most unholy man, and one who

72. This brother is called "John" in I Maccabees 2:2 and 9:36.
73. Eleazar was another brother, whose death is recorded in I Maccabees 6:43-6.
74. Generals fighting for Antiochus.

had greatly troubled the Jews. 33 While they were cele-
brating the victory in the city of their fathers, they burned
those who had set fire to the sacred gates, Callisthenes and some
others, who had fled into one little house; so these received the
proper recompense for their impiety.
34 The thrice-accursed Nicanor, who had brought the thou-
sand merchants to buy the Jews, 35 having been humbled
with the help of the Lord by opponents whom he regarded as
of the least account, took off his splendid uniform and made
his way alone like a runaway slave across the country till he
reached Antioch, having succeeded chiefly in the destruction of
his own army! 36 Thus he who had undertaken to secure
tribute for the Romans by the capture of the people of Jeru-
salem proclaimed that the Jews had a Defender, and that
therefore the Jews were invulnerable, because they followed
the laws ordained by him.

Introduction to Philo Judaeus

Philo Judaeus (*ca.* 20 B.C.-54 A.D.) is among the best-known examples of that intermingling of Greek with Oriental ways of thought which characterized the Hellenistic age. Born into a prominent Jewish priestly family and later a student of Jewish law, he wrote far better in Greek than in Hebrew; and he made it his life's work to reconcile Greek philosophy with the Old Testament. Little is known of him otherwise, except that he was a distinguished member of the Jewish community of Alexandria, and once served as chief of a delegation sent to Rome to protest the Emperor Caligula's order for a statue of himself to be placed within the temple precincts at Jerusalem.

Alexandria in Philo's day was one of the great crossroads of the Mediterranean world. There the intellectual currents of the age met and mingled. Traders from all corners of the known earth thronged its markets; it was home to men of many nations, and of varied persuasions. Alexandria's world-famous library contained the collected learning of the ancient world; in philosophical distinction the city ranked second only to Athens. It was no wonder that the Jews of this thriving metropolis, exposed to a wide variety of traditions and doctrines, felt the necessity of bringing into harmony their ancient religion with the philosophy of the Greeks. Examined in the light of reason, the tales of the Old Testament were difficult to accept at face value, though piety forbade their absolute rejection. Philo's solution to this dilemma was to explain the holy scriptures as symbolizing esoteric truths hardly accessible to reason.

Allegorical interpretation had been practiced long before Philo by Sophists and Stoics with regard to the myths of Greece. The method rested upon the assumption that religious tradition, based upon divine revelation, could not possibly be contrary to reason. The reason of the philosophers and the assertions of the holy scriptures must be manifestations of the same divine power; tradition must be susceptible of a rational explanation. Thus Philo found no anomaly in asserting that Moses, the Hebrew patriarch of an uncultured age, had "attained the very summit of philosophy."*

Philo's interest in number-mysticism shows the influence of Pythagoras, the Greek mathematician and mystic (d. *ca* 500 B.C.). The Pythagoreans, who were well versed in astronomy, had observed that the heavenly bodies move at intervals expressible in numerical relations. It was but a short step to regard number as the ultimate, permanent essence of the universe. Numbers are eternal, not subject to change; yet through them both movement and order can be expressed. The fantastic excesses to which some of the Pythagoreans carried these ideas hardly detracts from the plausibility of the basic conception.

Philo has also been termed the first of the Neo-Platonists, i.e., one of the school which sought to harmonize the philosophy of Plato with religious belief. He adopted the Platonic concept of Ideas as permanent, other-worldly archetypes which serve as models for the things of this world. By postulating a hierarchy of Ideas—which he sometimes identified with the angels of the Old Testament—he attempted to explain how an incorporeal, eternal, indescribable God can involve himself with this imperfect world without detracting from his majesty and goodness. But Philo did not clothe the Ideas with form and personality. Rather they represent for him the thoughts or characteristics of God, sometimes his messengers and servants, by which God makes himself known to mankind.

The highest of these Ideas—the sum of all the others—is the *logos*, or the wisdom of God. This *logos*-concept did not originate

* *On the Creation,* II.

with Philo. The philosopher Heracleitus (flourished *ca.* 500 B.C.), who had stressed the eternal flux and movement of things, called the order and rhythm of events the Reason (*logos*) of the universe; the Stoics of the third and second centuries B.C. applied the term to the natural necessity, or Providence, which they believed ruled the cosmos. But the concept of the *logos* as mediator between man and God, as God's foremost messenger to mankind, is first fully developed by Philo. From him it passed into the Gospel of Saint John.

Philo's approach to scriptural problems, and especially his allegorical method, made him a valuable model for Christian thinkers of the first several centuries A.D. He is one of the principal channels by which Greek concepts passed into Christianity; his influence upon Christian thought is incalculable.

PHILO JUDAEUS: FROM THE ALLEGORICAL INTERPRETATION OF GENESIS

Book 1

I. "And the heaven and the earth and all their world were completed" (Genesis 2:1). He[1] had already told of the creation of mind and sense-perception;[2] he now fully sets forth the consummation of both. He does not say that either the individual mind or the particular sense-perception have reached completion, but that the originals[3] have done so, that of mind and that of sense-perception. For using symbolical language he calls the mind heaven, since heaven is the abode of natures discerned only by mind, but sense-perception he calls earth, because sense-perception possesses a composition of a more earthly and body-like sort. "World,"[4] in the case of mind, means all in-

From *Philo*, trans. by F. H. Colson and G. H. Whitaker, London: William Heinemann Ltd.; New York: G. P. Putnam's Sons, 1929, Loeb Classical Library Series, I, 147-9, 151-61, 167-9, 175-7, 183-7, 213-19, with omissions. Reprinted by permission of Harvard University Press.

1. Moses.
2. In his earlier treatise, *On the Creation*, Philo argued that the "heaven" of the first chapter of Genesis is a symbol of mind (*nous*), "earth" a symbol of sense-perception.
3. I.e., the Ideas, the other-worldly archetypes of which visible things are the images.
4. The Greek word *kosmos* means both "order" and "world."

corporeal things, things discerned by mind alone: in the case of sense-perception it denotes things in bodily form and generally whatever sense perceives.[5]

II. "And God finished on the sixth day His works which He had made" (Genesis 2:2). It is quite foolish to think that the world was created in six days or in a space of time at all. Why? Because every period of time is a series of days and nights, and these can only be made such by the movement of the sun as it goes over and under the earth: but the sun is a part of heaven, so that time is confessedly more recent than the world. It would therefore be correct to say that the world was not made in time, but that time was formed by means of the world, for it was heaven's movement that was the index of the nature of time. When, then, Moses says, "He finished His work on the sixth day," we must understand him to be adducing not a quantity of days, but a perfect number, namely six, since it is the first that is equal to the sum of its own fractions ½, ⅓, and ⅙, and is produced by the multiplication of two unequal factors, 2 × 3; and see, the numbers two and three have left behind the incorporeal character that belongs to one, two being an image of matter, and being parted and divided as that is, while three is the image of a solid body, for the solid is patient of a threefold division. Nay more, the number six is akin to the movements of animals provided with instrumental limbs, for the body equipped with such instruments is so constituted by nature that it can move in six directions, forwards and backwards, upwards and downwards, to the right and to the left. Moses' wish, therefore, is to exhibit alike the things created of mortal kind and those that are incorruptible as having been formed in a way corresponding to their proper numbers. As I have just said, he makes mortal things parallel with the number six, the happy and blessed things with the number seven.[6]

First of all, then, on the seventh day the Creator, having

5. Philo argued previously (*On the Creation*, II) that because corporeal things are changeable they cannot be eternal, i.e., God must have created them. But he also asserts that God created the unchangeable Ideas.

6. Elsewhere Philo argued also that, while God did not require time for his work, nonetheless "for the things coming into existence there was need of order," and "order involves number" (*On the Creation*, III).

brought to an end the formation of mortal things, begins the shaping of others more divine.

. . . .

IV. Nature takes delight in the number seven. Thus there are seven planets,[7] the counterpoise to the uniform movement of the fixed stars. It is in seven stars that the bear[8] reaches completeness, and gives rise not to commerce only but to fellowship and unity among men. The changes of the moon, again, occur by sevens:[9] this is the luminary most sympathetic to earthly matters. And such changes as Nature produces in the atmosphere, she effects mainly by the influence of figures dominated by seven.[10] Indeed, all that concerns us mortals has a divine origin drawn from heaven and is for our weal when its movement is ruled by seven. Who does not know that seven months' infants come to the birth, while those that have taken a longer time, remaining in the womb eight months, are as a rule stillborn? And they say that man becomes a reasoning being during his first seven years, by which time he is already capable of expressing ordinary nouns and verbs through having acquired the reasoning faculty; and that during his second period of seven years he reaches complete consummation; consummation meaning the power of reproducing his like; for at about the age of fourteen we are able to beget offspring like ourselves. The third period of seven years, again, is the end of growth, for till the age of twenty-one years men increase in height, and by many this time is called his prime. Furthermore the unreasoning side of the soul consists of seven parts, five senses, and the organ of speech, and the genital organ. The body again has seven movements, six mechanical,[11] the seventh circular. Seven also are the internal organs, stomach, heart, spleen, liver, lung, two kidneys. Of equal number in like number are the

7. The sun, the moon, and the five planets known in Philo's day.

8. The constellation called Little Bear (Ursa Minor) contains the pole star which serves as a guide in navigation.

9. The new moon becomes full in 2 x 7 days, and completes its cycle to become new again after another fourteen days.

10. The reference is to the planets and the Pleiades, which regulated the time of sowing and reaping, and to the Equinoxes.

11. Presumably the six directions, as above.

divisions of the body—head, neck, breast, hands, belly, abdomen, feet. And the face, the living creature's noblest part, is pierced by seven apertures, by two eyes, and two ears, as many nostrils, and the mouth, which make up seven.

[Further examples follow of the power of the number seven.]

Further, seven is the first number after the perfect number six, and the same in some sort with the number one. Whereas other numbers within the decade are either produced by or produce those within the decade and the decade itself, the number seven neither produces any of the numbers within the decade nor is produced by any. By reason of this the Pythagoreans, indulging in myth, liken seven to the motherless and ever-virgin Maiden, because neither was she born of the womb nor shall she ever bear.

VI. "He rested therefore on the seventh day from all His works which He had made" (Genesis 2:2). This is as much as to say that God ceases moulding the masses that are mortal, whenever He begins to make those that are divine and in keeping with the nature of seven. But the interpretation of the statement in accordance with its bearing on human life and character is this, that, whenever there comes upon the soul the holy Reason of which Seven is the keynote, six together with all mortal things that the soul seems to make therewith comes to a stop.

. . . .

VIII. "This book is that of the origin of heaven and earth, when it came into being" (Genesis 2:4).[12] (That is to say): "This perfect Reason,[13] moving in accord with the number seven, is the primal origin both of mind ordering itself after the original patterns, and of sense-perception in the domain of mind[14] (if the expression is permissible) ordering itself after

12. The King James Bible translates this as, "These are the generations of the heavens and of the earth." A modern translation of the Greek Bible has: "This is the story of the generation . . ."

13. *Logos* in Greek means both "reason" and "word"; thus Philo identifies "book" with "reason."

14. Sense-perception functions in the material world; strictly speaking, it does not act in the sphere of mind (intellect).

those originals." "Book" is Moses' name for the Reason of God, in which have been inscribed and engraved the formation of all else. But that you may not suppose that the Deity makes anything in definite periods of time, but may know that to mortal kind the process of creation is unobserved, undescried, incomprehensible, he adds, "When it came into being," not defining "when" by a determining limit, for the things that come into being under the hand of the First Cause come into being with no determining limit. There is an end, then, of the notion that the universe came into being in six days.

IX. "In the day in which God made the heaven and the earth and every green thing of the field before it appeared upon the earth and all grass of the field before it sprang up; for God had not sent rain on the earth, and there was no man to till the earth" (Genesis 2:4,5). Above he has called this day a book, for he delineates the creation of heaven and earth as wrought in both: for by His own supremely manifest and far-shining Reason God makes both of them, both the original of the mind, which in symbolic language he calls "heaven," and the original of sense-perception, to which by a figure he gave the name of "earth." And he compares the original of the mind and the original of sense-perception to two fields; for they bear fruit, the mind all that is done in thinking, sense-perception all that is done in perceiving. What he means is something of this sort. As before the particular and individual mind[15] there subsists a certain original as an archetype and pattern of it, and again before the particular sense-perception, a certain original of sense-perception related to the particular as a seal making impression is to the form which it makes; just so, before the individual objects of intellectual perception came into being, there was existing as a genus the "intellectually-perceptible" itself,[16] by participation[17] in which the name has been given to the

15. "Before" in the sense of "prior to" (logically, if not actually) rather than "present to," though the individual mind might also be regarded as viewing its archetype.

16. I.e., the Idea or concept of mental perception *per se*, as opposed to particular ideas.

17. This notion of "participation" is essential to the theory of Ideas. Individual things exist because they "participate" in the genus or class-concept, which is the Idea.

members of the genus; and before the individual objects of sense-perception came into existence, there was existing as a genus the "sensibly-perceptible" itself,[18] by sharing in whose being all other objects of sense have become such. "Green of the field," then, is what he terms the "intellectually-perceptible" of the mind; for as in a field the green things spring up and bloom, even so the "intellectually-perceptible" is a growth springing from the mind. Before, then, the particular "intellectually-perceptible" came into being,[19] the Creator produced the solely abstract "intellectually-perceptible," as a generic existence. This he rightly calls "all," for the particular "intellectually-perceptible," being a fragment, is not all, but the generic is so, being a full whole.

. . . .

XII. "And God formed the man by taking clay from the earth, and breathed into his face a breath of life, and the man became a living soul" (Genesis 2:7).[20] There are two types of men: the one a heavenly man, the other an earthly. The heavenly man, being made after the image of God, is altogether without part or lot in corruptible and terrestrial substance; but the earthly one was compacted out of the matter scattered here and there, which Moses calls "clay."[21] For this reason he says that the heavenly man was not moulded, but was stamped with the image of God; while the earthly is a moulded work of the Artificer, but not His offspring.[22] We must account the man made out of the earth to be mind mingling with, but not yet blended with, body.[23] But this earthlike mind is in reality also corruptible, were not God to breathe into it a power of real life;

18. The Idea of sense-perception *per se*, as opposed to the individual objects perceived.
19. The Ideas of individual things.
20. According to the King James version, man was formed out of dust, not clay.
21. Genesis 1:26-7 states that God "created man in his own image." Through this distinction between heavenly man (created in God's image) and earthly man (created from clay), Philo is able to reconcile the two Biblical texts.
22. Since God is incorporeal, a corporeal being like earthly man cannot have been formed in God's image.
23. Note that mind is regarded as corporeal.

when He does so, it does not any more undergo moulding, but becomes a soul,[24] not an inefficient and imperfectly formed soul, but one endowed with mind and actually alive; for he says, "man became a living soul."

. . . .

XIV. "And God planted a pleasaunce in Eden toward the sun-rising,[25] and placed there the man whom He had formed" (Genesis 2:8). By using many words for it Moses has already made it manifest that the sublime and heavenly wisdom is of many names;[26] for he calls it "beginning" and "image" and "vision of God"; and now by the planting of the pleasaunce he brings out the fact that earthly wisdom is a copy of this as of an archetype. Far be it from man's reasoning to be the victim of so great impiety as to suppose that God tills the soil and plants pleasaunces. We should at once be at a loss to tell from what motive He could do so. Not to provide Himself with pleasant refreshment and comfort. Let not such fables even enter our mind. For not even the whole world would be a place fit for God to make His abode, since God is His own place, and He is filled by Himself, and sufficient for Himself, filling and containing all other things in their destitution and barrenness and emptiness, but Himself contained by nothing else, seeing that He is Himself One and the Whole.

Well then, God sows and plants earthly excellence for the race of mortals as a copy and reproduction of the heavenly. For pitying our race and noting that it is compact of a rich abundance of ills, He caused earthly excellence to strike root, to bring succour and aid to the diseases of the soul. It is, as I said before, a copy of the heavenly and archetypal excellence, to which Moses gives many names. Virtue is figuratively called "pleasaunce," and the locality specially suited to the pleasaunce "Eden," which means "luxury";[27] excellence to be sure has for its fit adjuncts peace and welfare and joy, in which true luxury

24. I.e., it is no longer subject to formation; it is finished.
25. Note that the ancient Mesopotamians also placed their paradise, Dilmun, in the east.
26. Paradise is a symbol of the heavenly wisdom, or virtue. See below.
27. The word "Eden" actually means "delight."

consists. Again the planting of the pleasaunce is "towards the sun-rising," for right reason does not set nor is quenched, but its nature is ever to rise, and, I take it, just as the sun when it has risen fills the gloom of the atmosphere with light, so virtue also, when it has risen in the soul, illumines its mist and disperses its deep darkness. "And He placed there" it says, "the man whom He had formed." For God, being good and training our race to virtue as the operation most proper to it, places the mind amid virtue, evidently to the end that as a good gardener it may spend its care on nothing else but this.

. . . .

XVII. "And God caused to spring out of the ground every tree fair to behold and good for food, and the tree of life in the midst of the garden, and the tree of knowledge of good and evil" (Genesis 2:9). Moses now indicates what trees of virtue God plants in the soul. These are the several particular virtues, and the corresponding activities, and the complete moral victories, and what philosophers call common duties. These are the plants of the garden. . . .

XVIII. Now the tree of life is virtue in the most comprehensive sense, which some term goodness. From it the particular virtues derive their existence.[28] That is why it is also set in the midst of the garden, occupying the central all-embracing position, that it may, like a king, be attended by those on either side as by body-guards. But some say that it is the heart that is called the tree of life, since it is the cause of life and has been allotted the central place in the body, as it naturally would, being in their view the dominating principle. But these people should remember that they are setting forth a view worthy of the physician rather than of the philosopher, while we, as we have said, maintain that virtue in its most generic aspect is called the tree of life. Of this he expressly says that it is in the midst of the garden, but as to the other tree, that of knowing good and evil, he has not made it clear whether it is within or without the garden, but immediately after the words, "and the

28. Like Plato, Philo arranges the Ideas hierarchically, with goodness as the highest and most comprehensive virtue.

tree of the knowledge of good and evil," he comes to a stop without making it clear where it was. His silence is due to his desire to prevent the man unversed in natural philosophy from regarding with wonder the spot where that knowledge dwells. What then must we say? That this tree is both in the garden and outside it, in literal fact in it, virtually outside it. How so? Our dominant part is all-receptive and resembles wax that receives all impressions fair and ugly; accordingly the supplanter Jacob makes acknowledgement saying, "Upon me came all these things" (Genesis 42:36); for upon the soul, one as it is, the countless impressions of all things in the universe are borne. Whenever, then, it shall have received the stamp of perfect virtue, it straightway becomes the tree of life, but when it receives that of wickedness, it straightway becomes the tree of knowledge of good and evil. . . .

. . . .

XXXII. "But of the tree of the knowledge of good and evil ye shall not eat" (Genesis 2:17). Therefore this tree is not in the garden: for if He bids them to eat of every tree in the garden, but not to eat of this one, it is evident that it is not in the garden: and this is quite naturally so: for actually, as I have said, it is there, and virtually it is not.[29] For as all the impressions are virtually in the wax, but actually only the one that has been made, so in the soul, whose nature is waxlike, all the types are contained virtually, but not in actual execution, and the single one engraved in it is in possession, so long as it has not been obliterated by another seal which has made over it a clearer and bolder impression.

Next there is this further question to be raised. When He is giving the charge to eat of every tree of the garden, He addresses the command to a single person, but when He issues the prohibition against making any use of that which causes evil and good, He speaks to more than one: for in the former case He says, "Thou shalt eat from every tree"; but in the latter, "ye shall not eat, and in the day that ye eat" not "that thou

29. I.e., to all appearances, this tree is inside the garden; but its powers (to grant the knowledge of good and evil) take effect only outside.

eatest," and "ye shall die" not "thou shalt die."[30] We must accordingly remark in the first place that the good is scarce, the evil abundant. Hence it is hard to find a single wise man, while of inferior men there is a countless multitude. Quite fitly, therefore, does He bid a single man to find nourishment in the virtues, but many to abstain from evil-doing, for myriads practise this. In the second place, for the acquisition and practice of virtue a single thing only, namely our understanding, is requisite:[31] but the body not only fails to co-operate to this end, but is an actual hindrance; for we may almost make it an axiom that the business of wisdom is to become estranged from the body and its cravings:[32] but for the enjoyment of evil it is necessary not only that the mind be in a certain condition, but also the power of perception and of speech, in fact the body; for all these the inferior man requires for the full satisfaction of his particular form of wickedness. For how shall he divulge sacred and hidden truths unless he have an organ of speech?[33] And how is he to indulge in pleasures, if he be bereft of a stomach and the organs of taste? So it is in accordance with the necessities of the case that He addresses the understanding alone about gaining virtue; for, as I said, it alone is needed for its acquisition; whereas in the pursuit of evil several faculties are needed, soul, speech, senses, body, for wickedness employs all these in displaying itself.

XXXIII. And further he says, "In the day that ye eat thereof, ye shall die the death" (Genesis 2:17). And yet after they have eaten, not merely do they not die, but they beget children and become authors of life to others. What, then, is to be said to this? That death is of two kinds, one that of the man in general, the other that of the soul in particular. The death of the man is the separation of the soul from the body,[34] but the

30. This distinction between the singular and plural "you" has not been preserved in modern translations of this passage. Even the King James version has "thou" in all these cases.

31. This is the Platonic view that knowledge is virtue; the possibility of an evil will (knowing the good but doing evil) is not considered.

32. An idea also found in Plato's *Phaedo*.

33. Revealing the sacred mysteries was regarded as a particularly heinous offense.

34. Plato's definition.

death of the soul is the decay of virtue and the bringing in of wickedness. It is for this reason that God says not only "die" but "die the death," indicating not the death common to us all, but that special death properly so called, which is that of the soul becoming entombed in passions and wickedness of all kinds. And this death is practically the antithesis of the death which awaits us all. The latter is a separation of combatants that had been pitted against one another, body and soul, to wit. The former, on the other hand, is a meeting of the two in conflict. And in this conflict the worse, the body, overcomes, and the better, the soul, is overcome. But observe that wherever Moses speaks of "dying the death," he means the penalty-death, not that which takes place in the course of nature. That one is in the course of nature in which soul is parted from body; but the penalty-death takes place when the soul dies to the life of virtue, and is alive only to that of wickedness. That is an excellent saying of Heracleitus, who on this point followed Moses' teaching, "We live," he says, "their death, and are dead to their life." He means that now, when we are living, the soul is dead and has been entombed in the body as in a sepulchre; whereas, should we die, the soul lives forthwith its own proper life, and is released from the body, the baneful corpse to which it was tied.

Introduction to the Gospel of Mark

In the first half-century after the death of Jesus, his followers presumably had little reason to commit to writing the story of his life. Many of them had known him personally; the oral tradition about him must have been still vivid. More importantly, they expected the imminent end of the world, when Jesus would reappear on earth to inaugurate a new era. But as the years passed and Jesus did not return, his followers became concerned to prevent the loss of the tradition, strengthen the faith, and answer the objections of opponents. The gospel narratives which were composed in response to this need recount the incidents of Jesus' life as remembered some fifty to eighty years afterward. But these books are more than biographies: they are also theological treatises which seek to explain the deeper meaning of Jesus' life and death.

The word "gospel" means "good news"—the news being that the "Day of the Lord," when all souls would be judged and the reign of the Messiah inaugurated on earth, was now close at hand. Four gospels—the books of Matthew, Mark, Luke, and John—are included in the canonical New Testament, though others exist in the apocryphal literature. The gospel of Mark is the earliest and shortest of the four, though it cannot have been written much before A.D. 75, twenty or more years after the early letters of Paul or the Epistle of James. Unlike the latter, which were composed in response to a specific practical issue, the gospels present an account and an interpretation of the Master's entire life.

Nothing within the New Testament identifies the writer of Mark's gospel. Tradition assigns the authorship to the John Mark mentioned in the Book of Acts as belonging to the early circle of believers at Jerusalem. This John Mark is supposed to have served as Peter's interpreter when Peter, who knew no Greek, spoke to Gentile communities. Perhaps Mark actually did take notes which later became a source for the gospel called by his name, though this cannot be proven. The book is written not in literary Greek, but in a popular form of the language as spoken by ordinary people. Though containing some Semitic expressions, it is not a translation from Aramaic, the language spoken by Jesus and his Galilean disciples. The book of Mark was used extensively as a source by other gospel writers.

Scholars have long been aware that the four canonical gospels do not tell exactly the same story, and that some of the divergencies are of major significance. Traditional Christian piety, which regards the entire Bible as directly inspired by God, asserts that these differences are somehow reconcilable even if mere humans cannot discover the key to the explanation. But from a historical standpoint, the gospels are products of a particular age and milieu; and differences of fact and emphasis are attributable to the varying backgrounds, characters, and purposes of their authors.

It is indisputable that Christianity did not arise in a vacuum, but in a time and place where numerous religious faiths competed with one another. Jesus and his followers were Jews who accepted the Jewish law and tradition; there is no evidence that they intended to form a new church. Various differences are evident, however, between the usual form of Judaism practiced in Jesus' day (insofar as we can reconstruct it) and the message preached by Jesus. It is possible that Jesus and his followers belonged to a Jewish monastic sect such as the Essenes, who stressed a high moral standard and expected the imminent arrival of a divine Redeemer announcing the end of the world. Scrolls found near the Dead Sea in the late 1940's lend substance to this supposition. The Dead Sea Scrolls, which date back to Jesus' time, describe the practices of a sect showing close affinities to the teaching of Jesus. It is possible that John the Baptist was an Essene and that Jesus—who was baptized by John—was originally John's disciple.

Some of the Gnostic and mystery cults which flourished around the Mediterranean in Jesus' day worshipped divine redeemers which in many respects resemble the figure of Jesus. The exact character of these faiths is difficult to reconstruct; for the Christian Church managed to suppress most of their scriptures. But the similarities were well known to the early Christians, who felt impelled to explain them away as the work of the devil. Like Jesus, the gods Attis in Asia Minor and Osiris in Egypt symbolized death and resurrection. The Persian sun-god Mithras, who was widely worshipped throughout the Roman empire, was represented as a divine bull whose fertility symbolized the continuity of all life. These religions of redemption, like Christianity, were organized around a rite of purification (baptism) and a sacrament granting unity with the god (Eucharist). Many incidents in the traditional story of Jesus resemble those told of other gods, e.g., the immaculate conception, which was attributed to many divine figures (and even to extraordinary human beings); or the remarkable natural phenomena accompanying the birth itself. The similarities extend to minor matters as well, e.g., the Lord's Day is called Sun-day after Mithras, and December 25th is Mithras' birthday.

These redeemers of the mystery religions, however, bore little resemblance to the usual Jewish conception of the Messiah. In some of the Jewish apocalyptic books the Messiah is a superhuman figure; but for the most part he was not expected to be the son of God. The Messiah was envisioned as a man of extraordinary powers, favored by God, who would restore the Jewish kingdom on earth. To the ordinary Jew of the first century A.D., the fact that Jesus died ignominiously on a cross was proof positive that he was not the Messiah.

Mark's gospel seeks to reconcile the two concepts of the Messiah. Wherever possible, it relates the life of Jesus to Old Testament prophecies concerning the Messiah or the Son of Man. It justifies the suffering and death of Jesus by asserting that they were accepted voluntarily. Crucifixion and death were necessary to Jesus' mission, which was to redeem the world from its sins; his death was followed by a triumphant resurrection. Similarly, those who believed in him might suffer in this life, but would attain happiness in the life hereafter.

The fact must have been well known that Jesus' own disciples did not recognize him as the Messiah during his lifetime. Some believers evidently thought that his Messiahship had begun only at the resurrection (as asserted, for instance, by the apocryphal *Apocalypse of Peter*). But Mark's gospel regards the Messiahship as having begun at the baptism. Jesus' disciples did not know his identity because Jesus deliberately kept it a secret, speaking in parables so that his hearers would not comprehend.

The gospel of Mark omits certain stories which have since become an inseparable part of the Christian tradition. Most notably, it begins with John the Baptist and makes no mention of the birth and childhood of Jesus. Also absent are the elaborate genealogies showing the direct descent of Jesus from King David, the temptation by Satan in the wilderness, and the appearances of Jesus after death to his disciples. The author of Mark's gospel was evidently much concerned with the conflict between those who asserted that faith in Jesus was sufficient for salvation and those who insisted on strict observance of Jewish law, for he records numerous instances of Jesus' replies to the Pharisees. The first eight chapters of the book consist very largely of accounts of Jesus' miracles—acts probably considered necessary to prove his divinity. But Mark's story is more straightforward than that of the other gospels, and shows less evidence of theological interpretation. Historically it is especially valuable as the gospel closest in time to the actual life of Jesus.

FROM THE GOSPEL OF MARK

Chapter 1

1 The beginning[1] of the gospel of Jesus Christ, the Son of
God; 2 As it is written in the prophets,

Mark 1:1-28, 6:1-16; 7:5-23; 8:27–9:13; 10:13-27; 12:13-31; 13:1–14:28, 32-64; 15:1-15, 27-38; 16:1-20. King James Bible.

1. "Beginning": compare Genesis 1:1; John 1:1.

Behold, I send my messenger before thy face, which shall
prepare thy way before thee.
3 The voice of one crying in the wilderness,
Prepare ye the way of the Lord,
Make his paths straight.[2]

4 John did baptize in the wilderness, and preach the baptism
of repentance for the remission of sins. 5 And there went
out unto him all the land of Judea,[3] and they of Jerusalem, and
were all baptized of him in the river of Jordan, confessing their
sins.[4] 6 And John was clothed with camel's hair, and with
a girdle of a skin about his loins; and he did eat locusts and
wild honey;[5] 7 And preached, saying, There cometh one
mightier than I after me, the latchet of whose shoes I am not
worthy to stoop down and unloose. 8 I indeed have bap-
tized you with water: but he shall baptize you with the Holy
Ghost.[6]
9 And it came to pass in those days, that Jesus came from
Nazareth[7] of Galilee,[8] and was baptized of John in Jordan.[9]

2. This quotation is a combination of two Old Testament verses, Malachi 3:1: "Behold, I will send my messenger, and he shall prepare the way before me . . ." and Isaiah 40:3: "The voice of him that crieth in the wilderness, Prepare ye the way of the Lord, make straight in the desert a highway for our God."

3. The southernmost division of Roman Palestine.

4. The rite of baptism had long been required of Gentiles who became converted to Judaism. The baptism performed by John, however, was evidently a preparation for the coming of the Messiah.

5. This description of John matches that of the Old Testament prophet Elijah in II Kings 1:8: "He was an hairy man, and girt with a girdle of leather about his loins." Elijah, who lived in the ninth century B.C., was known for his exhortations to the Hebrews to extirpate heathen worship and maintain a higher ethical standard. In the New Testament he appears as the herald of the Messiah in accordance with the prophecy of Malachi 4:3: "Behold, I will send you Elijah the prophet before the coming of the great and dreadful day of the Lord."

6. Or "Holy Spirit."

7. Recent scholarship seriously questions whether a place called Nazareth ever existed. It is nowhere mentioned in the Old Testament, in the Jewish Talmud, or by the historian Josephus in his detailed account of the Jewish revolt against Rome in A.D. 67-70. The word probably means "Nazorean" or "Nazarene." The evidence of the Dead Sea Scrolls suggests that a Jewish sect of that name existed in Palestine before Jesus' time. Paul in his appearance

10 And straightway coming up out of the water, he saw the
heavens opened, and the Spirit like a dove[10] descending upon
him: 11 And there came a voice from heaven, saying,

Thou art my beloved Son,
In whom I am well pleased.

12 And immediately the Spirit driveth him into the wilder-
ness. 13 And he was there in the wilderness forty days
tempted of Satan;[11] and was with the wild beasts; and the
angels ministered unto him.

14 Now after that John was put in prison, Jesus came into
Galilee, preaching the gospel of the kingdom of God, 15 And
saying, The time is fulfilled, and the kingdom of God is at
hand: repent ye, and believe the gospel. 16 Now as he
walked by the sea of Galilee, he saw Simon and Andrew his
brother casting a net into the sea: for they were fishers.
17 And Jesus said unto them, Come ye after me, and I will
make you to become fishers of men. 18 And straightway
they forsook their nets, and followed him. 19 And when he
had gone a little further thence, he saw James the son of Zebe-
dee, and John his brother, who also were in the ship mending
their nets. 20 And straightway he called them: and they
left their father Zebedee in the ship with the hired servants,
and went after him.

21 And they went into Capernaum;[12] and straightway on
the sabbath day he entered into the synagogue, and taught.

---

before the Roman governor is accused of being "a ringleader of the sect of the Nazarenes" (Acts 24:5).

8. Inland region of northern Palestine.

9. The sources diverge as to whether Jesus was actually baptized by John (which might be taken to mean that he was John's disciple). In the period when the gospels were written, the followers of Jesus were engaged in polemics with certain sects which honored John the Baptist and insisted that the Messiah preached by John had not yet appeared. According to the gospel of Matthew, when Jesus came to John to be baptized John answered, "I have need to be baptized of thee, and comest thou to me?" and Jesus replied, "Suffer it to be so now" (Matthew 3:14-15). Luke's gospel fails to state by whom Jesus was baptized.

10. The dove (or pigeon) is a symbol of innocence and harmlessness.

11. The word in Hebrew means "adversary," i.e., of God.

12. A town on the northern shore of the Sea of Galilee (Lake Tiberias).

22 And they were astonished at his doctrine: for he taught
them as one that had authority, and not as the scribes.[13]
23 And there was in their synagogue a man with an unclean
spirit;[14] and he cried out, 24 Saying, Let us alone; what
have we to do with thee, thou Jesus of Nazareth? art thou come
to destroy us? I know thee who thou art, the Holy One of God.
25 And Jesus rebuked him, saying, Hold thy peace, and come
out of him. 26 And when the unclean spirit had torn him,
and cried with a loud voice, he came out of him. 27 And
they were all amazed, insomuch that they questioned among
themselves, saying, What thing is this? what new doctrine is
this? for with authority commandeth he even the unclean
spirits, and they do obey him. 28 And immediately his
fame spread abroad throughout all the region round about
Galilee.

. . . .

Chapter 6

1 And he went out from thence, and came into his own coun-
try; and his disciples follow him. 2 And when the sabbath
day was come, he began to teach in the synagogue: and many
hearing him were astonished, saying, From whence hath this
man these things? and what wisdom is this which is given unto
him, that even such mighty works are wrought by his hands? 3
Is not this the carpenter, the son of Mary, the brother of James,
and Joses, and of Juda, and Simon? and are not his sisters here
with us? And they were offended at him. 4 But Jesus said
unto them, A prophet is not without honor, but in his own
country, and among his own kin, and in his own house. 5 And
he could there do no mighty work, save that he laid his hands
upon a few sick folk, and healed them. 6 And he marveled
because of their unbelief.

And he went round about the villages, teaching. 7 And he
called unto him the twelve, and began to send them forth by

13. The scribes were legal experts responsible for interpreting and applying the Jewish law.

14. Demons exerting evil influences were believed to be the cause of various mental aberrations.

two and two; and gave them power over unclean spirits;
8 And commanded them that they should take nothing for their
journey, save a staff only; no scrip,[15] no bread, no money in their
purse; 9 But be shod with sandals; and not put on two
coats. 10 And he said unto them, In what place soever ye
enter into a house, there abide till ye depart from that place.
11 And whosoever shall not receive you, nor hear you, when
ye depart thence, shake off the dust under your feet for a testi-
mony against them. Verily I say unto you, It shall be more
tolerable for Sodom and Gomorrah[16] in the day of judgment,
than for that city. 12 And they went out, and preached
that men should repent. 13 And they cast out many devils,
and anointed with oil many that were sick, and healed them.
14 And king Herod[17] heard of him; (for his name was spread
abroad;) and he said, That John the Baptist was risen from the
dead, and therefore mighty works do show forth themselves in
him. 15 Others said, That it is Elias.[18] And others said,
That it is a prophet, or as one of the prophets. 16 But when
Herod heard thereof, he said, It is John, whom I beheaded: he
is risen from the dead.[19]

. . . .

Chapter 7

5 Then the Pharisees[20] and scribes asked him, Why walk not
thy disciples according to the tradition of the elders, but eat
bread with unwashen hands? 6 He answered and said unto
them, Well hath Esaias[21] prophesied of you hypocrites, as it is
written,

15. Provision bag.

16. Cities south of the Dead Sea which, according to Genesis 19:24, God destroyed for their sins by sending a rain of fire and brimstone from heaven.

17. Herod I (called "the Great"), who ruled Judea as a Roman client-state from 37 to 4 B.C.

18. New Testament form of "Elijah" (see note 5 above).

19. According to both the historian Josephus (*Antiquities* XVIII, 5, 4) and the gospel of Mark (6:17-28), Herod beheaded John the Baptist at the request of his niece Salome, whose dancing had pleased him.

20. The Pharisees were a group of Jewish laymen who upheld religious puritanism, stressed conformity to ceremonial rules, and opposed secular trends.

21. New Testament form of "Isaiah."

This people honoreth me with their lips,
But their heart is far from me.
7 Howbeit in vain do they worship me, teaching for doctrines
the commandments of men.[22]

8 For laying aside the commandment of God, ye hold the tra-
dition of men, as the washing of pots and cups: and many other
such like things ye do. 9 And he said unto them, Full well
ye reject the commandment of God, that ye may keep your own
tradition. 10 For Moses said, Honor thy father and thy
mother; and, Whoso curseth father or mother, let him die the
death: 11 But ye say, If a man shall say to his father or
mother, It is Corban,[23] that is to say, a gift, by whatsoever thou
mightest be profited by me; he shall be free. 12 And ye
suffer him no more to do aught for his father or his mother;
13 Making the word of God of none effect through your tra-
dition, which ye have delivered: and many such like things do
ye.[24]
14 And when he had called all the people unto him, he said
unto them, Hearken unto me every one of you, and understand:
15 There is nothing from without a man, that entering into
him can defile him: but the things which come out of him, those
are they that defile the man. 16 If any man have ears to
hear, let him hear. 17 And when he was entered into the
house from the people, his disciples asked him concerning the
parable. 18 And he saith unto them, Are ye so without un-
derstanding also? Do ye not perceive, that whatsoever thing
from without entereth into the man, it cannot defile him;
19 Because it entereth not into his heart, but into the belly,
and goeth out into the draught, purging all meats? 20 And
he said, That which cometh out of the man, that defileth the
man. 21 For from within, out of the heart of men, proceed
evil thoughts, adulteries, fornications, murders, 22 Thefts,
covetousness, wickedness, deceit, lasciviousness, an evil eye,

22. These lines paraphrase Isaiah 29:13.
23. Hebrew technical term for "sacrifice" or "offering."
24. Although the Law enjoined honoring one's parents, tradition permitted a man to declare his property a gift to God and thereby keep it for himself.

blasphemy, pride, foolishness: 23 All these evil things come
from within, and defile the man.

. . . .

Chapter 8

27 And Jesus went out, and his disciples, into the towns of
Cæsarea Philippi:[25] and by the way he asked his disciples, say-
ing unto them, Whom do men say that I am? 28 And they
answered, John the Baptist: but some say, Elias; and others,
One of the prophets. 29 And he saith unto them, But whom
say ye that I am? And Peter answereth and saith unto him,
Thou art the Christ.[26] 30 And he charged them that they
should tell no man of him.
31 And he began to teach them, that the Son of man[27] must
suffer many things, and be rejected of the elders, and of the
chief priests, and scribes, and be killed, and after three days rise
again. 32 And he spake that saying openly. And Peter took
him, and began to rebuke him. 33 But when he had turned
about and looked on his disciples, he rebuked Peter, saying, Get
thee behind me, Satan: for thou savorest not the things that be
of God, but the things that be of men. 34 And when he had
called the people unto him with his disciples also, he said unto
them, Whosoever will come after me, let him deny himself,
and take up his cross, and follow me. 35 For whosoever will
save his life shall lose it; but whosoever shall lose his life for my
sake and the gospel's, the same shall save it. 36 For what
shall it profit a man, if he shall gain the whole world, and lose
his own soul? 37 Or what shall a man give in exchange for
his soul? 38 Whosoever therefore shall be ashamed of me
and of my words, in this adulterous and sinful generation, of

25. Caesarea Philippi (not to be confused with Caesarea, the capital of Roman Palestine) was a Gentile city north of the Sea of Galilee built by Herod I's son Philip while tetrarch (governor) of the region (4 B.C.-A.D. 34).

26. The word "Christ" in Greek and "Messiah" in Hebrew both mean "the anointed one." Kings in Israel were always anointed.

27. The term "Son of Man" has a dual meaning in the Bible. In the Old Testament it is usually a poetic expression for "man," though in certain Jewish apocalyptic books it refers to a superhuman being who will appear at the end of the world as ruler of the kingdom of God. Jesus uses the term in the latter sense.

him also shall the Son of man be ashamed, when he cometh in the glory of his Father with the holy angels.

Chapter 9

1 And he said unto them, Verily I say unto you, That there be some of them that stand here, which shall not taste of death, till they have seen the kingdom of God come with power.
2 And after six days Jesus taketh with him Peter, and James,
and John, and leadeth them up into a high mountain apart by
themselves: and he was transfigured[28] before them. 3 And
his raiment became shining, exceeding white as snow; so as no
fuller on earth can white them. 4 And there appeared unto
them Elias with Moses:[29] and they were talking with Jesus.
5 And Peter answered and said to Jesus, Master, it is good for
us to be here: and let us make three tabernacles,[30] one for thee,
and one for Moses, and one for Elias. 6 For he wist not
what to say; for they were sore afraid. 7 And there was a
cloud that overshadowed them: and a voice came out of the
cloud, saying, This is my beloved Son: hear him. 8 And
suddenly, when they had looked round about, they saw no man
any more, save Jesus only with themselves. 9 And as they
came down from the mountain, he charged them that they
should tell no man what things they had seen, till the Son of
man were risen from the dead. 10 And they kept that say-
ing with themselves, questioning one with another what the
rising from the dead should mean. 11 And they asked him,
saying, Why say the scribes that Elias must first come?
12 And he answered and told them, Elias verily cometh first,
and restoreth all things; and how it is written of the Son of
man, that he must suffer many things, and be set at nought.
13 But I say unto you, That Elias is indeed come, and they
have done unto him whatsoever they listed, as it is written of
him.

. . . .

28. I.e., transformed.
29. Symbolizing prophecy and the law.
30. The tabernacle (or tent) covered the ark and other sacred objects of the Hebrews in their nomadic days.

Chapter 10

13 And they brought young children to him, that he should
touch them; and his disciples rebuked those that brought them.
14 But when Jesus saw it, he was much displeased, and said
unto them, Suffer the little children to come unto me, and forbid
them not; for of such is the kingdom of God. 15 Verily I
say unto you, Whosoever shall not receive the kingdom of God
as a little child,[31] he shall not enter therein. 16 And he took
them up in his arms, put his hands upon them, and blessed
them.
17 And when he was gone forth into the way, there came one
running, and kneeled to him, and asked him, Good Master,
what shall I do that I may inherit eternal life? 18 And
Jesus said unto him, Why callest thou me good? there is none
good but one, that is, God. 19 Thou knowest the command-
ments, Do not commit adultery, Do not kill, Do not steal, Do not
bear false witness, Defraud not, Honor thy father and mother.
20 And he answered and said unto him, Master, all these have
I observed from my youth. 21 Then Jesus beholding him
loved him, and said unto him, One thing thou lackest: go thy
way, sell whatsoever thou hast, and give to the poor, and thou
shalt have treasure in heaven: and come, take up the cross, and
follow me. 22 And he was sad at that saying, and went
away grieved: for he had great possessions. 23 And Jesus
looked round about, and saith unto his disciples, How hardly
shall they that have riches enter into the kingdom of God!
24 And the disciples were astonished at his words. But Jesus
answereth again, and saith unto them, Children, how hard is it
for them that trust in riches to enter into the kingdom of God!
25 It is easier for a camel to go through the eye of a needle,
than for a rich man to enter into the kingdom of God.
26 And they were astonished out of measure, saying among
themselves, Who then can be saved? 27 And Jesus looking
upon them saith, With men it is impossible, but not with God:
for with God all things are possible.

. . . .

31. I.e., with the innocence and trust of a child.

Chapter 12

13 And they send unto him certain of the Pharisees and of the
Herodians,[32] to catch him in his words. 14 And when they
were come, they say unto him, Master, we know that thou art
true, and carest for no man; for thou regardest not the person
of men, but teachest the way of God in truth: Is it lawful to
give tribute to Cæsar,[33] or not? 15 Shall we give, or shall
we not give? But he, knowing their hypocrisy, said unto them,
Why tempt ye me?[34] bring me a penny, that I may see it.
16 And they brought it. And he saith unto them, Whose is
this image and superscription? And they said unto him,
Cæsar's. 17 And Jesus answering said unto them, Render to
Cæsar the things that are Cæsar's, and to God the things that
are God's. And they marveled at him.
18 Then come unto him the Sadducees,[35] which say there is
no resurrection; and they asked him, saying, 19 Master,
Moses wrote unto us, If a man's brother die, and leave his wife
behind him, and leave no children, that his brother should take
his wife, and raise up seed unto his brother.[36] 20 Now there
were seven brethren: and the first took a wife, and dying left no
seed. 21 And the second took her, and died, neither left he
any seed: and the third likewise. 22 And the seven had her,
and left no seed: last of all the woman died also. 23 In the
resurrection therefore, when they shall rise, whose wife shall
she be of them? for the seven had her to wife.[37] 24 And
Jesus answering said unto them, Do ye not therefore err, be-
cause ye know not the Scriptures, neither the power of God?
25 For when they shall rise from the dead, they neither
marry, nor are given in marriage; but are as the angels which

32. The political party among the Jews which supported the dynasty of Herod.
33. I.e., to the Roman government.
34. This was a trap: if Jesus should advise against paying tribute, he could be executed as a rebel against Rome.
35. The party of the priests, who represented the conservative tendencies in the nation.
36. In Deuteronomy 25:5.
37. By this example the Sadducees demonstrated their belief that the idea of resurrection was absurd.

are in heaven. 26 And as touching the dead, that they rise;
have ye not read in the book of Moses, how in the bush God
spake unto him, saying, I am the God of Abraham, and the God
of Isaac, and the God of Jacob?[38] 27 He is not the God of
the dead, but the God of the living: ye therefore do greatly err.[39]
28 And one of the scribes came, and having heard them rea-
soning together, and perceiving that he had answered them
well, asked him, Which is the first commandment of all?[40]
29 And Jesus answered him, The first of all the command-
ments is, Hear, O Israel; The Lord our God is one Lord:
30 And thou shalt love the Lord thy God with all thy heart,
and with all thy soul, and with all thy mind, and with all thy
strength: this is the first commandment.[41] 31 And the sec-
ond is like, namely this, Thou shalt love thy neighbor as thy-
self.[42] There is none other commandment greater than these.

. . . .

Chapter 13

13 And as he went out of the temple, one of his disciples saith
unto him, Master, see what manner of stones and what build-
ings are here! 2 And Jesus answering said unto him, Seest
thou these great buildings? there shall not be left one stone upon
another, that shall not be thrown down.[43] 3 And as he sat
upon the mount of Olives,[44] over against the temple, Peter and
James and John and Andrew asked him privately, 4 Tell
us, when shall these things be? and what shall be the sign when
all these things shall be fulfilled? 5 And Jesus answering
them began to say, Take heed lest any man deceive you:

38. In Exodus 3:6.
39. Jesus interprets Exodus 3:6 to mean that the patriarchs were alive long after their (bodily) death on earth.
40. The Jewish law was supposed to consist of more than six hundred commandments. The rabbis liked to discuss which one of them was the greatest.
41. Deuteronomy 6:4-5.
42. Leviticus 19:18.
43. Some authorities regard this passage as predicting the Jewish revolt against Rome of A.D. 67-70, in which the Temple was destroyed. More probably it refers to the end of the world.
44. The heights east of Jerusalem.

6 For many shall come in my name, saying, I am Christ,[45]
and shall deceive many. 7 And when ye shall hear of wars
and rumors of wars, be ye not troubled: for such things must
needs be; but the end shall not be yet. 8 For nation shall
rise against nation, and kingdom against kingdom: and there
shall be earthquakes in divers places, and there shall be famines
and troubles: these are the beginnings of sorrows.
9 But take heed to yourselves: for they shall deliver you up
to councils; and in the synagogues ye shall be beaten: and ye
shall be brought before rulers and kings for my sake, for a tes-
timony against them. 10 And the gospel must first be pub-
lished among all nations. 11 But when they shall lead you,
and deliver you up, take no thought beforehand what ye shall
speak, neither do ye premeditate: but whatsoever shall be given
you in that hour, that speak ye: for it is not ye that speak, but
the Holy Ghost. 12 Now the brother shall betray the
brother to death, and the father the son; and children shall rise
up against their parents, and shall cause them to be put to
death. 13 And ye shall be hated of all men for my name's
sake: but he that shall endure unto the end, the same shall be
saved.
14 But when ye shall see the abomination of desolation,
spoken of by Daniel the prophet,[46] standing where it ought not,
(let him that readeth understand,) then let them that be in
Judea flee to the mountains: 15 And let him that is on the
housetop not go down into the house, neither enter therein, to
take any thing out of his house: 16 And let him that is in
the field not turn back again for to take up his garment.
17 But woe to them that are with child, and to them that give
suck in those days! 18 And pray ye that your flight be not
in the winter. 19 For in those days shall be affliction, such
as was not from the beginning of the creation which God
created unto this time, neither shall be. 20 And except that

45. Undoubtedly there were men both before and after Jesus' day who claimed to be the Messiah. In II Corinthians 11:4 Paul complains of competition from apostles who preach "another Jesus."

46. "Abomination of desolation" may refer, as in Daniel 9:27 and 12:11, to the desecration of the Temple by a pagan foe.

the Lord had shortened those days, no flesh should be saved: but
for the elect's[47] sake, whom he hath chosen, he hath shortened
the days. 21 And then if any man shall say to you, Lo, here
is Christ; or, lo, he is there; believe him not: 22 For false
Christs and false prophets shall rise, and shall show signs
and wonders, to seduce, if it were possible, even the elect.
23 But take ye heed: behold, I have foretold you all things.
24 But in those days, after that tribulation, the sun shall be
darkened, and the moon shall not give her light, 25 And
the stars of heaven shall fall, and the powers that are in heaven
shall be shaken. 26 And then shall they see the Son of man
coming in the clouds with great power and glory.[48] 27 And
then shall he send his angels, and shall gather together his elect
from the four winds, from the uttermost part of the earth to the
uttermost part of heaven. 28 Now learn a parable of the fig
tree: When her branch is yet tender, and putteth forth leaves,
ye know that summer is near: 29 So ye in like manner,
when ye shall see these things come to pass, know that it is
nigh, even at the doors. 30 Verily I say unto you, that this
generation shall not pass, till all these things be done.
31 Heaven and earth shall pass away: but my words shall not
pass away.

32 But of that day and that hour knoweth no man, no, not the
angels which are in heaven, neither the Son, but the Father.
33 Take ye heed, watch and pray: for ye know not when the
time is. 34 For the Son of man is as a man taking a far
journey, who left his house, and gave authority to his servants,
and to every man his work, and commanded the porter to watch.
35 Watch ye therefore: for ye know not when the master of

47. This use of the term "elect" is one of a number of similarities between the early believers in Jesus and the sect of Essenes (or Nazoreans—the terms may have been interchangeable) which produced the Dead Sea Scrolls. Gnostic sects also were frequently divided into an elect—those who observed the rules of the faith more strictly than others and were considered particularly holy—and the ordinary laity.

48. Jesus' vision of the end of the world is similar to the dream of Daniel (in Daniel 7:13-14): "I saw in the night visions, and, behold, one like the Son of Man came with the clouds of heaven . . . And there was given him dominion, and glory, and a kingdom, that all people, nations, and languages should serve him. . . ."

the house cometh, at even, or at midnight, or at the cockcrow-
ing, or in the morning: 36 Lest coming suddenly he find
you sleeping. 37 And what I say unto you I say unto all,
Watch.

Chapter 14

1 After two days was the feast of the passover,[49] and of un-
leavened bread: and the chief priests and the scribes sought how
they might take him by craft, and put him to death. 2 But
they said, Not on the feast day, lest there be an uproar of the
people. 3 And being in Bethany,[50] in the house of Simon
the leper, as he sat at meat, there came a woman having an
alabaster box of ointment of spikenard[51] very precious; and she
brake the box, and poured it on his head. 4 And there were
some that had indignation within themselves, and said, Why
was this waste of the ointment made? 5 For it might have
been sold for more than three hundred pence, and have been
given to the poor. And they murmured against her. 6 And
Jesus said, Let her alone; why trouble ye her? she hath wrought
a good work on me. 7 For ye have the poor with you al-
ways, and whensoever ye will ye may do them good: but me ye
have not always. 8 She hath done what she could: she is
come aforehand to anoint my body to the burying. 9 Verily
I say unto you, Wheresoever this gospel shall be preached
throughout the whole world, this also that she hath done shall
be spoken of for a memorial of her.
10 And Judas Iscariot, one of the twelve, went unto the chief
priests, to betray him unto them. 11 And when they heard
it, they were glad, and promised to give him money. And he
sought how he might conveniently betray him.
12 And the first day of unleavened bread, when they killed the
passover,[52] his disciples said unto him, Where wilt thou that we

49. I.e., two days later. The feast of the Passover commemorated the escape of the Jews from Egypt under Moses' leadership.

50. A village a mile and a half from Jerusalem.

51. Spikenard was an Indian plant, the oil of which was made into a valuable perfume.

52. Killing the passover lamb marked the beginning of a seven-day period during which the Jews ate only unleavened bread in memory of the fact that their ancestors were unable to bake bread while in flight out of Egypt.

go and prepare that thou mayest eat the passover? 13 And
he sendeth forth two of his disciples, and saith unto them, Go ye
into the city, and there shall meet you a man bearing a pitcher
of water: follow him. 14 And wheresoever he shall go in,
say ye to the goodman of the house, The Master saith, Where is
the guest chamber, where I shall eat the passover with my dis-
ciples? 15 And he will show you a large upper room fur-
nished and prepared: there make ready for us. 16 And his
disciples went forth, and came into the city, and found as he had
said unto them: and they made ready the passover. 17 And
in the evening he cometh with the twelve. 18 And as they
sat and did eat, Jesus said, Verily I say unto you, One of you
which eateth with me shall betray me. 19 And they began
to be sorrowful, and to say unto him one by one, Is it I? and
another said, Is it I? 20 And he answered and said unto
them, It is one of the twelve, that dippeth with me in the dish.
21 The Son of man indeed goeth, as it is written of him:[53] but
woe to that man by whom the Son of man is betrayed! good
were it for that man if he had never been born.

22 And as they did eat, Jesus took bread, and blessed, and
brake it, and gave to them, and said, Take, eat; this is my body.
23 And he took the cup, and when he had given thanks, he
gave it to them: and they all drank of it. 24 And he said
unto them, This is my blood of the new testament, which is shed
for many. 25 Verily I say unto you, I will drink no more
of the fruit of the vine, until that day that I drink it new in the
kingdom of God.

26 And when they had sung a hymn, they went out into the
mount of Olives. 27 And Jesus saith unto them, All ye shall
be offended because of me this night: for it is written, I will
smite the shepherd, and the sheep shall be scattered. 28 But
after that I am risen, I will go before you into Galilee. . . .

32 And they came to a place which was named Gethsemane:[54]

53. Nowhere does the Old Testament state that the Son of Man must suffer and die. Perhaps Jesus was thinking of the suffering servant described in Isaiah, chapter 53, as "a man of sorrows . . . wounded for our transgressions . . . brought as a lamb to the slaughter."

54. On the western side of the Mount of Olives.

and he saith to his disciples, Sit ye here, while I shall pray.
33 And he taketh with him Peter and James and John, and
began to be sore amazed, and to be very heavy,[55] 34 And
saith unto them, My soul is exceeding sorrowful unto death:
tarry ye here, and watch. 35 And he went forward a little,
and fell on the ground, and prayed that, if it were possible, the
hour might pass from him. 36 And he said, Abba,[56] Father,
all things are possible unto thee; take away this cup from me:
nevertheless, not what I will, but what thou wilt. 37 And
he cometh, and findeth them sleeping, and saith unto Peter,
Simon,[57] sleepest thou? couldest not thou watch one hour?
38 Watch ye and pray, lest ye enter into temptation. The
spirit truly is ready, but the flesh is weak. 39 And again he
went away, and prayed, and spake the same words. 40 And
when he returned, he found them asleep again, (for their eyes
were heavy,) neither wist they what to answer him. 41 And
he cometh the third time, and saith unto them, Sleep on now,
and take your rest: it is enough, the hour is come; behold, the
Son of man is betrayed into the hands of sinners. 42 Rise
up, let us go; lo, he that betrayeth me is at hand.
43 And immediately, while he yet spake, cometh Judas, one
of the twelve, and with him a great multitude with swords and
staves, from the chief priests and the scribes and the elders.
44 And he that betrayed him had given them a token, saying,
Whomsoever I shall kiss, that same is he; take him, and lead
him away safely. 45 And as soon as he was come, he goeth
straightway to him, and saith, Master, Master; and kissed him.
46 And they laid their hands on him, and took him. 47 And
one of them that stood by drew a sword, and smote a servant of
the high priest, and cut off his ear. 48 And Jesus answered
and said unto them, Are ye come out, as against a thief, with
swords and with staves to take me? 49 I was daily with you
in the temple teaching, and ye took me not: but the Scriptures
must be fulfilled. 50 And they all forsook him, and fled.

55. I.e., disturbed, distressed.
56. Aramaic word for "father."
57. Simon was Peter's given name. According to John 1:42, Jesus called him Peter, which means "rock."

51 And there followed him a certain young man, having a
linen cloth cast about his naked body; and the young men laid
hold on him: 52 And he left the linen cloth, and fled from
them naked.
53. And they led Jesus away to the high priest: and with him
were assembled all the chief priests and the elders and the
scribes.[58] 54 And Peter followed him afar off, even into the
palace of the high priest: and he sat with the servants, and
warmed himself at the fire. 55 And the chief priests and all
the council sought for witness against Jesus to put him to death;
and found none. 56 For many bare false witness against
him, but their witness agreed not together. 57 And there
arose certain, and bare false witness against him, saying,
58 We heard him say, I will destroy this temple that is made
with hands, and within three days I will build another made
without hands. 59 But neither so did their witness agree
together. 60 And the high priest stood up in the midst, and
asked Jesus, saying, Answerest thou nothing? what is it which
these witness against thee? 61 But he held his peace, and
answered nothing. Again the high priest asked him, and said
unto him, Art thou the Christ, the Son of the Blessed?[59]
62 And Jesus said, I am: and ye shall see the Son of man
sitting on the right hand of power,[59] and coming in the clouds
of heaven. 63 Then the high priest rent his clothes, and
saith, What need we any further witness? 64 Ye have
heard the blasphemy: what think ye?[60] And they all condemned
him to be guilty of death.[61]

. . . .

58. This group was the Sanhedrin—the council which claimed authority over all Jews. Rome recognized its jurisdiction only for violations of the Jewish religious law by Jews. The Sanhedrin could pass the death sentence, but only Romans could carry it out.

59. "The Blessed," "power," are titles used to avoid pronouncing the name of God.

60. I.e., Jesus has convicted himself out of his own mouth by claiming (blasphemously) to be the Messiah.

61. According to Jewish law, the penalty for blasphemy was stoning (Leviticus 24:16; Acts 6:13, 7:59).

Chapter 15

1 And straightway in the morning the chief priests held a
consultation with the elders and scribes and the whole council,[62]
and bound Jesus, and carried him away, and delivered him to
Pilate.[63] 2 And Pilate asked him, Art thou the King of the
Jews?[64] And he answering said unto him, Thou sayest it.
3 And the chief priests accused him of many things; but he
answered nothing. 4 And Pilate asked him again, saying,
Answerest thou nothing? behold how many things they witness
against thee. 5 But Jesus yet answered nothing; so that
Pilate marveled. 6 Now at that feast he released unto them
one prisoner, whomsoever they desired. 7 And there was
one named Barabbas, which lay bound with them that had
made insurrection with him, who had committed murder in the
insurrection. 8 And the multitude crying aloud began to
desire him to do as he had ever done unto them.[65] 9 But
Pilate answered them, saying, Will ye that I release unto you
the King of the Jews? 10 For he knew that the chief priests
had delivered him for envy. 11 But the chief priests moved
the people, that he should rather release Barabbas unto them.[66]
12 And Pilate answered and said again unto them, What
will ye then that I shall do unto him whom ye call the King
of the Jews? 13 And they cried out again, Crucify him.
14 Then Pilate said unto them, Why, what evil hath he done?
And they cried out the more exceedingly, Crucify him.
15 And so Pilate, willing to content the people, released Barabbas unto them, and delivered Jesus, when he had scourged
him, to be crucified.[67] . . .
. . . 27 And with him they crucify two thieves; the one on
his right hand, and the other on his left. 28 And the Scrip-

62. The Sanhedrin could not decide a capital case at night.
63. Pontius Pilate was the Roman procurator (governor) of Judea, A.D. 26-36. Jesus could not be executed without his order.
64. Whereas the Messiah was a religious figure, the claim to be "king" of the Jews would constitute a political offence, an act of rebellion against Rome.
65. It was usual to release one prisoner at the time of the passover.
66. Barabbas, the insurrectionist, was probably popular with those Jews who hated Roman authority.
67. According to Acts 5:30 and 10:39, Jesus was "hanged on a tree."

ture was fulfilled, which saith, And he was numbered with the
transgressors.[68] 29 And they that passed by railed on him,
wagging their heads, and saying, Ah, thou that destroyest the
temple, and buildest it in three days, 30 Save thyself, and
come down from the cross. 31 Likewise also the chief priests
mocking said among themselves with the scribes, He saved
others; himself he cannot save. 32 Let Christ the King of
Israel descend now from the cross, that we may see and believe.
And they that were crucified with him reviled him.
33 And when the sixth hour was come, there was darkness
over the whole land until the ninth hour. 34 And at the
ninth hour Jesus cried with a loud voice, saying,

Eloi, Eloi, lama sabachthani?[69]

which is, being interpreted,

My God, my God, why hast thou forsaken me?

35 And some of them that stood by, when they heard it, said,
Behold, he calleth Elias. 36 And one ran and filled a sponge
full of vinegar, and put it on a reed, and gave him to drink, say-
ing, Let alone; let us see whether Elias will come to take him
down.[70] 37 And Jesus cried with a loud voice, and gave up
the ghost. 38 And the veil of the temple[71] was rent in twain
from the top to the bottom.

. . . .

Chapter 16

1 And when the sabbath was past, Mary Magdalene,[72] and
Mary the mother of James, and Salome,[73] had bought sweet

68. Scholars regard this verse as a later addition to the gospel, perhaps from Luke 22:37. It makes Jesus' career accord with the prophecy about the suffering servant in Isaiah 53:12.
69. Quotation from Psalm 22:1 in the Aramaic language.
70. The man wishes to prolong Jesus' life to see whether Elias (Elijah) will come to save him.
71. The veil which hid the ark of the tabernacle from view, as commanded in Exodus 26:31-2.
72. Possibly this is the same "sinner" who anointed Jesus' feet at the house of Simon the Pharisee (Luke 7:37-8), if the "seven demons" which Jesus cast from her may be taken to mean mental or moral aberration.
73. Not to be confused with the Salome responsible for the beheading of John the Baptist.

spices, that they might come and anoint him.[74] 2 And very
early in the morning, the first day of the week, they came unto
the sepulchre at the rising of the sun. 3 And they said
among themselves, Who shall roll us away the stone from the
door of the sepulchre? 4 And when they looked, they saw
that the stone was rolled away: for it was very great. 5 And
entering into the sepulchre, they saw a young man[75] sitting on
the right side, clothed in a long white garment; and they were
affrighted. 6 And he saith unto them, Be not affrighted: ye
seek Jesus of Nazareth, which was crucified: he is risen; he is
not here: behold the place where they laid him. 7 But
go your way, tell his disciples and Peter that he goeth before
you into Galilee: there shall ye see him, as he said unto
you. 8 And they went out quickly, and fled from the sepul-
chre; for they trembled and were amazed: neither said they any
thing to any man; for they were afraid.[76]
9 Now when Jesus was risen early the first day of the week,
he appeared first to Mary Magdalene, out of whom he had cast
seven devils. 10 And she went and told them that had been
with him, as they mourned and wept. 11 And they, when
they had heard that he was alive, and had been seen of her,
believed not. 12 After that he appeared in another form
unto two of them, as they walked, and went into the coun-
try. 13 And they went and told it unto the residue: neither
believed they them. 14 Afterward he appeared unto the
eleven as they sat at meat, and upbraided them with their un-
belief and hardness of heart, because they believed not them
which had seen him after he was risen. 15 And he said
unto them, Go ye into all the world, and preach the gospel
to every creature. 16 He that believeth and is baptized shall

74. Anointing was the customary preparation for burial.

75. According to Luke 24:4, "two men in shining garments"; in John 20:12, "two angels."

76. The oldest and best manuscripts of Mark all end with verse 16:8. Verses 9-20 are a later addition, drawn mainly from Luke and John. In Luke 24:13-15 the disciples see Jesus not in Galilee, but at Emmaeus in Judea. In John, chapter 20, Jesus appears first to Mary Magdalene at the sepulchre, then to the disciples assembled in a room and afterward to "doubting" Thomas alone; finally to the disciples at the Sea of Tiberias (Sea of Galilee).

be saved; but he that believeth not shall be damned. 17 And
these signs shall follow them that believe; In my name shall
they cast out devils; they shall speak with new tongues;
18 They shall take up serpents; and if they drink any deadly
thing, it shall not hurt them; they shall lay hands on the sick,
and they shall recover. 19 So then, after the Lord had
spoken unto them, he was received up into heaven, and sat on
the right hand of God. 20 And they went forth, and
preached every where, the Lord working with them, and con-
firming the word with signs following. Amen.

Introduction to the Gospel of John

The gospels of Matthew, Mark, and Luke, despite their differences, regard the person of Jesus from essentially the same point of view (thus their designation as "Synoptic" gospels). But the gospel of John takes us into another world of thought, and gives a quite different picture of the events and the meaning of Jesus' life.

The New Testament itself gives no clue to the identity of the writer of John's gospel. But the character of the book makes evident that he cannot have been the "beloved disciple" of Jesus, John the son of Zebedee, to whom tradition ascribes the authorship. The Galilean fisherman cannot have moved in the gospel writer's sophisticated world of Hellenistic speculation and symbolism. The *logos*-idea propounded in the first chapter of John has obvious antecedents in Greek philosophy, especially as developed at Alexandria (e.g., by Philo Judaeus). The *logos,* or divine reason of the Greeks, becomes for John the messenger of God, the Holy Spirit. The gospel likewise applies to Jesus the Greek idea that divinity is uncreated, unchanging, and pre-existent from all eternity.

Composed probably between A.D. 90 and 100, the gospel of John is far more homogeneous in structure than the Synoptic gospels. We cannot tell what sources the writer drew upon, though probably he used Mark to some extent. John's gospel is not a collection of loosely related anecdotes; everything it says is based upon a consistent view of the character of Jesus. By his own account (John

21:35), the author selected only certain incidents of Jesus' life for presentation and omitted many others.

John's gospel stresses the unity of Father and Son, who are bound by the Holy Spirit—a conception which evolved into the theological doctrine of the Trinity. According to John, it was Jesus' mission to reveal the will of God to the world. Jesus was conscious from the beginning of his Messiahship; neither he nor his disciples ever questioned it. Everything he did was an integral part of God's plan. His miracles were performed not out of spontaneous compassion, but with a didactic purpose as evidence of God's power. He underwent no spiritual struggles; the devil never tempted him; he did not search his soul at Gethsemane prior to the crucifixion. His fate had always been known to him, and he met it serenely.

In contrast to the Synoptic gospels, the book of John denies that the kingdom of God on earth will be established only at some future date. God's kingdom is timeless: it exists already in the eternal here-and-now. It is not a form of external order, but rather the inward presence of Jesus in the hearts of those who believe in him.

FROM THE GOSPEL OF JOHN

Chapter 1

1 In the beginning was the Word,[1] and the Word was with
God, and the Word was God. 2 The same was in the begin-
ning with God. 3 All things were made by him; and with-
out him was not any thing made that was made.[2] 4 In him
was life,[3] and the life was the light[4] of men. 5 And the light
shineth in darkness; and the darkness comprehended[5] it not.
6 There was a man sent from God, whose name was John.
7 The same came for a witness, to bear witness of the Light,
that all men through him might believe. 8 He was not that
Light, but was sent to bear witness of that Light. 9 That

John 1:1-14; 3:1-21; 8:51-9; 14:1-20. King James Bible.

1. *Logos* in Greek means both "word" and "reason."
2. God created through the word. As in Genesis, "God said . . ."
3. I.e., the word of God is the source of life.
4. Light is the symbol of truth, as opposed to the darkness of sin.
5. Overwhelmed, mastered.

was the true Light, which lighteth every man that cometh into
the world. 10 He[6] was in the world, and the world was
made by him, and the world[7] knew him not. 11 He came
unto his own,[8] and his own received him not. 12 But as
many as received him, to them gave he power to become the sons
of God, even to them that believe on his name: 13 Which
were born, not of blood, nor of the will of the flesh, nor of the
will of man, but of God.[9]
14 And the Word was made flesh,[10] and dwelt among us, (and
we[11] beheld his glory, the glory as of the only begotten of the
Father,) full of grace and truth.

. . . .

Chapter 3

1 There was a man of the Pharisees, named Nicodemus, a
ruler of the Jews: 2 The same came to Jesus by night, and
said unto him, Rabbi, we know that thou art a teacher come
from God: for no man can do these miracles that thou doest, ex-
cept God be with him. 3 Jesus answered and said unto him,
Verily, verily, I say unto thee, Except a man be born again, he
cannot see the kingdom of God. 4 Nicodemus saith unto
him, How can a man be born when he is old? can he enter the
second time into his mother's womb, and be born? 5 Jesus
answered, Verily, verily, I say unto thee, Except a man be born
of water and of the Spirit, he cannot enter into the kingdom of
God. 6 That which is born of the flesh is flesh; and that which
is born of the Spirit is spirit. 7 Marvel not that I said unto
thee, Ye must be born again. 8 The wind[12] bloweth where
it listeth, and thou hearest the sound thereof, but canst not tell
whence it cometh, and whither it goeth: so is every one that is
born of the Spirit. 9 Nicodemus answered and said unto

6. The Light, i.e., Jesus, who is one in essence with God.
7. I.e., mankind.
8. I.e., to his own people, the Jews.
9. The new chosen people are to be selected not according to race or nation or through any human plan, but by the will of God.
10. I.e., the divine reason was embodied in the human form of Jesus.
11. I.e., the eyewitnesses to Jesus' life.
12. The Greek word *pneuma* means both "wind" and "spirit."

him, How can these things be? 10 Jesus answered and said
unto him, Art thou a master of Israel, and knowest not these
things? 11 Verily, verily, I say unto thee, We speak that
we do know, and testify that we have seen;[13] and ye receive not
our witness. 12 If I have told you earthly things, and ye
believe not, how shall ye believe, if I tell you of heavenly
things? 13 And no man hath ascended up to heaven, but
he that came down from heaven, even[14] the Son of man which
is in heaven. 14 And as Moses lifted up the serpent in the
wilderness, even so must the Son of man be lifted up:[15]
15 That whosoever believeth in him should not perish, but
have eternal life.
16 For God so loved the world, that he gave his only begotten
Son, that whosoever believeth in him should not perish, but
have everlasting life. 17 For God sent not his Son into the
world to condemn the world; but that the world through him
might be saved. 18 He that believeth on him is not con-
demned: but he that believeth not is condemned already, be-
cause he hath not believed in the name of the only begotten
Son of God. 19 And this is the condemnation, that light is
come into the world, and men loved darkness rather than light,
because their deeds were evil. 20 For every one that doeth
evil hateth the light, neither cometh to the light, lest his deeds
should be reproved. 21 But he that doeth truth cometh to
the light, that his deeds may be made manifest, that they are
wrought in God.

. . . .

Chapter 8

51 Verily, verily, I say unto you, If a man keep my saying,
he shall never see death. 52 Then said the Jews unto him,
Now we know that thou hast a devil. Abraham[16] is dead, and
the prophets; and thou sayest, If a man keep my saying, he
shall never taste of death. 53 Art thou greater than our

13. Jesus here refers to himself as one of the prophets.
14. Namely; in other words.
15. I.e., on the cross.
16. The ancestor of the Hebrews, who in Jesus' time had been dead for nearly two thousand years.

father Abraham, which is dead? and the prophets are dead:
whom makest thou thyself? 54 Jesus answered, If I honor
myself, my honor is nothing: it is my Father that honoreth me;
of whom ye say, that he is your God: 55 Yet ye have not
known him; but I know him: and if I should say, I know him
not, I shall be a liar like unto you: but I know him, and keep
his saying. 56 Your father Abraham rejoiced to see my
day:[17] and he saw it, and was glad. 57 Then said the Jews
unto him, Thou art not yet fifty years old, and hast thou seen
Abraham? 58 Jesus said unto them, Verily, verily, I say
unto you, Before Abraham was, I am. 59 Then took they
up stones to cast at him: but Jesus hid himself, and went out
of the temple, going through the midst of them, and so passed
by.

. . . .

Chapter 14

1 Let not your heart be troubled: ye believe in God, believe
also in me. 2 In my Father's house are many mansions: if
it were not so, I would have told you. I go to prepare a place for
you. 3 And if I go and prepare a place for you, I will come
again, and receive you unto myself; that where I am, there ye
may be also. 4 And whither I go ye know, and the way ye
know. 5 Thomas saith unto him, Lord, we know not whither
thou goest; and how can we know the way? 6 Jesus saith
unto him, I am the way, the truth, and the life: no man cometh
unto the Father, but by me. 7 If ye had known me, ye
should have known my Father also: and from henceforth ye
know him, and have seen him.
8 Philip saith unto him, Lord, show us the Father, and it suf-
ficeth us. 9 Jesus saith unto him, Have I been so long time
with you, and yet hast thou not known me, Philip? he that hath
seen me hath seen the Father; and how sayest thou then, Show
us the Father? 10 Believest thou not that I am in the Father,
and the Father in me? the words that I speak unto you I speak
not of myself: but the Father that dwelleth in me, he doeth the

17. "My day": Jesus' coming.

works. 11 Believe me that I am in the Father, and the Fa-
ther in me: or else believe me for the very works' sake.[18]
12 Verily, verily, I say unto you, He that believeth on me, the
works that I do shall he do also; and greater works than these
shall he do; because I go unto my Father. 13 And whatso-
ever ye shall ask in my name, that will I do, that the Father
may be glorified in the Son. 14 If ye shall ask any thing in
my name, I will do it.
15 If ye love me, keep my commandments. 16 And I will
pray the Father, and he shall give you another Comforter,[19] that
he may abide with you for ever; 17 Even the Spirit of truth;
whom the world cannot receive, because it seeth him not, nei-
ther knoweth him: but ye know him; for he dwelleth with you,
and shall be in you.
18 I will not leave you comfortless: I will come to you.
19 Yet a little while, and the world seeth me no more; but
ye see me: because I live, ye shall live also. 20 At that
day ye shall know that I am in my Father, and ye in me, and
I in you. . . .

18. I.e., the disciples are enjoined to believe that Jesus' works (miracles) came from God.
19. The Paraclete, or Holy Spirit (in later Christian theology, the third person of the Trinity).

Introduction
to the Book of Acts and the Letter to the Galatians

Although Jesus had counted himself among the Jewish prophets, it was not long before significant numbers of non-Jews came to regard him as the divine Redeemer through whom they could gain happiness after death. The status of these Gentiles was one of the principal points of conflict among the early followers of Jesus. The Jerusalem community of believers, led by James, regarded faith in Jesus' Messiahship as merely an addition to Judaism which in no way modified the requirements of the Mosaic law. Converts were asked in effect to join the Jewish nation, which meant observing all the Jewish ritual and dietary regulations and submitting to circumcision. To non-Jews, however, the requirement of observing Jewish law was a major hindrance to their acceptance of Jesus.

The apostle Paul, who was a Jew from the cosmopolitan port of Tarsus in Asia Minor, realized that the spread of the belief in Jesus to the Gentiles demanded a relaxation of Jewish regulations. He asserted that faith alone was the sign of a Christian. This standpoint naturally irritated the "Judaizers," who regarded the law of Moses as an essential part of their religion. In his emphasis on faith rather than law Paul apparently went farther than any of the other apostles. The book of Acts and the letter to the Galatians both tell of a conference at Jerusalem—presumably the same one—at which Paul and James attempted to resolve the conflict.

The account in Galatians is the testimony of Paul himself, written some forty years earlier than the version in Acts. It is addressed to a community of believers in Galatia in Asia Minor, presumably one which he himself had founded. Evidently the dispute between Judaizers and Gentiles threatened the harmony of the Galatian community. Paul wrote his letter in order to meet this specific situation, and he took care to emphasize his veracity by taking a solemn oath.

The book of Acts, in recounting the events of the conference, represents the viewpoint of the leaders at Jerusalem, who claimed authority over the entire Christian movement. The author of Acts regarded belief in Jesus not as a new religion, but as a development of Judaism. Christianity to him was the true Judaism, which fulfilled the Messianic prophecies of the Old Testament. This was an important point politically as well as religiously; for Judaism was a legal religion recognized by the Roman empire, whereas Christianity was not. Acts denies that any serious conflict had ever arisen between the Jewish and Gentile believers. The only dispute was between believers in Jesus and non-believers. Those questions which arose were settled amicably, on a basis which recognized the pre-eminence of the Jerusalem community in the Christian movement.

Acts was first published about A.D. 105. The identity of the author is unknown; but he almost certainly also wrote the gospel of Luke. Acts was written as a sequel to that gospel; and originally both were published together as a single work. According to tradition, the writer was Luke, a physician and co-worker of Paul in the apostle's later years. But a companion of Paul, unless he was very young at the time, could scarcely have lived to write Luke-

Acts. Moreover, the fact that Acts frequently contradicts the testimony of Paul's own letters makes it unlikely that the author was one of Paul's associates.

In relating the events of the conference at Jerusalem, Acts and Galatians give rather different accounts. In Galatians, Paul makes no attempt to conceal the bitterness of the conflict; Acts reads as though the dispute was of minor significance. According to Acts, it was James who laid down the conditions of fellowship between Jewish and Gentile Christians. The conflict was settled by James' decree, which Paul then carried to the church at Antioch. In the letter to the Galatians, Paul mentions only that the Jerusalem leaders gave him "the right hand of fellowship" and enjoined him to remember the poor. He regarded the results of the conference as merely a modus vivendi whereby Jewish and Gentile believers could eat together without undue offense to Jewish sensibilities. The regulations which the Gentile believers agreed to observe were merely an accommodation and in no way indispensable to salvation.

Paul, in fact, never accepted the claim of the Jerusalem leaders to pre-eminence. Though he wished to remain on good terms with them, he regarded himself as equal to James in status and an equal partner in the negotiations. His apostleship was not derived from Jerusalem, but from his own direct experience of the presence of Jesus Christ. It is clear from both versions of the conference that James partially acceded to Paul's point of view. He relaxed the dietary restrictions for Gentile believers and did not insist on circumcision. In view of Paul's considerable success in proselytizing among the Gentiles, perhaps he could scarcely have done otherwise without destroying all semblance of unity within the movement. Nonetheless, the Judaic-Gentile conflict raged throughout the first century A.D. among the various groups who accepted Jesus' Messiahship, and subsided only as the Gentile element became preponderant in the emerging Christian church.

FROM THE BOOK OF ACTS

Chapter 15

1 And certain men which came down from Judea taught the
brethren, and said, Except ye be circumcised after the manner

Acts 15:1-35. King James Bible.

of Moses, ye cannot be saved. 2 When therefore Paul and
Barnabas had no small dissension and disputation with them,
they determined that Paul and Barnabas, and certain other of
them, should go up to Jerusalem unto the apostles and elders
about this question. 3 And being brought on their way by
the church, they passed through Phenice[1] and Samaria, declar-
ing the conversion of the Gentiles: and they caused great joy
unto all the brethren. 4 And when they were come to
Jerusalem, they were received of the church, and of the apostles
and elders, and they declared all things that God had done with
them. 5 But there rose up certain of the sect of the Pharisees
which believed,[2] saying, That it was needful to circumcise them,
and to command them to keep the law of Moses.
6 And the apostles and elders came together for to consider of
this matter. 7 And when there had been much disputing,
Peter rose up, and said unto them, Men and brethren, ye know
how that a good while ago God made choice among us, that the
Gentiles by my mouth should hear the word of the gospel, and
believe.[3] 8 And God, which knoweth the hearts, bare them
witness, giving them the Holy Ghost, even as he did unto
us; 9 And put no difference between us and them, purify-
ing their hearts by faith. 10 Now therefore why tempt ye
God, to put a yoke upon the neck of the disciples, which neither
our fathers nor we were able to bear?[4] 11 But we believe
that through the grace of the Lord Jesus Christ we shall be
saved, even as they.
12 Then all the multitude kept silence, and gave audience to
Barnabas and Paul, declaring what miracles and wonders God
had wrought among the Gentiles by them.
13 And after they had held their peace, James answered, say-
ing, Men and brethren, hearken unto me: 14 Simeon[5] hath

1. Phoenicia.
2. Pharisees who joined the Jerusalem church. The Pharisees were a Jewish group which stressed the exact observance of the law.
3. According to Acts, chapter 10, God in a vision commanded Peter not to regard any man as unclean.
4. I.e., the law (because of its minute regulations) has proved a burden even to the Jews; it is unreasonable to expect the Gentiles to observe it.
5. A member of the Jerusalem community.

declared how God at the first did visit the Gentiles, to take out
of them a people for his name.[6] 15 And to this agree the
words of the prophets; as it is written,

16 After this I will return,
And will build again the tabernacle of David, which
is fallen down;
And I will build again the ruins thereof,
And I will set it up:
17 That the residue of men might seek after the Lord,
And all the Gentiles, upon whom my name is called,
Saith the Lord, who doeth all these things.[7]
18 Known unto God are all his works from the beginning
of the world.

19 Wherefore my sentence is, that we trouble not them, which
from among the Gentiles are turned to God: 20 But that we
write unto them, that they abstain from pollutions of idols, and
from fornication, and from things strangled, and from blood.[8]
21 For Moses of old time hath in every city them that preach
him, being read in the synagogues every sabbath day.[9]
22 Then pleased it the apostles and elders, with the whole
church, to send chosen men of their own company to Antioch
with Paul and Barnabas; namely, Judas surnamed Barsabas,
and Silas, chief men among the brethren: 23 And they
wrote letters by them after this manner; The apostles and elders
and brethren send greeting unto the brethren which are of the
Gentiles in Antioch and Syria and Cilicia:[10] 24 Forasmuch
as we have heard, that certain which went out from us have
troubled you with words, subverting your souls, saying, Ye
must be circumcised, and keep the law; to whom we gave no

6. Possibly a reference to the fact that Galilee was Gentile country.
7. Amos 9:11-12.
8. The Mosaic law forbade eating animals offered to pagan gods, or strangled things (because this involved eating blood, which was forbidden). Fornication probably means temple prostitution—a feature of certain pagan cults.
9. The Jews already know the law of Moses; these regulations are addressed to the Gentiles.
10. Antioch was the chief city of Syria, former capital of the Seleucid empire. Cilicia was the province of southern Asia Minor immediately north of Syria.

such commandment: 25 It seemed good unto us, being as-
sembled with one accord, to send chosen men unto you with our
beloved Barnabas and Paul, 26 Men that have hazarded
their lives for the name of our Lord Jesus Christ. 27 We
have sent therefore Judas and Silas, who shall also tell you the
same things by mouth. 28 For it seemed good to the Holy
Ghost, and to us, to lay upon you no greater burden than these
necessary things; 29 That ye abstain from meats offered to
idols, and from blood, and from things strangled, and from forni-
cation: from which if ye keep yourselves, ye shall do well. Fare
ye well.
30 So when they were dismissed, they came to Antioch: and
when they had gathered the multitude together, they delivered
the epistle: 31 Which when they had read, they rejoiced
for the consolation. 32 And Judas and Silas, being prophets
also themselves, exhorted the brethren with many words, and
confirmed them. 33 And after they had tarried there a
space, they were let go in peace from the brethren unto the
apostles. 34 Notwithstanding it pleased Silas to abide there
still. 35 Paul also and Barnabas continued in Antioch,
teaching and preaching the word of the Lord, with many others
also.

FROM THE LETTER TO THE GALATIANS

Chapter 2

1 Then fourteen years after[1] I went up again to Jerusalem
with Barnabas, and took Titus with me also. 2 And I went
up by revelation,[2] and communicated unto them that gospel
which I preach among the Gentiles,[3] but privately to them
which were of reputation,[4] lest by any means I should run, or

Galatians 2:1-21. King James Bible.

1. Either fourteen years after his earlier visit to Jerusalem (recounted in Galatians 1:18) or after his conversion.
2. I.e., by the direct command of God.
3. The Antioch church included both Jewish and Gentile believers; Paul had not required the Gentiles to observe Jewish law.
4. I.e., the leaders of the Jerusalem community.

had run, in vain. 3 But neither Titus, who was with me,
being a Greek, was compelled to be circumcised: 4 And
that because of false brethren unawares brought in, who came
in privily to spy out our liberty which we have in Christ Jesus,
that they might bring us into bondage: 5 To whom we gave
place by subjection, no, not for an hour; that the truth of the
gospel might continue with you. 6 But of those who seemed
to be somewhat,[5] (whatsoever they were, it maketh no matter
to me: God accepteth no man's person:) for they who seemed
to be somewhat in conference added nothing to me.[6] 7 But
contrariwise, when they saw that the gospel of the uncircum-
cision was committed unto me, as the gospel of the circumcision
was unto Peter; 8 (For he that wrought effectually in Peter
to the apostleship of the circumcision, the same was mighty in
me toward the Gentiles;) 9 And when James, Cephas, and
John, who seemed to be pillars, perceived the grace that was
given unto me, they gave to me and Barnabas the right hands
of fellowship; that we should go unto the heathen, and they
unto the circumcision. 10 Only they would that we should
remember the poor; the same which I also was forward to do.
11 But when Peter was come to Antioch, I withstood him to
the face, because he was to be blamed. 12 For before that
certain[7] came from James, he did eat with the Gentiles:[8] but
when they were come, he withdrew and separated himself, fear-
ing them which were of the circumcision. 13 And the other
Jews dissembled likewise with him; insomuch that Barnabas
also was carried away with their dissimulation. 14 But
when I saw that they walked not uprightly according to the
truth of the gospel, I said unto Peter before them all, If thou,
being a Jew, livest after the manner of Gentiles, and not as do
the Jews, why compellest thou the Gentiles to live as do the
Jews? 15 We who are Jews by nature, and not sinners of
the Gentiles, 16 Knowing that a man is not justified by the

5. Persons of importance.

6. I.e., the Jerusalem leaders did not require Paul to add anything to what he already was preaching.

7. Before that time certain persons . . .

8. I.e., Peter had observed the practice of the Antioch community in which Jewish and Gentile Christians ate together.

works of the law, but by the faith of Jesus Christ, even we have
believed in Jesus Christ, that we might be justified by the faith
of Christ, and not by the works of the law: for by the works of
the law shall no flesh be justified. 17 But if, while we seek
to be justified by Christ, we ourselves also are found sinners,[9]
is therefore Christ the minister of sin? God forbid. 18 For
if I build again the things which I destroyed, I make myself a
transgressor.[10] 19 For I through the law am dead to the law,
that I might live unto God.[11] 20 I am crucified with Christ:
nevertheless I live; yet not I, but Christ liveth in me:[12] and the
life which I now live in the flesh I live by the faith of the Son
of God, who loved me, and gave himself for me. 21 I do not
frustrate[13] the grace of God: for if righteousness come by the
law, then Christ is dead in vain.

9. I.e., sinners in Jewish eyes, as having transgressed the Mosaic law.
10. I.e., it would be wrong to insist on observing the law after having declared that salvation is through faith in Christ.
11. The Jewish law has become irrelevant to his new faith in Christ.
12. I.e., the spirit of Christ grants eternal life.
13. Reject.

Introduction to Lucian of Samosata

A notable feature of the Hellenistic age was the frequent self-conscious effort by men of Near Eastern antecedents to transform themselves into Greeks. One outstanding example of this was Lucian, the famous satirist and orator of the second century A.D. Born in the provincial town of Samosata in Syria, perhaps around A.D. 120, he was originally apprenticed to a stonemason. But, as he tells us in one of his rare autobiographical references, his inclinations were toward the liberal arts, which meant a Greek education. As a young man he migrated to one of the flourishing Greek cities of Asia Minor, where he mastered the Greek language and acquired that basic knowledge of Greek literature which was considered the indispensable mark of the educated man.

In Asia Minor Lucian became what was called a sophist, or practitioner of various traditional forms of rhetoric. He spent some time as a pleader in law courts, but soon abandoned this profession for that of itinerant orator. He traveled widely throughout the lands of the Mediterranean, and for a time held a post as public orator (in the Greek language) in a town in Gaul. At about age forty he seems to have tired of the standard rhetorical themes, and began to address himself to philosophical and religious questions. During some twenty years his principal residence was Athens; but late in life he accepted a post with the Roman administration of Egypt, where presumably he died, perhaps around 200 A.D.

To the educated class of Lucian's day, the classical Greek language and literature represented the highest possible ideal of culture. But the rhetorical art as practiced in the second century A.D. had little in common with the sophistic movement of the fifth century B.C. The old Greek sophists, as they appear, for example, in Plato, taught the art of persuasive argument with the goal of preparing students for a political career. But in Lucian's day politics was the sphere of the Romans, and sophism had nothing to do with civic responsibility. The sophists exercised their rhetorical skill in public performances, the purpose of which was to entertain rather than to instruct or persuade. A talented performer might win considerable wealth and popular acclaim; but the themes of his discourses often were trivial in the extreme. It was an article of faith that all great authors had belonged to the classical age of Hellas (Latin literature was disdained). Fifth- and fourth-century Greece represented the high point of human history; the sophist was expected to praise the past and fill his speeches with classical allusions.

Lucian's fame rests upon his mordant wit, vivid imagery, and fine sense of drama. He himself invented the form of satiric comedy-dialogue which he used so successfully—though he felt compelled to apologize for its novelty. He handles a variety of themes, mostly taken from classical Greek literature; all of them—whether serious or frivolous—he treats with lofty irreverence. But his pieces are not topical; unlike the comic poets of the fifth century whom he so admired, he does not address himself to the personalities or events of his own century, which by implication he dismisses as unworthy of consideration. His greatest pride was his astonishing mastery of the Greek language and the polished style in which he was unsurpassed in his own day. He is a linguistic purist, complaining of the intrusion of Asiatic words into Attic, and seeking to arrest the decline of Greek into an unsophisticated vernacular spoken by foreigners as a second language.

Lucian is supposed to have admired the Cynic philosophy more than any other. One of his models was the third-century Cynic philosopher, Menippus. But in the main he is uncommitted to any school; his standpoint is that of critical rationalism. Though in his later period he often dealt with philosophy and religion, it is unlikely that he regarded either as a serious approach to life. Politics he scarcely touched. Life, he seems to suggest, is not worth taking seriously; all creeds and dogmas are essentially ridiculous; and the intelligent man will take care not to be duped by any of them.

In *The Sale of Creeds* Lucian presents the Greek gods Zeus and Hermes auctioning off various philosophers, some of whom represent actual historical individuals, others a composite doctrine. Even the gods, Lucian seems to say, find philosophy laughable—though in other dialogues he pokes cruel fun at gods, too. Some philosophers bring better prices than others—a fact probably indicating Lucian's estimate of their popular appeal rather than his opinion of their actual worth. But it is noteworthy that the creeds he satirizes are all between three and five centuries old; some were moribund in his day; others, like Platonism and Stoicism, had become so modified that they bore little resemblance to their originals. *The Sale of Creeds,* like Lucian's other works, is not a critique of contemporary beliefs, but a humorous composition drawing its material from the past.

LUCIAN OF SAMOSATA: THE SALE OF CREEDS

1 ZEUS. Now get those benches straight there, and make the place fit to be seen. Bring up the lots, one of you, and put them in line. Give them a rub up first, though; we must have them looking their best, to attract bidders. Hermes, you can declare the sale-room open, and a welcome to all comers.—*For Sale! A varied assortment of Live Creeds. Tenets of every description.—Cash on delivery; or credit allowed on suitable security.*

HERMES. Here they come, swarming in. No time to lose; we must not keep them waiting.

ZEUS. Well, let us begin.

2 HERMES. What are we to put up first?

From *The Works of Lucian of Samosata,* trans. by H. W. Fowler and F. G. Fowler, Oxford: At the Clarendon Press, 1905, I, 190-206. Reprinted by permission of the Clarendon Press.

ZEUS. The Ionic fellow, with the long hair. He seems a showy piece of goods.

HERMES. Step up, Pythagoreanism, and show yourself.

ZEUS. Go ahead.

HERMES. Now here is a creed of the first water. Who bids for this handsome article? What gentleman says Superhumanity? Harmony of the Universe! Transmigration of souls! Who bids?

FIRST DEALER. He looks all right. And what can he do?

HERMES. Magic, music, arithmetic, geometry, astronomy, jugglery. Prophecy in all its branches.

FIRST DEALER. Can I ask him some questions?

HERMES. Ask away, and welcome.

3 FIRST DEALER. Where do you come from?

PYTHAGORAS. Samos.[1]

FIRST DEALER. Where did you get your schooling?

PYTHAGORAS. From the sophists in Egypt.[2]

FIRST DEALER. If I buy you, what will you teach me?

PYTHAGORAS. Nothing. I will remind you.[3]

FIRST DEALER. Remind me?

PYTHAGORAS. But first I shall have to cleanse your soul of its filth.[4]

FIRST DEALER. Well, suppose the cleansing process complete. How is the reminding done?

PYTHAGORAS. We shall begin with a long course of silent contemplation. Not a word to be spoken for five years.

FIRST DEALER. You would have been just the creed for Croesus's son![5] But *I* have a tongue in my head; I have no ambition to be a statue. And after the five years' silence?

PYTHAGORAS. You will study music and geometry.[6]

1. Greek island off the coast of Asia Minor between Ephesus and Miletus.
2. I.e., the priests, from whom Pythagoras may have learned some astronomy and geometry.
3. According to this doctrine, found also in Plato, the soul acquires knowledge by remembering what it knew in a former existence.
4. I.e., from the contaminations of the body.
5. According to Herodotus, Croesus' son was dumb.
6. Both music and geometry are based upon numerical relations, and were therefore of great interest to the Pythagoreans.

FIRST DEALER. A charming recipe! The way to be wise: learn the guitar.

4 PYTHAGORAS. Next you will learn to count.

FIRST DEALER. I can do that already.

PYTHAGORAS. Let me hear you.

FIRST DEALER. One, two, three, four,—

PYTHAGORAS. There you are, you see. *Four* (as you call it) is *ten*. Four the perfect triangle.[7] Four the oath of our school.

FIRST DEALER. Now by Four, most potent Four!—higher and holier mysteries than these I never heard.

PYTHAGORAS. Then you will learn of Earth, Air, Fire, and Water; their action, their movement, their shapes.

FIRST DEALER. Have Fire and Air and Water *shapes?*

PYTHAGORAS. Clearly. That cannot move which lacks shape and form. You will also find that God is a number; an intelligence; a harmony.[8]

FIRST DEALER. You surprise me.

5 PYTHAGORAS. More than this, you have to learn that you yourself are not the person you appear to be.

FIRST DEALER. What, I am some one else, not the I who am speaking to you?

PYTHAGORAS. You are that you now: but you have formerly inhabited another body, and borne another name. And in course of time you will change once more.[9]

6 FIRST DEALER. Why then I shall be immortal, and take one shape after another? But enough of this. And now what is your diet?

PYTHAGORAS. Of living things I eat none. All else I eat, except beans.[10]

FIRST DEALER. And why no beans? Do you dislike them?

PYTHAGORAS. No. But they are sacred things. Their nature

7. $1 + 2 + 3 + 4 = 10$. The triangle is 

8. Since number is the essence of things, even God must work through mathematical relations.

9. Transmigration of the soul into various bodies was a cardinal Pythagorean doctrine.

10. Meat, eggs, and beans were forbidden to members of the Pythagorean community.

is a mystery. Consider them first in their generative aspect; take a green one and peel it, and you will see what I mean. Again, boil one and expose it to moonlight for a proper number of nights, and you have—blood. What is more, the Athenians use beans to vote with.

FIRST DEALER. Admirable! A very feast of reason. Now just strip, and let me see what you are like. Bless me, here is a creed with a golden thigh![11] He is no mortal, he is a God. I must have him at any price. What do you start him at?

HERMES. Forty pounds.[12]

FIRST DEALER. He is mine for forty pounds.

ZEUS. Take the gentleman's name and address.

HERMES. He must come from Italy, I should think; Croton[13] or Tarentum, or one of the Greek towns in those parts. But he is not the only buyer. Some three hundred of them have clubbed together.

ZEUS. They are welcome to him. Now up with the next.

7 HERMES. What about yonder grubby Pontian?[14]

ZEUS. Yes, he will do.

HERMES. You there with the wallet and cloak;[15] come along, walk round the room. Lot No. 2. A most sturdy and valiant creed, free-born.[16] What offers?

SECOND DEALER. Hullo, Mr. Auctioneer, are you going to sell a free man?

HERMES. That was the idea.

SECOND DEALER. Take care, he may have you up for kidnapping. This might be matter for the Areopagus.[17]

HERMES. Oh, he would as soon be sold as not. He feels just as free as ever.

11. Some of Pythagoras' followers identified their master with the god Apollo, who was supposed to have a golden thigh.
12. In the Greek: ten minas. One mina equaled about a pound and a quarter of silver.The translators have converted the Greek monetary units into their approximate British equivalents, based upon the price of silver in 1905.
13. Crotona was the city in southern Italy where Pythagoras founded his religious community and where he lived for the latter part of his life.
14. Pontus was a kingdom on the southeastern shore of the Black Sea.
15. The Cynic philosophers wore rough garments and carried knapsacks.
16. Man becomes free by reducing his desires to the barest necessities.
17. The supreme court.

SECOND DEALER. But what is one to do with such a dirty fellow?[18] He is a pitiable sight. One might put him to dig perhaps, or to carry water.

HERMES. That he can do and more. Set him to guard your house, and you will find him better than any watch-dog.—They call him Dog for short.[19]

SECOND DEALER. Where does he come from? and what is his method?

HERMES. He can best tell you that himself.

SECOND DEALER. I don't like his looks. He will probably snarl if I go near him, or take a snap at me, for all I know. See how he lifts his stick, and scowls; an awkward-looking customer!

HERMES. Don't be afraid. He is quite tame.

8 SECOND DEALER. Tell me, good fellow, where do you come from?

DIOGENES. Everywhere.

SECOND DEALER. What does that mean?

DIOGENES. It means that I am a citizen of the world.[20]

SECOND DEALER. And your model?

DIOGENES. Heracles.[21]

SECOND DEALER. Then why no lion's-skin? You have the orthodox club.

DIOGENES. My cloak is my lion's-skin. Like Heracles, I live in a state of warfare, and my enemy is Pleasure;[22] but unlike him I am a volunteer. My purpose is to purify humanity.

SECOND DEALER. A noble purpose. Now what do I understand to be your strong subject? What is your profession?

DIOGENES. The liberation of humanity,[23] and the treatment

18. The Cynic Diogenes (412-323 B.C.), seeking to live as simply as animals do, slept on the ground.
19. This is a play on words. The term "Cynic" is derived from "Cynosarges" (Dogfish), the gymnasium where the original Cynics gathered.
20. The Cynics refused to respect the laws of any state, but called themselves cosmopolitans.
21. Or Hercules, the mythical hero known for his great strength, who killed a lion and afterward wore its skin.
22. The Cynics believed that happiness is to be found not in the pursuit of pleasure but in a simple and natural life.
23. I.e., liberation from bondage to pleasure and the passions.

of the passions. In short, I am the prophet of Truth and Candour.[24]

9 SECOND DEALER. Well, prophet; and if I buy you, how shall you handle my case?

DIOGENES. I shall commence operations by stripping off your superfluities, putting you into fustian,[25] and leaving you closeted with Necessity. Then I shall give you a course of hard labour. You will sleep on the ground, drink water, and fill your belly as best you can. Have you money? Take my advice and throw it into the sea. With wife and children and country you will not concern yourself; there will be no more of that nonsense. You will exchange your present home for a sepulchre, a ruin, or a tub.[26] What with lupines[27] and close-written tomes, your knapsack will never be empty; and you will vote yourself happier than any king. Nor will you esteem it any inconvenience, if a flogging or a turn of the rack should fall to your lot.

SECOND DEALER. How! Am I a tortoise, a lobster, that I should be flogged and feel it not?

DIOGENES. You will take your cue from Hippolytus;[28] *mutatis mutandis.*

SECOND DEALER. How so?

10 DIOGENES. "The heart may burn, the tongue knows nought thereof."[29] Above all, be bold, be impudent; distribute your abuse impartially to king and commoner. They will admire your spirit. You will talk the Cynic jargon with the true Cynic snarl, scowling as you walk, and walking as one should who scowls; an epitome of brutality. Away with modesty, good-nature, and forbearance. Wipe the blush from your cheek for ever. Your hunting-ground will be the crowded city. You will live alone in its midst, holding communion with none, admitting neither friend nor guest; for such would undermine your

24. Diogenes called free speech the greatest of all goods; he was known for his blunt language.
25. A coarse cloth of cotton and linen.
26. Diogenes lived for a time in a tub or barrel in the courtyard of a temple at Athens.
27. Seeds of a plant belonging to the pea family; the traditional fare of impecunious philosophers.
28. Character in a play of that name by Euripides.
29. Hippolytus' reply (in the play) when reproached with having broken an oath.

power. Scruple not to perform the deeds of darkness in broad daylight: select your love-adventures with a view to the public entertainment: and finally, when the fancy takes you, swallow a raw cuttle-fish, and die.[30] Such are the delights of Cynicism.

11 SECOND DEALER. Oh, vile creed! Monstrous creed! Avaunt!

DIOGENES. But look you, it is all so easy; it is within every man's reach. No education is necessary, no nonsensical argumentation. I offer you a short cut to Glory. You may be the merest clown—cobbler, fishmonger, carpenter, money-changer; yet there is nothing to prevent your becoming famous. Given brass and boldness, you have only to learn to wag your tongue with dexterity.

SECOND DEALER. All this is of no use to me. But I might make a sailor or a gardener of you at a pinch; that is, if you are to be had cheap. Three-pence[31] is the most I can give.

HERMES. He is yours, to have and to hold. And good riddance to the brawling foul-mouthed bully. He is a slanderer by wholesale.

12 ZEUS. Now for the Cyrenaic,[32] the crowned and purple-robed.

HERMES. Attend please, gentlemen all. A most valuable article, this, and calls for a long purse. Look at him. A sweet thing in creeds. A creed for a king. Has any gentleman a use for the Lap of Luxury?[33] Who bids?

THIRD DEALER. Come and tell me what you know. If you are a practical creed, I will have you.

HERMES. Please not to worry him with questions, sir. He is drunk, and cannot answer; his tongue plays him tricks, as you see.

THIRD DEALER. And who in his senses would buy such an abandoned reprobate? How he smells of scent! And how he slips and staggers about! Well, you must speak for him, Hermes. What can he do? What is his line?

HERMES. Well, for any gentleman who is not strait-laced,

30. Diogenes was supposed to have died in this way.
31. In Greek: two obols. The obol was the smallest unit of Greek coinage.
32. From Cyrene, the African port which gave its name to a school of philosophy.
33. The Cyrenaics believed that pleasure was the aim of life and that the keenest pleasures are physical or sensual.

who loves a pretty girl, a bottle, and a jolly companion, he is the very thing. He is also a past master in gastronomy, and a connoisseur in voluptuousness generally. He was educated at Athens, and has served royalty in Sicily,[34] where he had a very good character. Here are his principles in a nutshell: Think the worst of things: make the most of things: get all possible pleasure out of things.

THIRD DEALER. You must look for wealthier purchasers. My purse is not equal to such a festive creed.

HERMES. Zeus, this lot seems likely to remain on our hands.

13 ZEUS. Put it aside, and up with another. Stay, take the pair from Abdera and Ephesus;[35] the creeds of Smiles and Tears. They shall make one lot.

HERMES. Come forward, you two. Lot No. 4. A superlative pair. The smartest brace of creeds on our catalogue.

FOURTH DEALER. Zeus! What a difference is here! One of them does nothing but laugh, and the other might be at a funeral; he is all tears.—You there! what is the joke?

DEMOCRITUS. You ask? You and your affairs are all one vast joke.

FOURTH DEALER. So! You laugh at us? Our business is a toy?

DEMOCRITUS. It is. There is no taking it seriously. All is vanity.[36] Mere interchange of atoms in an infinite void.

14 FOURTH DEALER. *Your* vanity is infinite, if you like. Stop that laughing, you rascal.—And you, my poor fellow, what are you crying for? I must see what I can make of you.

HERACLITUS. I am thinking, friend, upon human affairs; and well may I weep and lament, for the doom of all is sealed. Hence my compassion and my sorrow. For the present, I think not of it; but the future!—the future is all bitterness. Conflagration and destruction of the world. I weep to think that nothing

34. Aristippus (435-356 B.C.), founder of the Cyrenaic school, sought the patronage of Dionysius I, tyrant of Sicily.
35. Democritus of Abdera (460-362 B.C.) was the originator of the atomist theory of matter; Heraclitus of Ephesus (flourished around 500 B.C.) taught that everything is constantly in flux.
36. Lucian puts this conclusion into Democritus' mouth. Democritus himself taught that the wise man should aspire to a tranquil frame of mind corresponding to the gentle movement of the atoms.

abides.[37] All things are whirled together in confusion. Pleasure and pain, knowledge and ignorance, great and small; up and down they go, the playthings of Time.

FOURTH DEALER. And what is Time?

HERACLITUS. A child; and plays at draughts and blindman's-buff.

FOURTH DEALER. And men?

HERACLITUS. Are mortal Gods.

FOURTH DEALER. And Gods?

HERACLITUS. Immortal men.

FOURTH DEALER. So! Conundrums, fellow? Nuts to crack? You are a very oracle for obscurity.[38]

HERACLITUS. Your affairs do not interest me.

FOURTH DEALER. No one will be fool enough to bid for you at that rate.

HERACLITUS. Young and old, him that bids and him that bids not, a murrain[39] seize you all!

FOURTH DEALER. A sad case. He will be melancholy mad before long. Neither of these is the creed for my money.

HERMES. No one bids.

ZEUS. Next lot.

15 HERMES. The Athenian there? Old Chatterbox?

ZEUS. By all means.

HERMES. Come forward!—A good sensible creed this. Who buys Holiness?[40]

FIFTH DEALER. Let me see. What are you good for?

SOCRATES. I teach the art of love.[41]

FIFTH DEALER. A likely bargain for me! I want a tutor for my young Adonis.[42]

37. Heraclitus thought that fire was the basic element of the universe. Since everything is constantly transforming itself into its opposite, fire is constantly changing into things and things into fire.

38. Heraclitus was called "the obscure" even in antiquity because of the enigmatic nature of his assertions. Oracles were likewise known for their obscure utterances which could be interpreted in various ways.

39. Pestilence, plague.

40. Reference to Socrates' concern with the virtuous life.

41. Love to Socrates meant love of goodness and justice, rather than physical love. His views on the subject are recorded in Plato's *Symposium*.

42. Here a proper name; but in Greek mythology Adonis was the handsome youth who was loved by Aphrodite (Venus), the goddess of love.

SOCRATES. And could he have a better? The love I teach is of the spirit, not of the flesh. Under my roof, be sure, a boy will come to no harm.

FIFTH DEALER. Very unconvincing that. A teacher of the art of love, and never meddle with anything but the spirit? Never use the opportunities your office gives you?

16 SOCRATES. Now by Dog and Plane-tree,[43] it is as I say!

FIFTH DEALER. Heracles! What strange Gods are these?

SOCRATES. Why, the Dog is a God, I suppose? Is not Anubis[44] made much of in Egypt? Is there not a Dog-star[45] in Heaven, and a Cerberus[46] in the lower world?

17 FIFTH DEALER. Quite so. My mistake. Now what is your manner of life?

SOCRATES. I live in a city of my own building; I make my own laws, and have a novel constitution of my own.[47]

FIFTH DEALER. I should like to hear some of your statutes.

SOCRATES. You shall hear the greatest of them all. No woman shall be restricted to one husband. Every man who likes is her husband.[48]

FIFTH DEALER. What! Then the laws of adultery are clean swept away?

SOCRATES. I should think they were! and a world of hair-splitting with them.

FIFTH DEALER. And what do you do with the handsome boys?

SOCRATES. Their kisses are the reward of merit, of noble and spirited actions.[49]

43. The plane-tree is a small tree resembling a sycamore. Perhaps this is a reference to Socrates' love of discoursing in the open air.
44. Anubis was an Egyptian god with the head of a jackal and the body of a man. The Greeks identified him with their own Hermes.
45. The dog-star (Sirius) is the brightest star in the sky, forming part of the constellation Canis Major.
46. Cerberus was the watchdog stationed at the gate of Hell to prevent the living from entering and the dead from escaping.
47. Plato described an ideal community in his *Republic*, the inspiration for which came to some extent from Socrates.
48. A distortion of Socrates' view (see note 41).
49. Pederasty was forbidden both by law and general opinion at Athens, but nonetheless was cultivated by the upper classes.

18 FIFTH DEALER. Unparalleled generosity!—And now, what are the main features of your philosophy?

SOCRATES. Ideas and types of things. All things that you see, the earth and all that is upon it, the sea, the sky,—each has its counterpart in the invisible world.

FIFTH DEALER. And where are they?

SOCRATES. Nowhere.[50] Were they anywhere, they were not what they are.

FIFTH DEALER. I see no signs of these "types" of yours.

SOCRATES. Of course not; because you are spiritually blind. *I* see the counterparts of all things; an invisible you, an invisible me; everything is in duplicate.

FIFTH DEALER. Come, such a shrewd and lynx-eyed creed is worth a bid. Let me see. What do you want for him?

HERMES. Five hundred.[51]

FIFTH DEALER. Done with you. Only I must settle the bill another day.

19 HERMES. What name?

FIFTH DEALER. Dion; of Syracuse.[52]

HERMES. Take him, and much good may he do you. Now I want Epicureanism. Who offers for Epicureanism? He is a disciple of the laughing creed and the drunken creed, whom we were offering just now.[53] But he has one extra accomplishment—impiety.[54] For the rest, a dainty, lickerish creed.

SIXTH DEALER. What price?

HERMES. Eight pounds.[55]

SIXTH DEALER. Here you are. By the way, you might let me know what he likes to eat.[56]

50. I.e., in the supernatural, or in the mind, not in a *place*.
51. In Greek: two talents. The talent was the heaviest Greek unit of weight and currency, equal to 60 minas.
52. Dion was an admirer of Plato. It was at his instigation that Plato went to Syracuse as tutor to Dion's nephew, Dionysius II.
53. Epicurus derived his atomism from Democritus (see section 13, above) and his hedonism from the Cyrenaics (section 12).
54. The Epicureans believed that the world was created through natural causes, not by the gods.
55. Two minas.
56. Some of the later Epicureans claimed that all good things have reference to the stomach.

HERMES. Anything sweet. Anything with honey in it. Dried figs are his favourite dish.

SIXTH DEALER. That is all right. We will get in a supply of Carian fig-cakes.

20 ZEUS. Call the next lot. Stoicism; the creed of the sorrowful countenance, the close-cropped creed.[57]

HERMES. Ah yes, several customers, I fancy, are on the look-out for him.[58] Virtue incarnate! The very quintessence of creeds! Who is for universal monopoly?

SEVENTH DEALER. How are we to understand that?

HERMES. Why, here is monopoly of wisdom, monopoly of beauty, monopoly of courage, monopoly of justice. Sole king, sole orator, sole legislator, sole millionaire.[59]

SEVENTH DEALER. And I suppose sole cook, sole tanner, sole carpenter, and all that?

HERMES. Presumably.

21 SEVENTH DEALER. Regard me as your purchaser, good fellow, and tell me all about yourself. I dare say you think it rather hard to be sold for a slave?

CHRYSIPPUS.[60] Not at all. These things are beyond our control. And what is beyond our control is indifferent.

SEVENTH DEALER. I don't see how you make that out.

CHRYSIPPUS. What! Have you yet to learn that of *indifferentia* some are *praeposita* and others *rejecta*?[61]

SEVENTH DEALER. Still I don't quite see.

CHRYSIPPUS. No; how should you? You are not familiar with our terms. You lack the *comprehensio visi*.[62] The earnest student of logic knows this and more than this. He understands the nature of subject, predicate, and contingent, and the distinctions between them.[63]

SEVENTH DEALER. Now in Wisdom's name, tell me, pray,

57. Stoicism stressed the patient endurance of adversity.
58. Stoicism was popular with men of affairs.
59. The Stoics believed that their philosophy produced these virtues.
60. Chrysippus (280-206 B.C.) was the third head of the Stoic school, who sought to give Stoicism a foundation in logic.
61. I.e., though all things are indifferent, some are preferable to others.
62. Faculty of conceptual thinking.
63. Lucian is making fun of the Stoics' preoccupation with technical logic.

what is a predicate? what is a contingent? There is a ring about those words that takes my fancy.

CHRYSIPPUS. With all my heart. A man lame in one foot knocks that foot accidentally against a stone, and gets a cut. Now the man is *subject* to lameness; which is the *predicate*. And the cut is a *contingency*.

22 SEVENTH DEALER. Oh, subtle! What else can you tell me?

CHRYSIPPUS. I have verbal involutions, for the better hampering, crippling, and muzzling of my antagonists. This is performed by the use of the far-famed syllogism.[64]

SEVENTH DEALER. Syllogism! I warrant him a tough customer.

CHRYSIPPUS. Take a case. You have a child?

SEVENTH DEALER. Well, and what if I have?

CHRYSIPPUS. A crocodile catches him as he wanders along the bank of a river, and promises to restore him to you, if you will first guess correctly whether he means to restore him or not. Which are you going to say?

SEVENTH DEALER. A difficult question. I don't know which way I should get him back soonest. In Heaven's name, answer for me, and save the child before he is eaten up.

CHRYSIPPUS. Ha, ha. I will teach you far other things than that.

SEVENTH DEALER. For instance?

CHRYSIPPUS. There is the "Reaper." There is the "Rightful Owner." Better still, there is the "Electra" and the "Man in the Hood."[65]

SEVENTH DEALER. Who was he? and who was Electra?

CHRYSIPPUS. She was *the* Electra, the daughter of Agamemnon, to whom the same thing was known and unknown at the same time. She knew that Orestes was her brother: yet when he stood before her she did not know (until he revealed himself) that her brother was Orestes.[66] As to the Man in the Hood, he

64. The syllogism is a form of argument in which a conclusion is drawn from two premises.

65. The names for certain (logical) fallacies.

66. In Greek mythology (and the plays of Sophocles and Euripides), Electra and Orestes kill their mother Clytaemnestra in revenge for Clytaemnestra's murder of their father Agamemnon.

will surprise you considerably. Answer me now: do you know your own father?

SEVENTH DEALER. Yes.

CHRYSIPPUS. Well now, if I present to you a man in a hood, shall you know him? eh?

SEVENTH DEALER. Of course not.

23 CHRYSIPPUS. Well, but the Man in the Hood is your father. You don't know the Man in the Hood. Therefore you don't know your own father.

SEVENTH DEALER. Why, no. But if I take his hood off, I shall get at the facts. Now tell me, what is the end of your philosophy? What happens when you reach the goal of virtue?

CHRYSIPPUS. In regard to things external, health, wealth, and the like, I am then all that Nature intended me to be. But there is much previous toil to be undergone. You will first sharpen your eyes on minute manuscripts, amass commentaries, and get your bellyful of outlandish terms. Last but not least, it is forbidden to be wise without repeated doses of hellebore.[67]

SEVENTH DEALER. All this is exalted and magnanimous to a degree. But what am I to think when I find that you are also the creed of cent-per-cent, the creed of the usurer?[68] Has *he* swallowed his hellebore? is *he* made perfect in virtue?

CHRYSIPPUS. Assuredly. On none but the wise man does usury sit well. Consider. His is the art of putting two and two together, and usury is the art of putting interest together.[69] The two are evidently connected, and one as much as the other is the prerogative of the true believer; who, not content, like common men, with simple interest, will also take interest *upon* interest. For interest, as you are probably aware, is of two kinds. There is simple interest, and there is its offspring, compound interest.[70] Hear Syllogism on the subject. "If I take simple interest, I shall also take compound. But I *shall* take simple interest: therefore I shall take compound."

67. The poisonous roots of the hellebore plant were used as a heart stimulant. Chrysippus was supposed to have taken this medicine.
68. This refers to the popularity of Stoicism among businessmen.
69. In Greek, the verb for "put two and two together" (i.e., draw conclusions) is a compound of the simple verb meaning "to draw interest."
70. *Tokos,* "interest," literally means "offspring."

24 SEVENTH DEALER. And the same applies to the fees you take from your youthful pupils? None but the true believer sells virtue for a fee?

CHRYSIPPUS. Quite right. I take the fee in my pupil's interest, not because I want it. The world is made up of diffusion and accumulation.[71] I accordingly practise my pupil in the former, and myself in the latter.

SEVENTH DEALER. But it ought to be the other way. The pupil ought to accumulate, and you, "sole millionaire," ought to diffuse.

CHRYSIPPUS. Ha! you jest with me? Beware of the shaft of insoluble syllogism.

SEVENTH DEALER. What harm can that do?

25 CHRYSIPPUS. It cripples; it ties the tongue, and turns the brain. Nay, I have but to will it, and you are stone this instant.

SEVENTH DEALER. Stone! You are no Perseus,[72] friend?

CHRYSIPPUS. See here. A stone is a body?

SEVENTH DEALER. Yes.

CHRYSIPPUS. Well, and an animal is a body?

SEVENTH DEALER. Yes.

CHRYSIPPUS. And you are an animal?

SEVENTH DEALER. I suppose I am.

CHRYSIPPUS. Therefore you are a body. Therefore a stone.[73]

SEVENTH DEALER. Mercy, in Heaven's name! Unstone me, and let me be flesh as heretofore.

CHRYSIPPUS. That is soon done. Back with you into flesh! Thus: Is every body animate?

SEVENTH DEALER. No.

CHRYSIPPUS. Is a stone animate?

SEVENTH DEALER. No.

CHRYSIPPUS. Now, you are a body?

SEVENTH DEALER. Yes.

CHRYSIPPUS. And an animate body?

SEVENTH DEALER. Yes.

71. Of the atoms.
72. Perseus was supposedly the builder of Mycenae, the pre-historic Greek capital noted for its heavy stone buildings.
73. Lucian is ridiculing the proofs of formal logic.

CHRYSIPPUS. Then being animate, you cannot be a stone.

SEVENTH DEALER. Ah! thank you, thank you. I was beginning to feel my limbs growing numb and solidifying like Niobe's.[74] Oh, I must have you. What's to pay?

HERMES. Fifty pounds.[75]

SEVENTH DEALER. Here it is.

HERMES. Are you sole purchaser?

SEVENTH DEALER. Not I. All these gentlemen here are going shares.

HERMES. A fine strapping lot of fellows, and will do the "Reaper" credit.

26 ZEUS. Don't waste time. Next lot,—the Peripatetic![76]

HERMES. Now, my beauty, now, Affluence! Gentlemen, if you want Wisdom for your money, here is a creed that comprises all knowledge.

EIGHTH DEALER. What is he like?

HERMES. He is temperate, good-natured, easy to get on with; and his strong point is, that he is twins.

EIGHTH DEALER. How can that be?

HERMES. Why, he is one creed outside, and another inside. So remember, if you buy him, one of him is called Esoteric, and the other Exoteric.[77]

EIGHTH DEALER. And what has he to say for himself?

HERMES. He has to say that there are three kinds of good: spiritual, corporeal, circumstantial.[78]

EIGHTH DEALER. *There's* something a man can understand. How much is he?

HERMES. Eighty pounds.[79]

EIGHTH DEALER. Eighty pounds is a long price.

74. In Greek mythology Niobe, the mortal mother of twelve children, arrogantly compared herself to the goddess Leto, who had only two. For this presumption the gods slew her children and changed her into stone.

75. Twelve minas.

76. The Aristotelians were called Peripatetics from the shaded walks (*peripatoi*) of the Lyceum where Aristotle walked as he discoursed with his students.

77. Traditionally, Aristotle's works were divided into "popular" (non-technical) and "esoteric" (for serious students of philosophy).

78. Reference to Aristotle's love of definitions.

79. Twenty minas.

HERMES. Not at all, my dear sir, not at all. You see, there is some money with him, to all appearance. Snap him up before it is too late. Why, from him you will find out in no time how long a gnat lives, to how many fathoms' depth the sunlight penetrates the sea, and what an oyster's soul is like.[80]

EIGHTH DEALER. Heracles! Nothing escapes him.

HERMES. Ah, these are trifles. You should hear some of his more abstruse speculations, concerning generation and birth and the development of the embryo; and his distinction between man, the laughing creature, and the ass, which is neither a laughing nor a carpentering nor a shipping creature.[78]

EIGHTH DEALER. Such knowledge is as useful as it is ornamental. Eighty pounds be it, then.

27 HERMES. He is yours.

ZEUS. What have we left?

HERMES. There is Scepticism. Come along, Pyrrhias,[81] and be put up. Quick's the word. The attendance is dwindling; there will be small competition. Well, who buys Lot 9?

NINTH DEALER. Tell me first, though, what do you know?

SCEPTIC. Nothing.[82]

NINTH DEALER. But how's that?

SCEPTIC. There does not appear to me to *be* anything.

NINTH DEALER. Are not *we* something?

SCEPTIC. How do I know that?

NINTH DEALER. And you yourself?

SCEPTIC. Of that I am still more doubtful.

NINTH DEALER. Well, you *are* in a fix! And what have you got those scales for?

SCEPTIC. I use them to weigh arguments in, and get them evenly balanced. They must be absolutely equal—not a featherweight to choose between them; then, and not till then, can I make uncertain which is right.[83]

80. Aristotle conducted many scientific experiments, especially in biology.
81. This is a play on the words "pyrrhias" (copper-head) and "Pyrrho." Pyrrho was the founder of the Sceptic philosophy.
82. The principal tenet of Scepticism was that all so-called knowledge is untrustworthy.
83. The Sceptics doubted man's ability to make valid judgments; they held that for every opinion another equally valid one can be found.

NINTH DEALER. What else can you turn your hand to?

SCEPTIC. Anything; except catching a runaway.

NINTH DEALER. And why not that?

SCEPTIC. Because, friend, everything eludes my grasp.[84]

NINTH DEALER. I believe you. A slow, lumpish fellow you seem to be. And what is the end of your knowledge?

SCEPTIC. Ignorance. Deafness. Blindness.

NINTH DEALER. What! sight and hearing both gone?

SCEPTIC. And with them judgement and perception, and all, in short, that distinguishes man from a worm.

NINTH DEALER. You are worth money!—What shall we say for him?

HERMES. Four pounds.[85]

NINTH DEALER. Here is is. Well, fellow; so you are mine?

SCEPTIC. I doubt it.

NINTH DEALER. Nay, doubt it not! You are bought and paid for.

SCEPTIC. It is a difficult case. . . . I reserve my decision.

NINTH DEALER. Now, come along with me, like a good slave.

SCEPTIC. But how am I to know whether what you say is true?

NINTH DEALER. Ask the auctioneer. Ask my money. Ask the spectators.

SCEPTIC. Spectators? But can we be sure there are any?

NINTH DEALER. Oh, I'll send you to the treadmill. That will convince you with a vengeance that I am your master.

SCEPTIC. Reserve your decision.

NINTH DEALER. Too late. It is given.

HERMES. Stop that wrangling and go with your purchaser. Gentlemen, we hope to see you here again to-morrow, when we shall be offering some lots suitable for plain men, artisans, and shopkeepers.

84. I.e., everything is doubtful; there is no absolute certainty.
85. One mina.

Introduction to Plotinus

Plotinus (A.D. 203-270) is a prime example of that synthesis of many traditions which was so common among Hellenistic thinkers. A native Egyptian, he was born in Lycopolis in central Egypt, but received a basic Greek education. At Alexandria—that melting-pot of the Mediterranean world—he studied philosophy with Ammonius Saccas, a Christian turned pagan. After ten years with Ammonius, he joined the Roman emperor Gordian's expedition to India (A.D. 244), where he hoped to learn at first hand the doctrines of the Persian Magi and Indian Brahmins. But Gordian's army turned back in Persia; and Plotinus went to Rome, where he spent the remainder of his life as a teacher of philosophy.

Plotinus is the best-known thinker of the Neo-Platonist school, which sought to re-interpret Plato in a religious sense. Although his own faith was not confined to the doctrines of any church, the intensity of his religious feeling can scarcely be doubted. He appears to have been a mystic; in one of his rare autobiographical references he alludes to his personal experience of God. As a thinker, he did not organize his ideas in any systematic manner, and only late in life did he commit them to writing. His *Enneads* ("Nine Books")—each of which regards his whole system from a particular viewpoint—are among the most difficult literature in the whole history of Western philosophy. Nonetheless, until modern times Neo-Platonism was the channel through which the philosophy of Plato reached the West and exerted its enormous influence on Western thought.

Plotinus' attempt to find order and reason in the universe was in the best Greek tradition. But he could not have been unaware of the religious ferment—the competition of many diverse creeds—which existed in his day at Alexandria and Rome. His concept of a series of emanations proceeding from the highest to the lowest principle, and his emphasis on knowledge rather than faith as the way to salvation, resemble the ideas of the Gnostics. Though he never reached India, it is quite conceivable that even in Alexandria—which maintained commercial contacts with India at that time—he was able to learn something of Hinduism. His belief in the transmigration of souls and his ascetic morality had antecedents in Gnosticism and even in Plato, though they are fundamental to Indian religion as well. But his identification of the individual human soul with the World Soul, and his exaltation of a contemplative state in which the individual consciousness is extinguished, offer clearer examples of possible Indian influence.

In Plotinus' cosmology everything has its assigned place, arranged in order of rank. The source and unifying principle of all that exists in the universe is the One, or God. The second principle is the Intelligence, or the world known to the mind—corresponding roughly to Plato's world of Ideas, though Plotinus strongly resisted the suggestion that the Ideas somehow exist outside of the world. The third of his principles is the World Soul, of which all individual souls form a part. Each of these principles is spiritual in nature as well as logical. In Plotinus' system the spiritual component necessary to religion merges with the logical element demanded by reason.

The One is a unity, without distinction or variety within itself. Creation occurs spontaneously and continuously through emanation from the One. The process may be visualized by comparing the One to a kind of inexhaustible energy-source whose emissions flow outward and weaken in direct proportion to their distance from the center. There are no breaks in nature—each entity merges imperceptibly into the next.

The rational principle of the universe is the Intelligence, which is the model for the world of visible phenomena. The Intelligence is unchanging and incorporeal; the specific Ideas of things are within it. As the second in rank, it mediates between the principle immediately above it—the One—and the World Soul, which is directly below it. In turn, the World Soul acts as intermediary between the Intelligence and the material world of things. The organizing force of each body is an individual soul. These souls are part of the World Soul just as individual bodies are part of the material universe. Every active force in nature is a soul or attaches itself to a soul. Thereby the World Soul both contains and directs the universe.

Through contemplation—looking inward upon itself—the individual soul becomes conscious of its unity with the World Soul. Through the World Soul it advances to contemplation of the Intelligence, and ultimately to union with the One. The soul proceeds on this journey through its own advance in knowledge. There is no place in Plotinus' system for a Saviour who enlightens mankind and leads the way. Through its own contemplative activity, the soul knows (and thus becomes) Intelligence and is reabsorbed into its original source, the One.

PLOTINUS: FROM THE ENNEADS

It has happened often.

1 Roused into myself from my body[1]—outside everything else and inside myself—my gaze has met a beauty wondrous and great. At such moments I have been certain that mine was the better part,[2] mine the best of lives lived to the fullest, mine identity with the divine. Fixed there firmly, poised above everything in the intellectual[3] that is less than the highest,[4] utter actuality was mine.[5]

But then there has come the descent, down from intellection to the discourse of reason.[6] And it leaves me puzzled. Why this descent?

Indeed, why did my soul ever enter my body since even when in the body it remains what it has shown itself to be when by itself?[7]

. . . .

2 . . . One is driven to questions about soul in general: How has soul been brought into association with body? Of what sort is this world in which soul (freely or necessarily or in any other way) lives? Did the demiurge[8] do right in making this world? Or as our souls do?[9]

It would seem that our souls, charged with the managing of bodies less perfect than they, had to penetrate into them if they were to manage them truly. For such bodies have a tendency to

1. Or: out of my body and into myself; an apparent paradox, describing the contemplative state.
2. The better part of life.
3. The realm of Ideas.
4. Apparently: the highest, or unified Intelligence, as distinct from individual Ideas.
5. A sense of complete reality; unity with the divine One.
6. I.e., the rational observation of individual things.
7. I.e., it remains the divine thing which it was outside of the body.
8. In Plato, the demiurge is the direct creator of the universe. Plotinus uses the term even though it fits imperfectly into his scheme of things.
9. Scholars dispute the interpretation of this passage. The translator takes it to mean: Did the demiurge act freely in making this world, or did it act out of necessity, like our souls do?

come apart, their parts struggling to return to their natural places (since everything in the cosmos has its natural place). More than that, such bodies require a knowing management that is both extensive and detailed because they are forever exposed to the assaults of alien bodies, are forever oppressed by wants; they need help, unremittingly, in the multiple adversities that beset them.

The body of The Soul,[10] on the other hand, is perfect. It is complete. It is self-sufficient. It is not subject to influences that prevent its expressing its own nature. It requires, accordingly, only a light control.[11] That is why The Soul remains free of care and molestations, its native disposition intact—"nothing going out, nothing coming in." Hence Plato says that the human soul, when it is with this perfect one, becomes perfect itself and "journeys on high and controls the whole world," and, so long as it does not withdraw (to enter a body, to be attached to something individual), exercises a control as effortless as that of The Soul. That it gives body existence is not necessarily to the soul's hurt: providing for a lower nature does not necessarily prevent the agency that exercises it from remaining itself in a state of perfection. Providence is of two kinds: it is directed to the whole and regulates everything after the fashion of kings, giving orders to be executed by others, or it is involved with detail and operates directly, adapting agent and acted upon one to the other. The Soul, divine, administers the heavens in the first way: transcending them in its highest phases and immanent to them solely in its lowest.[12] One cannot accordingly accuse divinity of having assigned an inferior place to The Soul; it has never been deprived of its native status; this operation, which is not counter to its nature, it always possessed and always will.

In saying that the relation of the souls of the stars to their bodies is the same as that of The Soul of the world to the world[13] (since these starry bodies are encompassed in the circuit of The

10. The World Soul (capitalized), as distinct from individual human souls.
11. By the Intelligence.
12. This explains how the soul can be immanent in the body without detracting from its divinity: immanence is considered an inferior form of control; transcendence is higher.
13. I.e., the world of physical nature; the visible world of sense-perception.

Soul), Plato also accords the stars their appropriate happiness. Of the two objections against the interaction of soul and body—that it "hinders" the soul's intellective act and that it "fills" the soul with pleasure, "lust," fear—neither holds here. The soul has not penetrated deeply into body and is not dependent on the particular. Body is for it and not it for body. Its body lacks nothing, wants nothing.[14] Hence the soul is free from both desires and fears. Since the starry body is what it is, the soul has no cause for disturbance on its account. Nothing intrudes upon its repose and makes it incline downward, robbing it of the high happiness of contemplation. It is always with the things in the realm above and, empowered and undisturbed, governs the realm of sense.

3 Let us now consider the human soul, which while in the body is subject to ills and suffering, a prey to griefs, lusts, fears, and evils of every kind, whose body is a "chain" or a "tomb" and the realm of sense a "cave" or a "grotto."[15] That it should be thus does not go counter to the preceding; it is simply that the causes of its descent are different.

To begin with, The Intelligence dwells entire within that region of thought we call the intelligible realm,[16] yet it comprises within itself a variety of intellective powers and particular intelligences. The Intelligence is not merely one: it is one and many. In the same way is there both Soul and many souls. From the one Soul proceeds a multiplicity of different souls, as from one and the same genus proceed species of various ranks, some of which are more rational and others (at least in their actual existence) less rational in form.

Again, in the intelligible realm there is The Intelligence, which like some huge organism contains potentially all other intelligences, and there are the individual intelligences, each of them an actuality. Think of a city as having a soul. It would include inhabitants, each of whom would have a soul. The soul of the city would be the more perfect and more powerful. What would prevent the souls of the inhabitants from being of the

14. Plotinus is still speaking of starry bodies, not human ones.
15. The phrases derive from Plato.
16. Which includes both the Intelligence and the objects of its knowing.

same nature as the soul of the city? Or, again, take fire, the universal, from which proceed large and small particular fires; all of them have a common essence, that of universal fire—or, rather, all partake of that essence whence proceeds universal fire. The function of The Soul, as intellective, is intellection. But it is not limited to intellection. If it were, there would be no distinction between it and The Intelligence. It has functions besides the intellectual and these, by which it is not simply intelligence, determine its distinctive existence. In directing itself to what is above itself, it thinks. In directing itself to itself, it preserves itself. In directing itself to what is lower than itself, it orders, administers, and governs. The reason for such an existent as The Soul is that the totality of things cannot continue limited to the intelligible so long as a succession of further existents is possible; although less perfect, they necessarily are because the prior existent necessarily is.

4 Thus individual souls are possessed by a desire for the intelligible that would have them return there whence they came, and they possess, too, a power over the realm of sense much in the way that sunshine, although attached to the sun above, does not deny its rays to what is below. If the souls remain in the intelligible realm with The Soul, they are beyond harm and share in The Soul's governance. They are like kings who live with the high king and govern with him and, like him, do not come down from the palace.

Thus far all are in the one same place.

But there comes a point at which they come down from this state, cosmic in its dimensions, to one of individuality. They wish to be independent. They are tired, you might say, of living with someone else. Each steps down into its own individuality.

When a soul remains for long in this withdrawal and estrangement from the whole, with never a glance towards the intelligible, it becomes a thing fragmented, isolated, and weak. Activity lacks concentration. Attention is tied to particulars. Severed from the whole, the soul clings to the part; to this one sole thing, buffeted about by a whole worldful of things, has it turned and given itself. Adrift now from the whole, it manages even this particular thing with difficulty, its care of it compelling attention to externals, presence to the body, the deep penetration of the body.

Thus comes about what is called "loss of wings" or the "chaining" of the soul. Its no longer are the ways of innocence in which, with The Soul, it presided over the higher realms. Life above was better by far than this. A thing fallen, chained, at first barred off from intelligence and living only by sensation, the soul is, as they say, in tomb or cavern pent.

Yet its higher part remains. Let the soul, taking its lead from memory, merely "think on essential being"[17] and its shackles are loosed and it soars.

Souls of necessity lead a double life, partly in the intelligible realm and partly in that of sense, the higher life dominant in those able to commune more continuously with The Intelligence, the lower dominant where character or circumstance are the less favorable. . . .

5 . . . Everything that becomes worse does so unwillingly, yet when it becomes so through inherent tendency, that submission to the lower can be regarded as a penalty.[18] Then, too, these experiences and acts are determined by an eternal law of nature, so that it may be said, without being either inconsistent or untruthful, that a soul that descends from the world above to some lower being is sent by the divinity; for final effects, however far removed by intermediate effects, are always to be referred back to the starting point.

There are two wrongs the soul commits. The first is its descent; the second, the evil done after arrival here below. The first is punished by the very conditions of its descent. Punishment for the second is passage once more into other bodies, there to remain at greater or less length according to the judgment of its deserts. (The word "judgment" indicates that this takes place as a result of divine law.) If, however, its perversity goes beyond all measure, the soul incurs an even more severe penalty administered by avenging daimons.[19]

17. I.e., on the Intelligence.
18. For one's acts in a previous existence.
19. These are eternal beings intermediary between the three principles and man. Their task is to chastise the human soul.

Thus, too, The Soul enters body—although its nature is divine and its realm the intelligible. A lesser divinity, it is impelled by the stress of its powers and the attraction of governing the next below it. By voluntary inclination it plunges into this sphere. If it returns quickly, it will have suffered no harm in thus learning of evil and of what sin is, in bringing its powers into manifest play, in exhibiting activities and achievements that, remaining merely potentialities in the intelligible realm, might as well never have been if they were never meant to be actualized: The Soul itself would never really know these suppressed, inhibited potencies. Potencies are revealed by acts, for potencies in themselves are hidden and undetectable and, for all practical purposes, nonexistent. As it is, all now marvel at the inner greatness of The Soul exteriorly revealed in the richness of its acts.

6 The One must not be solely the solitary. If it were, reality would remain buried and shapeless since in The One there is no differentiation of forms. No beings would exist if The One remained shut up in itself. More than that, the multiplicity of beings issued from The One would not exist as they do if there did not issue from The One those beings that are in the rank of souls. Likewise, souls must not play the solitaries, their issue stifled. Every nature must produce its next, for each thing must unfold, seedlike, from indivisible principle into a visible effect. Principle continues unaltered in its proper place; what unfolds from it is the product of the inexpressible power that resides in it. It must not stay this power and, as though jealous, limit its effects. It must proceed continuously until all things, to the very last, have within the limits of possibility come forth. All is the result of this immense power giving its gifts to the universe, unable to let any part remain without its share.

Nothing hinders anything from sharing in the Good to the extent it is able. That statement holds true even for matter. If, on the one hand, matter is assumed to have existed from all eternity,[20] it is impossible that, having existence, it should not have a share in that which, in accord with each receptivity, communicates the Good to all. If, on the other hand, matter is

20. As in Zoroastrian dualism.

held to be the necessary consequence of anterior causes, it will not be separated from this principle either as though, having graciously given it existence, it was powerless to reach it.

The excellence, the power, and the goodness of the intelligible realm is revealed in what is most excellent in the realm of sense, for the realms are linked together. From the one, self-existent, the other eternally draws its existence by participation and, to the extent it reproduces the intelligible, by imitation.

7 As there are these two realms, the intelligible and that of sense, it is better for the soul to dwell in the intelligible. But, such is its nature, it is necessary that it live also in the realm of sense. Accordingly it occupies only an intermediate rank. Yet there is no cause for complaint that it is not in all respects the highest. By nature divine, it is located at the nethermost limit of the intelligible realm, bordering on the realm of sense, and there gives to the realm of sense something of its own. In turn it is itself affected when, instead of controlling the body without endangering its own security, it lets itself be carried away by an excessive zeal and plunges deep into the body and ceases to be wholly united to The Soul. Yet the soul can rise above this condition again and, turning to account the experience of what it has seen and suffered here below, can better appreciate the life that is above and can know more clearly what is the better by contrast with its opposite. Indeed, knowledge of good is sharpened by experience of evil in those incapable of any sure knowledge of evil unless they have experienced it.

For The Intelligence, to reason discursively[21] is to descend to its lowest level rather than to rise to the level of the existence beyond. But it cannot remain within itself. Of necessity it produces. Of necessity, then, by the very law of its nature, it proceeds to the level of The Soul. It goes no further. Entrusting the later stages of being to The Soul, it returns once more to the intelligible realm.

For The Soul it is much the same. Its lowest act is the realm of sense; its highest, contemplation of the supernal beings.

21. Logically rather than intuitively. Reason proceeds from the Intelligence into the soul.

For individual souls this contemplation is fragmentary and divided by time, so their conversion begins on a lower level. But The Soul never becomes involved in the activities of the lower world. Immune to evil, it comprehends intellectually what is below it while always cleaving to what is above it. Therefore is it able, at one and the same time, to be debtor to what is above and, since as soul it cannot escape touching this sphere, benefactor to what is below.

8 This, now, goes counter to current belief. But let us take our courage in our hands and say it: No soul, not even our own, enters into the body completely. Soul always remains united by its higher part to the intelligible realm. But if the part that is in the realm of sense dominates, or rather becomes dominated and disturbed, it keeps us unaware of what the higher part of the soul contemplates. . . .

Every soul has a lower part directed towards the bodily and a higher part directed towards the intelligible. The Soul, effortlessly, manages the universe by that part directed towards the bodily. For The Soul governs the bodily not by discursive reasoning, as we do, but by intuition (much as is done in the arts). Individual souls, each of which manages a part of the universe, also have a higher phase. But they are preoccupied with sensation and its impressions. Much they perceive is contrary to nature and troubles and confuses them. This is so because the body in their care is deficient, hedged about with alien influences, filled with desires, deceived in its very pleasures. Yet there is a part of the soul insensitive to the lure of these passing pleasures, whose living is correspondent to its reality.

Introduction to Gnosticism

"Gnosticism" is a general term for a broad spectrum of religious systems holding similar views of the origin and fate of mankind. Formerly regarded simply as a Christian heresy of the first several centuries A.D., Gnosticism is now known to have antedated the Christian period. Certain Gnostic sects—the Valentinians and the Hermetics in Egypt, the Mandaeans in southern Babylonia (who survive to this day)—were purely pagan in origin. Even in the early Christian church, the boundaries were fluid between orthodoxy and heresy. Some famous thinkers who were deeply marked by Gnosticism nevertheless considered themselves Christian, e.g. Marcion (2nd century A.D.) and Origen (early 3rd century), both of whom eventually were declared anathema by the Roman Church. Finally, Manichaeism—once a chief rival of Christianity—showed many similarities to Gnosticism.

All the Gnostic religions were religions of salvation, which focused on the fate of the human soul after bodily death. The instrument of salvation was *gnosis*, meaning "knowledge"; but the knowledge referred to had little in common with reason or logic. Rather, it signified the understanding of divine things: knowledge of God and of the secret lore required for salvation. This *gnosis* was attainable not through reason, but through a kind of inner illumination or revelation.

The God of the Gnostics was a remote and "alien" God, residing in a realm of Light far removed from the universe. He did not create the universe, nor even take any interest in it: involvement with an inferior world would infringe upon his perfection. The world was generated and governed by inferior deities. The creation of these lesser gods was a major theme of Gnostic speculation. In the Syro-Egyptian, or non-dualistic forms of Gnosticism, the necessity of reconciling God's omnipotence and goodness with the existence of evil gave rise to vast and subtle systems of mythology in which the details of the creation were minutely delineated. Iranian dualist Gnosticism had a simpler task: by assuming an eternal principle of Darkness co-equal with the Light, it could regard the world as evil without prejudicing the goodness of Light.

In the Gnostic myth, the earth resembles the innermost circle of a vast prison, analogous in many respects to the Greek Underworld or the Christian Hell. The earth is surrounded by a number of concentric spheres, usually counted as seven, though certain Gnostic thinkers postulated many more. Each of the seven spheres is ruled by one of the seven wicked Archons (identified with the seven planets); the eighth and outermost sphere is regulated by the fixed stars. The tyrannical rule of the Archons is termed Fate, or the law of Nature.

Just as the earth is surrounded by spheres, so the human spirit (*pneuma*) is enclosed in seven vestments, which are the carnal passions or appetites composing the soul. Like the body, the soul too is a creation of the Archons, who endowed it with their own evil natures. Only the *pneuma*, the divine spark consisting of Light-substance, is pure. In the vast upheaval which preceded the creation of the world, particles of this Light-substance became entrapped in the material universe. The human body was formed specifically to hold these particles and prevent their escape.

Salvation thus consists of liberating the *pneuma* from its bodily prison so that it may ascend to God. Association with the body has caused it to forget its high origin and true nature: in a word, it is ignorant. Ignorance is thus the Gnostic equivalent of sin. The escape from ignorance is knowledge, which leads to salvation. Unaided, man cannot attain this saving knowledge. He requires a Saviour who will show him the truth and lead his spirit out of its dark prison. The Saviour—who is an indirect creation of God—arrives on earth disguised in an earthly body in order to deceive the Archons. He awakens the entrapped particles of Light from their sleep. He teaches the secret passwords which are necessary to outwit the Archons and make possible the passage of the *pneuma* through the seven spheres; he himself leads the way. At the end of the world, all the lost particles of Light-substance will be reassembled above in the realm of Light.

The ethics of Gnosticism follow from this cosmic concept. The body and its desires are evil; for they prevent the *pneuma* from gaining release. Thus the Gnostic sects encouraged indifference to the body; their "Elect," or saints, practiced extreme forms of asceticism. To the Gnostics, the goal of human striving lay in another world, rather than in this one, which they regarded as by nature evil and unredeemable. Nonetheless, for the most part they considered virtuous conduct on this earth as pre-requisite to the freeing of the spirit.

Modern knowledge of Gnosticism is fragmentary; for its holy writings were largely destroyed through the vigilance of orthdox Christianity. But there can be no doubt that Gnosticism was a major religious force in the early Christian centuries. Certain striking resemblances between Gnostic and Christian doctrines—e.g. Saint Paul's division of man into spirit, soul, and flesh, which has no counterpart in Judaism—proved acutely embarrassing to the Fathers of the Christian Church. There was never a single Gnostic Church; indeed, in its emphasis on inner illumination, Gnosticism encouraged individual speculation and was productive of many sects. Perhaps this divisiveness—together with the persecuting zeal of the Christians—contributed to its eventual disappearance. But as a part of the thought-world in which Christianity originated, Gnosticism—with its relative, Manichaeism—left an undoubted mark upon the religious thought of the West.

Introduction to The Hymn of the Soul

"The Hymn of the Soul" is a Gnostic composition of the early third century A.D. It has come down to us as part of the *Acts of Saint Thomas*, an apocryphal work of Gnostic and ascetic tendencies which purports to describe the mission of the apostle Thomas in India. Though the "Hymn" is supposed to have been composed by Saint Thomas in an Indian prison, it actually has little connection with the rest of the *Acts*, which it almost certainly antedates. The poem is extant in both Greek and Syriac versions, though the Syriac is clearly the original. Its author may possibly have been the famous Syrian Gnostic Bardesanes (flourished *ca.* 200 A.D.), the creator of the literary Syriac language.

The hymn relates the central Gnostic salvation-doctrine in the guise of a fable. The prince is the Saviour who comes into the world to awaken the sleeping particles of Light. The pearl is a standard Gnostic symbol for the engulfed Light—a shining treasure surrounded by layers of animal shell and hidden in the dark depths. But with that duplication of symbols characteristic of Gnostic mythology, the prince himself soon comes to personify the existential condition of the engulfed *pneuma*. The evil world of matter—symbolized by Egypt, the home of the cult of the dead and death—has caused him to forget his true identity and sink into the slumber of ignorance.

The figure of the "saved Saviour"—the Saviour himself in need of redemption—is a familiar one in Gnostic mythology whenever divine personages are involved in the lower world. This duplication of identities is repeated in other symbols. The heavenly garments of the Saviour represent his eternal self—a kind of double or image of himself preserved in the upper realms while he is down below. This image is perfected by his good deeds; at the completion of his mission he is reunited with it. The twin brother, or next-in-rank, may also be a form of this eternal image.

The dress of the Egyptians, on the other hand, symbolizes the body—the transient earthly prison of the spirit. By putting on Egyptian dress, the prince clothes himself in evil matter. Similarly in the Gnostic myth, the Saviour assumes the burden of the world's sins. In a purely physical way, he incorporates these sins into his own flesh. Thereby he is able to exhaust their evil power; for at death he leaves his flesh behind and assumes his celestial body. Likewise the prince of our hymn sheds his Egyptian garments, puts on his glittering heavenly robe, and dwells forever after in his Father's kingdom.

THE HYMN OF THE SOUL

When I was a little child
Living in my kingdom, in my father's house,
Happy in the wealth and rank
Of those that reared me—
From the East, our home,
My parents sent me out.
The treasures of our store-room
They tied for me in a bundle;[1]
Large, yet so light
That I could carry it in my hands:
Gold of Beth-Ellaye,[2]
Silver of Gazzak the Great,[3]
Rubies of Hind,[4]
Agates of Beth Kashan;[5]

Trans. by Arthur Waley in the anthology *The Secret History of the Mongols,* London: George Allen & Unwin, 1963, pp. 297-302. Originally published in *Encounter* magazine, December 1953. Reprinted by permission of George Allen & Unwin, Ltd., and Barnes & Noble, Inc.

1. The bundle of provisions symbolizes the spiritual instruction, or *gnosis,* which the Saviour communicates to the faithful.

2. Or: land of the Ellaeans. Ellaea was an ancient port of northwest Asia Minor; at one time it served as harbor for the rich city of Pergamum.

3. Or Gazaca: the great palace of the Parthians in Upper Media, probably at Ecbatana.

4. India.

5. Or: the land of the Kushans, in modern Afghanistan.

And at my belt was tied *adamas*,[6]
That can crush iron.
And they took off the glittering robe
That in their love they had made for me,
And my purple cloak
That was measured and woven to my stature,
And they made a pact with me,
And lest I should forget
They wrote it on my heart:
"If you go down into Egypt
And bring that only pearl
That is in the midst of the sea,[7]
Guarded by the snorting dragon,[8]
Then you shall put on again your glittering robe
And the cloak that you delight in,
And with your brother, next in rank,
Be heir to our kingdom."
I left the East, and went down,
And there were two couriers with me,
For the way was dangerous and hard to find,
And I was young to take it.
I passed the borders of Maishan,[9] the meeting place
Of the merchants of the East.
I came to the land of Babel,[10]
I entered the walls of Sarbug.[11]
I went down into Egypt,
And my companions left me.
I went to the place of the dragon;

6. Adamant, a very hard stone.
7. "Sea" is a frequent Gnostic symbol for the world of matter or darkness.
8. The dragon is the ruler or evil principle of the world. Its mythological archetype is Tiamat, the monster slain by the Babylonian god Marduk.
9. Or Mesene, meaning "middle land." There were probably two districts in ancient Mesopotamia called by this name, one near the mouths of the Tigris, the other farther up the same river.
10. Babylonia.
11. Or the Labyrinth, a structure full of intricate passages. There were four principal labyrinths in the ancient world. The one in Egypt, located near the site of modern Cairo, was adorned with massive columns, gigantic statues, richly carved hieroglyphics, and every form of Egyptian art.

I lived close to his lair,
Waiting till he should be asleep,
So that I might take the pearl from him.
I was quite alone,
A stranger to those with whom I lived.
Then one of my own race, a freeman,
A man of the East I saw,[12]
A youth fresh and comely,
A son of chieftains.
He came to me and was my friend;
I made him partner in my quest,
Warning him against the Egyptians,
Against consorting with the unclean.
But I wore a dress like theirs
Lest they should scorn me as a stranger,
Lest when I went to take the pearl
They should rouse up the dragon against me.
But whether by this means or that
They saw I was not their countryman.
They dealt with me cunningly,
They gave me their food to eat.
Then I forgot I was a son of kings,
And served their king.
I forgot the pearl
For which my parents had sent me.
The burden of their food lay heavy on me,
And I fell into a deep sleep.
But all that had happened to me
My parents knew, and were very sad.
There was made a proclamation in our Kingdom
That all should hasten to our gate,
Kings and princes of Parthia—
All the nobles of the East.
They made a plan to save me,
That I might not be left in Egypt.
They wrote a letter[13] to me

12. This may be another instance of the duplication of symbols.
13. The "letter" or "call" which awakens the sleeping *pneuma* from its ignorance is a standard Gnostic symbol.

And every noble put his name to it:
"From your father, king of kings,
And your mother, mistress of the East,
From your brother next in rank,
To our son in Egypt, greeting!
Rise from your sleep and listen
To the words of our letter.
Remember that you are a son of kings;
See to what slavery you stoop!
Remember the pearl
For which you hurried to Egypt,
Think of the glittering robe,
Recall your glorious cloak
That you shall wear again as your finery
When in the list of the valiant
Your name is cited.
With your brother, our next of rank,
You shall be heir in our kingdom."
My letter! A letter from the king
Sealed with his own right hand
That it might be safe from the wicked,
The children of Babel and the cruel demons of Sarbug.
It flew in the likeness of an eagle,
King of all birds;
It flew and lighted beside me
And became all speech.
At its voice and the sound of its rustling
I started and rose from my sleep.
I took it up and kissed it
And loosened the seal and read;
And according to what was traced on my heart
Were the words of the letter written.
I remembered I was the son of kings;
I missed my free estate,
I remembered the pearl
For which I had been sent into Egypt,
And I laid a charm on the terrible one,[14]

14. The "charm" is effective because the Light is as much poison to the Darkness as the Darkness is to Light.

The snorting dragon;
I hushed him to sleep, lulled him to slumber,
For my father's name I named over him
And the name of our next-in-rank,
And of my mother, queen of the East.
I snatched away the pearl
And turned to go back to my father's house.
Their filthy and unclean dress
I stripped off and left in their country;
I took my way straight back
To the light of our home, the East.
And my letter, my awakener,
I found before me on the road;
And as with its voice it had aroused me
So with its light it led me on.
Dweller in silk,
It shone before me with its form;
With its voice and guidance
It quickened me on my path,
With its love it drew me on.
I went forth and passed by Sarbug,
I left Babel on my left hand
And reached Maishan the great,
The harbour of the merchants,
That sits upon the shore of the sea.
And my bright robe that I had stripped off
And the cloak it was wrapped in
From Ramtha-Reken[15] my parents sent to me
By the hand of treasurers
Whose faithfulness they trusted.
I had forgotten how it was fashioned,
For I was a child when I left it
At my father's house.
And now as I came towards it
The dress seemed to me
Like a mirror of myself.

15. "The heights," probably of Hyrcania, the province of the Persian empire southeast of the Caspian Sea.

I saw in it all my whole self;
I went to myself in going to it.
We were two in distinction,
Yet one in likeness.
And the treasurers, too, who brought it
I saw in like manner
That they were two, yet one in likeness;[16]
For one kingly sign was graven on them,
As on the hands of him that had restored it to me.
Here was my treasure, my wealth,
My bright embroidered robe,
Gay with many colours.
With gold, beryls, rubies and agates
And sardonyx of every hue,
Skilfully worked in its high home.
With stones of *adamas*
All its seams were fastened,
And the picture of the king of kings
Was embroidered all over it.
And like the sapphire stone
Were its many hues.
And again I saw that all over it
The motions of knowledge were quivering.
And I saw it making ready
As though it would speak to me.
I heard the sound of its voice
As it spoke to those that brought it down:
"I am the active in deeds
(Whom they reared for him before my father;)[17]
I perceived in myself that my nature
Grew according to his labours."
And in its kingly movements
It poured itself out over me,
And on the hand of the givers

16. The notion of the image in Gnosticism is probably derived from the Persian doctrine, found in the *Avesta*, that after the death of a believer his own conscience appears to his soul.
17. Unintelligible both in Greek and the Syriac [Tr.].

It hastened, that I might take it.
And love urged me on,
That I should run to meet it and receive it.
I stretched out my hand and took it,
With the beauty of its colours I clothed myself.
My cloak of bright colours
I cast round me in its whole breadth.
I dressed in it, I went up
To the gate of greeting and homage,
To the Majesty[18] of my father who sent it to me;
For I had done his commandment
And he too had done what he promised.
And at the gate of his princes
I mingled with his nobles,
For he rejoiced in me and welcomed me,
And I was back with him in his kingdom;
For with the voice of praise
All his servants glorify him.
And now they promised that to the door
Of the king of kings I should be brought;
That bringing my gift and my pearl
I should come before the king.

18. *Ziwa,* the sign of kingship [Tr.].

Introduction to Manichaeism

Manichaeism, like Gnosticism, was anchored upon the conviction that man is an exile in a world of Darkness. Both religions taught an immensely involved cosmology explaining the fall of Light in a great war with Darkness and the resultant incorporation of Light-substance into human bodies. With both, the goal of human life was to free the Light from its prison of Matter. But unlike the Gnostic sects, which were often primarily concerned with the salvation of an elite, Manichaeism sought to be a mass-religion devoted to the redemption of mankind. Though its core was Gnostic, it consciously attempted to synthesize the major religions of its time into a single all-embracing system which would be the culmination of all others. Mani, its founder, considered himself the fourth prophet in a series which included Buddha, Zoroaster, and Jesus.

Mani was born in A.D. 216 in Babylonia, which was then a part of the Parthian empire. Of Persian rather than native Babylonian parentage, he grew up amid two cultural traditions—a fact perhaps related to his later syncretistic efforts. Uncertain evidence suggests that his father was connected with the Mandaean sect, which, if so, could account for the Gnostic element in his teaching. In any event, Mani became a wide-ranging traveler acquainted with many religions. He received the call to preach in the reign of Ardashir, founder of the Sassanian dynasty; but his main prophetic activity occurred under Shapur I (reigned A.D. 241-72). Shapur protected him; and as long as the king lived Mani was free to propagate his doctrine. But the established Zoroastrian priesthood of the empire resented his success; and under Bahram I (reigned A.D. 273-76) their influence prevailed. In the year A.D. 275, Mani was crucified.

From Zoroastrianism Mani took his notion of two eternal and co-equal principles, which he called Light and Darkness. The nature of Light he described as harmony and peace; that of Darkness as discord, hate, and strife. The world came into being through an act of Darkness. Originally, the realm of Light had bordered on the realm of Darkness with no dividing wall. The Light wished only to enjoy its own tranquillity; it had no ambition either to challenge the Darkness or to transform it. But in one of the internal upheavals perpetually occurring within the lower realm, a son of Darkness was pushed to the edge of the Depths and caught a glimpse of the Light. Recognizing the superiority of the Light and admiring the wonderful Light-creations, he was filled with hate and envy. Desiring to possess the Light for itself, Darkness initiated the great war.

This was the starting-point for Manichaean cosmology—a vast and complicated epic in which countless mythological figures took part. Forced to take note of the threat from below, Light was roused from its tranquillity. The Father of Greatness—king of the realm of Light—began the process of emanation which brought forth a series of divine beings designed to do battle in his name. Through an outflow of his own substance, he created the first of these godly personages—the Mother of Life. She in turn produced Primal (First) Man, the central Saviour-figure of the system. Next to be created—in descending order of rank—were the Living Spirit, the Third Messenger, and the Luminous Jesus.

Primal Man was the first to combat the Darkness. In some versions of the myth he is defeated; in others, anticipating defeat, he sacrifices his five sons to the Darkness. By whatever means, the Darkness succeeds in devouring a portion of Primal Man's divine Light-substance. The swallowed Light has a numbing effect upon the Darkness, which is thereby deflected from its original goal—the conquest of the realm of Light itself. But the Light cannot rest until it has recovered all of its lost substance. An extensive series of further battles occurs, in which, as an incidental effect, the universe and mankind are created.

Primal Man is an archetypal figure as well as an actor in the divine drama. His five lost sons are the elements of man's soul. In the myth, Primal Man himself—without his soul—was restored to the realm of Light through the call of the Living Spirit. But the call of the Living Spirit and Primal Man's response live on in the human soul as the possibility of escape from Darkness and return to the world of Light. The recovery of all the lost Light will mean not only the end of the universe, but the final conquest of Darkness, which, separated from the captured Light, will be reduced to impotence forever.

The various portions of the Darkness hold unequal quantities of Light-substance. In the first step toward freeing the Light, the Living Spirit separates the mixed portions from the pure Darkness. He extracts that part of the Light which is least contaminated and forms it into physical Light, from which are created the sun, moon, and stars. From the bodies of the Archons—demons whose substance has become mixed with Light—he creates the earth.*

Then the Third Messenger appears to set the heavenly bodies in motion. Through the revolutions of sun, moon, and stars a portion of the Light automatically will be separated from the Darkness and transported upwards. At the same time, the Messenger reveals to the Archons his divine beauty, in both its male and female aspects. Excited by the sight, the Archons begin to release some of the captured Light; but a quantity of Dark substance escapes also. As the purer parts of Light rise upward, the contaminated portions fall to earth to form the vegetable world. Through their love for the Messenger, the daughters of Darkness produce abortions, offspring "born out of due time,"† which become the animal world.

The grand counter-strategy of Darkness is the creation of Adam

* Similarly, the god Marduk created the world out of the body of the dragon Tiamat in the Babylonian *Creation Epic.* (See Volume I of this series.)
† Saint Paul applies this expression to himself in I Corinthians, 15:8.

and Eve. With particularly devilish ingenuity he shapes them in the image of Primal Man, because in this form it will be easiest to retain a large quantity of the captured Light. The human body is thus of devilish design. Reproduction is Satan's most formidable weapon: not only does it indefinitely prolong the captivity of Light; but by dispersing the Light into many bodies it renders more difficult the work of recovery. The return of all the engulfed Light requires the salvation of each individual particle. The cosmic struggle between Light and Darkness thus centers on mankind; and the acts of the individual assume enormous significance.

The Saviour of earthly man is the Luminous Jesus—the heavenly personage produced by emanation from the Living Spirit. He personifies the Light which is entangled with Darkness. Because he is dispersed throughout the universe, in his passive aspect he suffers every day—he is the Jesus who "hangs from every tree."* In his active aspect he is the transmundane Reason, which liberates the captive Light-substance. In earthly history his revelation has been four times renewed, through the apostolates of Buddha, Zoroaster, the historical Jesus, and Mani. The Luminous Jesus rules over the New Paradise—the heavenly kingdom created by the Father of Greatness as a resting place for the Saviours during their struggle to redeem the lost Light. As soon as all souls have been saved and the universe is at an end, the liberated Light will return to the Father's Eternal Paradise.

Consistent with their low view of the world, the Manichaeans taught a sternly ascetic morality. Life on earth they regarded as merely a preparation for the liberation of Light-substance. Attachment to the pleasures and comforts of earthly existence was discouraged. All believers were expected to refrain from eating animal food, which was supposed to contain comparatively large amounts of Light. But the "Elect" formed a group apart who pledged themselves also to abstain from marriage and reproduction and deliberately to encourage poverty. By ministering to the needs of the Elect, laymen gained credit for good deeds performed.

One of the great attractions of Manichaeism was that it regarded man and Nature as forming a cosmic unity. It taught, for example, that the released particles of Light—whether from man or from plants and animals—mount to the moon during its waxing; in the waning of the moon they are guided to the sun. The same soul-substance is present in both earthly and heavenly bodies. The whole cosmic process has religious meaning, because everything that occurs

* Compare the New Testament: Acts 5:30 and 10:39.

is an integral part of the process of freeing Light from Darkness. Another element in Manichaeism's appeal was doubtless its syncretism. Rather than rejecting and vilifying other faiths, it recognized the provisional and partial validity of its chief competitors—Buddhism, Zoroastrianism, and Christianity. Missionaries were free to emphasize whatever aspect of Manichaeism was most congenial to their listeners.

Fostered by King Shapur, the religion of Mani spread outward in all directions from its Iranian base. Communities of believers sprang up not only throughout the Persian empire, but also in the Near East, Central Asia, and as far away as Europe and China. Manichaeism in its early centuries was a well-organized missionary Church which engaged in widespread proselytizing. At one time it rivaled Christianity for dominance within the Roman empire; in medieval Europe it still ranked as a dangerous heresy.

Inevitably, Manichaeism aroused the opposition of entrenched priesthoods in the lands to which it spread; and ultimately it fell victim to its persecutors. Today this once-powerful faith has utterly ceased to exist. Even as a historical phenomenon it is little known, for the Christian Church succeeded in destroying most of the sources on which a balanced evaluation of its influence must rest. But there can be no doubt of Manichaeism's historical importance or of its broad appeal to highly divergent segments of the society of the ancient world.

Introduction to the Kephalaia

Various ancient sources testify to the existence of flourishing Manichaean communities in Egypt in the late Roman period. But owing to the almost complete disappearance of the writings of the Manichaeans themselves, modern knowledge of their religion has been based largely upon Christian polemics against it. Thus the discovery in the 1930's of a bundle of original Manichaean papyri in the Coptic tongue represented a major archaeological find. Unearthed at Medinet Madi near Lycopolis in central Egypt, the collection includes various hymns and psalms, a book of homilies, and the cosmological explanations of the work known as *Kephalaia*, or "chapters."

The texts appear to be translations from the Syriac language into Coptic, the popular speech of the Egyptians. Probably the Syriac originals were carried to Egypt by Manichaean missionaries; it may be that Lycopolis was a center for the further dissemination of the faith. The papyri apparently were discovered accidentally by Egyptians in a wooden chest in the cellar of a ruin, then divided up and sold to various dealers in antiquities, who offered them to archaeologists. The location of the find is logical; for the Manichaeans were a persecuted group and the owner of the papyri presumably found it advisable to conceal them.

Though the wooden chest saved the papyri from complete disintegration, they were nonetheless found in an advanced stage of decay. Medinet Madi lies near a swamp, and the cellar where they lay was subject to flooding when rainfall was heavy. The salty water from the desert proved especially destructive. The papyrus acted as a filter for the salt, which caused the edges of the pages to stick firmly together and completely destroyed the writing wherever crystals formed. Only through long and delicate labor were archaeologists able to separate the leaves and restore a fair portion of the texts.

The *Kephalaia* originally included several hundred chapters; but at least a third of them have been lost. The author cannot be identified, though he may have been one of Mani's original disciples. In the preface to the work, Mani is represented as directing his disciples to remember his teaching and write it down. The various chapters consist of dialogue between Mani and these men. The latter ask questions; the prophet answers. In enormously involved detail, he explains the course of the battles between Darkness and Light, the manifold emanations from the Father of Greatness, and the eventual creation of the universe.

In this first chapter, Mani affirms his apostolic status and summarizes his entire career. But although he expressly declares himself to be the successor of three prophets, the *Kephalaia*—as might be expected of a Western Manichaean text—shows much greater familiarity with Christianity than with either Zoroastrianism or Buddhism.

FROM THE KEPHALAIA

I

On the [Coming] of the Apostle:

This is the first chapter, [in which] his disciples [asked him]
About his apostleship and his [coming into] the world
In [what] way it occurred. . . . .
To wander about in every city (and) in every land,
In what way he [was] sent. . . . . .
. . in the beginning, before he had chosen [his congregation]
The apostle spoke to them: I. . . . .
. . . . but I will make it known to you. . . . .
. . . .
. . . Know, O my beloved ones, that all apostles
Who are ever sent into the world [resemble]
Tillers of the soil, while their congregations, which they select,
Resemble (the months of) Parmuthi and Paophi.[1] . . . .

[Text too fragmentary for translation]

. . . Parmuthi, because (the tiller) comes and sows seed-grain
[then] and plants, and is busy from the first
. . . Grain and takes pains with them. But when harvest-time
[comes] in that year and his grain becomes ripe for mowing
[Then] the tiller comes forth and mows. Likewise the [fruit-gardener (?)] from the first
. . . . Busies himself with his fruits and cultivates them and he
. . . . and they get ripe, and he comes forth and plucks them from the tree.
[So also the] apostles, who come into the world . . .

From Hans J. Polotsky, *Manichaeische Handschriften der Staatlichen Museen Berlin*, published under the auspices of the Prussian Academy of Sciences, Stuttgart: W. Kohlhammer Verlag, 1940, Vol. I, Part 1. Reprinted by permission of W. Kohlhammer Verlag. This selection trans. from the German by J. Sedlar.

1. Compare John 15:1: "I am the true vine, and my Father is the husbandman."

[In the following seventy lines, harvesting the ripe fruit is compared to the choosing of the Elect and the catechumens.]

. . . . The coming of the apostle has occurred again and again
. . . . as I have told you: from Seth,
[the first-] born son of Adam, to Enos, also
[Enoch, from] Enoch to Shem, [the] son [of Noah][2]
. . . .
. . . . congregation, then [was sent]
. . . . Buddha to the East, and Aurentes[3] and the others. . . .
. . . . . . who were sent to the East. From the [coming]
Of Buddha and Aurentes until the coming of Za-
rathustra[4] to Persia, in those days when he came to King
Hystaspes,[5] from the coming of Zarathustra until the coming of Jesus
[Christ], the son of the Great One.[6]
[The coming] of Jesus Christ, our Lord. He came (?) . . .
. . . in spirit, in body.[7] . . .
As I have told you of him. . . . . .
He came without body.[8] His apostles announced anew
That he had assumed the form of a servant, an appearance like
Men.[9] He descended and revealed himself in the world in

2. This genealogy appears in Genesis, chapter 5.

3. Identity uncertain; possibly a corruption of Ananda, the name of Buddha's faithful disciple.

4. Modern scholarship considers it probable that Buddha and Zoroaster were contemporaries, or nearly so.

5. Presumably Darius I Hystaspes (reigned 521-486 B.C.), whose name was associated with that of Zarathustra.

6. According to Manichaean cosmology, Jesus was produced indirectly from the Father of Greatness by a process of emanation. The five Great Ones are, in order of rank: 1) the Father of Greatness himself, the supreme Deity; 2) the Mother of Life together with Primal Man; 3) the Living Spirit; 4) the Third Messenger; 5) the Luminous Jesus.

7. The word used is *soma,* meaning the (eternal) form of the body; not *sarx,* the flesh which perishes at death.

8. This line appears to contradict the statement of two lines previously, though possibly the condition of the text or a scribe's error is at fault.

9. Compare the verse in Paul's Epistle to the Philippians (2:7): "But [Jesus] made himself of no reputation and took upon him the form of a servant, and was made in the likeness of men." I.e., by assuming sinful flesh he put himself into the power of the demons.

The sect of the Jews. He chose his Twelve[10]
[and] his Seventy-two[11] and fulfilled the will of his Father, who
Had sent him into the world. Thereby the Evil One[12] aroused
Envy against the sect of the Jews. Satan entered
Into Judas Iscariot, one of the Twelve
Of Jesus.[13] He accused him to the sect [of the Jews],
Through his kiss he delivered [him into the hands]
Of the Jews and the cohorts of the soldiers.[14] [The Jews]
For their part seized the son of God, [declared]
Him outside of the law in an assembly and condemned him
Unjustly, although he had committed no sins. They raised him onto the wood of the
Cross, they crucified him together with robbers on the cross.[15]
They took him down from the cross and laid him in the grave, [and]
After three days he arose from the dead and he
Came to his disciples and appeared to them, he clothed them
With power and infused his holy spirit into them,[16] [he sent]
Them out into the whole world, so that they preached [the]
Great One.[17] But as for him he raised himself [to Heaven]
. . . . .

[Text too fragmentary for translation]

[While] the apostles were still in the world, [they were joined by Pau]l,
The apostle. He too went out and preached. . . . . .
. . . . he gave strength to the apostles and strengthened [them]

10. His twelve disciples. See Matthew 10:1; Mark 3:14; Luke 6:13.
11. Seventy, not seventy-two. According to Luke 10:1, "After these things the Lord appointed other seventy also, and sent them two and two before his face into every city and place, whither he himself would come."
12. Ruler of the realm of Darkness, Satan.
13. As recounted in Luke 22:3; John 13:7.
14. Told in Matthew 26:49; Mark 14:44; Luke 22:47.
15. Matthew 27:38, 44; Mark 15:27.
16. The infusion of the Holy Spirit occurs only in John (20:22): "he breathed on them, and saith unto them, Receive ye the Holy Ghost." In the other gospels the disciples are simply sent out into the world to preach (Mark 16:15; Matthew 28:19).
17. See note 6 above.

[Text very fragmentary]

After the apostle Paul, gradually, day by (?)
Day all of mankind was led astray [into sin]. They left [justice]
And the hard and narrow path behind them, and preferred . . . . .
[To] walk on the broad path.
At that time there appeared once again in the last congregation a just man
And a righteous man,[18] who belonged to the "realm";[19] he joined together with. . .
. . . . they managed (?) the church of our Lord according [to their]
[Strength, but] they too ascended to the land
[Of Light]. After them gradually
[The Church] again degenerated. The world remained without
Church, like a tree from which one picks and takes away the
Fruits that are on it, so that it remains without fruit.
[When?] the congregation of the Saviour had ascended to Heaven, then
My apostleship occurred, which you asked me about. From that time onward
The Paraclete was sent, the spirit of Truth, who
Has come to you in this last generation, as the Saviour
Said: When I go, I will send you the Paraclete,
[And when] the Paraclete comes, he will lead the world away [from]
[Sin and] will speak with you about justice and
[about sin and about the] Judgment.[20] . . . .

[Text very fragmentary]

18. Possibly Bardesanes and Marcion. Bardesanes (flourished about A.D. 200) was an outstanding Syrian Gnostic. Marcion (flourished 2nd century A.D.) attempted to eliminate the Judaic elements from Christianity and was excommunicated by the Christian Church. A number of "Marcionite" sects propagated his teachings.
19. Presumably the realm of the "Elect."
20. In John's gospel the Paraclete is the Holy Spirit (Ghost) who will come in Jesus' stead, the Comforter and the Spirit of truth.

. . . . in order to preach about the Paraclete of Truth. For he
. . . . he has come to reveal himself to him who has recognized him. . . .

[Text very fragmentary]

. . . . . and will make them free. But when the church
Had acquired flesh, then the time was come to save their souls, like
The [month] Parmuthi, in which the grass is ripe enough
To be mowed. At this same time he [created] my
Form, which I bear in the days of Artabanes,[21]
The king of Parthia. But in the years of Ardashir,[22] the
King of Persia, I grew and became greater and the time was fulfilled.
In the same year that Ardashir the King [was about to?]
[Receive] the crown, the living Paraclete came down [to me and] spoke
To me. He revealed to me the secret mystery
That was hidden from the worlds and the generations, the mystery of the Depth[23]
And the Height.[24] He revealed to me the mystery of the Light
And the Darkness, the mystery of the battle and the war (?)
And the great war— . . . which the Darkness stirred up.[25] [Afterward?]
He also revealed to me how the Light. . . .
The Darkness through their intermingling and how this world was established.
He enlightened me also about how the ships[26] were made firm so that

21. Artabanes V (reigned A.D. 208-26), the last of the Parthian (Arsacid) kings of the Persian empire, was overthrown by Ardashir in A.D. 226.
22. Ardashir I (reigned A.D. 224-41), or Artaxerxes, founded the Sassanian dynasty, extended the boundaries of the Persian empire to the Oxus and the Euphrates, and sought to restore Zoroastrianism.
23. The land of Darkness, Hell.
24. Heaven, the land of Light.
25. The aggressiveness of Darkness against Light which began the process of creation of the universe.
26. The sun and the moon.

[The gods] of the Light let themselves down in them, in order to purify the Light
[From out] of the creation, [to throw] the dregs and the refuse[27] [into]
The abyss; the mystery of the creation of Adam, the first man.
He taught me also about the mystery of the tree of knowledge
From which Adam ate, through which his eyes were opened.[28]
Also about the mystery of the apostles, who are sent into the world [to]
Choose the congregations; the mystery of the Elect [and their]
Commandments; the mystery of the sinners and their works;
The mystery of the catechumens, their helpers and [their]
Rules; the mystery of the sinners and their works
And the punishment which awaits them (?). In this manner everything which has come to pass
And will come to pass was revealed to me by the Paraclete. . .
Everything that the eye sees and the ear hears and the mind
Thinks and. . . . . Through him I have come to know
Everything. I have seen the universe through him and become a body
And a spirit.—In the last years of Ardashir,
The king, I went out to preach. I sailed to the land of the Indians and
Preached to them the hope of life and selected there
A good harvest.—But in the year that
King Ardashir died[29] and his son Shapur became king, he [sent? for me?].
I went from the land of the Indians to the land of the Persians, from the
Land of the Persians I arrived again in the land of Babylon, Maisan
And Susiana.[30] I appeared before King Shapur, he received

27. Matter.
28. This is a variation on the Biblical theme: the "awakening" is a positive step, not an awakening into sin.
29. 241 A.D.
30. Maisan (Mesene) was a district on the lower Tigris; Susiana (Elam) the region directly east of Babylonia.

Me with great honor and allowed me to travel about in [his]
[Territories and] preach the word of Life. I spent further years in
. . . . [with] him in his retinue, many years in
Persia, in the land of the Parthians as far as Adiabene[31] and
The border districts of the lands of the Roman empire.
[I have chosen (?)] you, the good harvest, the holy
Congregation, to which I was sent by the Father. I [have]
[Sown the] grain of Life and have. . . . .
. . from the East to the West, as you see
[My hope] has gone out to the East of the world and (to) the regions
[Of all] the globe, in the northerly direction and the
[southerly?]. Not one of the apostles ever did likewise. . .

[Text very fragmentary]

[For] it is [the] spirit of the Paraclete which was sent to me from
[The Father of Greatness (?). What] has come to pass and will come to pass
[Has been] revealed to me. I wrote in detail about this for you in my
Books formerly. Now you have asked me again, look, I have declared
The matter to you briefly. —Thereby, [when his]
Disciples had heard all this from him, they rejoiced greatly.
Their minds were enlightened and they spoke to him joyfully: "We thank
You, O Lord, that you have written for us about your coming in the
Scriptures. Just as it occurred, so we have accepted it and believed it.
But you have told it to us here in short synopsis; we
[However] have accepted it in full and believe that you are the
[Paraclete], who (comes) from the Father, the revealer
Of all secrets."

[End of Chapter I]

31. Adiabene was a fertile region of Assyria east of the Tigris.

Introduction to the Psalms of Thomas

The hymn-cycle called "Psalms of Thomas" is part of the rich treasure of Coptic Manichaean papyri discovered at Medinet Madi in Egypt. In their present form the psalms probably date from about 340 A.D. As with the *Kephalaia,* the original texts seem to have been composed in Syriac and translated into Coptic. The "Thomas" of the title is known to have been a propagator of Manichaean doctrine.

This hymn recounts merely the first episode of that cosmic war which, according to the Manichaeans, culminated in the creation of the universe.

FROM THE PSALMS OF THOMAS

I: [Concerning the Father and] all his Aeons and the Stirring of the Enemy

[My Father, the] glad Light, the glad Light,
the Glorious, my Father, the glad Light, the glad
and blessed Light, my Father, the glad Light,
the glad and honoured Light: he evoked
the Aeons[1] of Light, he appointed them to the joy of his
greatness. He evoked the Aeons of Peace, in whom
there is no waning or diminution. He evoked the Aeons
of Light, he summoned his sons and set them up
in them. He evoked the Aeons of Peace, he
summoned his Richnesses and set them up in them.
He evoked the Aeons of Rest, he summoned his
Angels and set them up in them. He established

From *A Manichaean Psalm-Book,* Part 2, ed. by C. R. C. Allberry, Stuttgart: W. Kohlhammer Verlag, 1938, pp. 203-7. Reprinted by permission of W. Kohlhammer Verlag.

1. Worlds.

dwellings of Life and set up living Images in
them, he set up living Images in them which
never perish. He evoked clouds
of Brightness, dropping down dew (?) and life, he summoned
a holy fire, giving a sweet burning.
He evoked a Wind and an Air, breathing the
breath of the Living. He evoked holy Mountains,
sending up fragrant roots. They are
all in agreement and concord: there is no waning or diminution
in them, they rejoicing and being glad in the glory (?), full,
abiding in Eternity. I know not
where the Son of Evil saw them: he rose
up saying, May I be one like them. [Where] did the Son of
Evil see them? He rose up saying, May I be one
like them. Where did the Son of Evil see them—the
poor one who has nothing, no riches
in his treasure, no Eternity in his
possession, no riches in his treasure? He rose
up saying, May I be one like them. He caught the hand of his
seven companions and his twelve helpers: [he]
caught the hand of his seven companions, he went, he looked (?)
to them in a moment (?), in order that, if any[2] should fall and come down,
he might go and be one like them. The Great (?) Father therefore
took the first step, he strengthened all his Angels, saying
"Assemble, all of you, and guard yourselves from the eye of the Evil one
which has looked up." One of the Sons of Light
looked from on high and saw him: he said to his rich
brethren: "O my brethren, the Sons of Light,
in whom there is no waning or diminution: I
looked down to the abyss, I saw the Evil one, the
Son of Evil, I saw the Evil one, the Son of
Evil, desiring to wage war. I saw his seven companions
also and his twelve ministers.
I saw the tent fixed, the fire kindled

2. Any of the divine emanations.

in its midst: I saw the poor wretches (?) at hand (?),
thinking to wage war. I
saw their cruel armour which is ready to make
the war, I saw snares set and
nets cast and spread, that the bird that should [come] might
[be] caught . . . . that (?) it might not escape from them. [I saw] them reclining, drinking
stolen wine, eating plundered flesh." . . .

. . . .

Concerning the coming of the Soul[3]

[They] that are not as I am made themselves like me, they that are
unworthy of me made me wroth. The wretches (?) that belong not to the house
of my Father rose, they took arms against me, they rose,
they took arms against me, making war with me, making
war with me, fighting (?) for my holy robe,[4]
for my enlightening Light, that it might lighten
their Darkness, for my sweet Fragrance, that it might
sweeten their foulness, because of my brethren, the Sons of
Light, that they might give a peace to their land, be-
cause of my sister, the hour of Light, that she might be
a strengthening of their building. A part therefore went forth from
my robe, it went, it lightened their Darkness; my
sweet fragrance went, it sweetened their stink;
my brethren, the Sons of Light, went, they gave a peace
to their land; my sister went, the hour of Light,
she was a strengthening of their building. They take arms
against me, making war with me, crying out
against me, like men going to subdue a camp
they drew the swords against me, like men
going to kill lions; they stretched their hands to the bow
against me, like thieves going to attack a man.

3. Here the Soul (or the First Man) is speaking.

4. Compare the symbolism of the heavenly garment in the "Hymn of the Soul," above.

. . . .
. . . . . My Father therefore sent
the aid to me, my brethren arose, they became one with [me.]
Through a cry only which my brethren uttered, their wall[5]
tottered and fell, their wall tottered and fell,
their watches were unable to (?) stop them, nor was he that
goes round with the bell and cries good fortune (?)
found, against the cry which my brethren uttered. The
demons ran to the Darkness, the demons ran to the
Darkness, trembling seized their Archon[6] entirely. But
I said to my brethren, "Suffer me yet this
hour." I was quieting my brethren that they might not
destroy their firmament; for I await my robe until
it comes and clothes him that shall wear it. I will await
my enlightening Light until it strips itself of their
Darkness. I will await my pleasant fragrance until
it returns to its place. I will await my sister,
the hour of Light, until she casts their corruption
away. I will await my brethren, the sons of Light, until
their stature (?) is completed for them. When therefore my shining
robe comes and clothes him that shall wear it: when my
pleasant fragrance strips itself of their stink and returns
[to its place:] when my lightening Light leaves
the Darkness: when my brethren, the sons of Light,
are complete in their stature: when my sister, the hour of
Light, goes up and sees the Land of Light:
then I will strike my foot on the earth and sink their Darkness
down, I will smite their height with my head and shake
their firmament and the stars shall fall down like
. . . . . I will uproot the Darkness and cast it out and plant
the Light in its place, I will uproot the Evil and cast it
out and plant the Good in its place. The world
[shall] be full of glory, the earth shall be without suspicion, the

5. The wall was constructed by the sons of Darkness as part of their strategy.

6. The ruler of the demons; heaven and earth will subsequently be formed out of the Archons' skins and carcasses.

whole world shall contain the Righteous, they of the earth shall dwell in peace,
there being no more rebel from henceforth, no name of sin shall be
uttered again, the Rich ones of Light shall rejoice on
every side without any grief. That which the Living ones took was
saved, they will return again to that which is their own.

Introduction to Huwidagman and Angad Rošnan

Among the texts brought back by an archaeological expedition to Chinese Turkestan in the early years of this century were fragments of the Manichaean hymn-cycles *Huwidagman* and *Angad Rosnan*. The hymns were written not in Chinese, but in Parthian, the language of northeastern Iran. It is known that Manichaean communities flourished for a time in western China; we may conjecture that these hymn-cycles were carried there by Iranian missionaries.

Both compositions have been preserved in highly fragmentary condition. Of hundreds of sheets of text, only five survive entirely intact; the rest have been pieced together laboriously, if at all. The two works are so alike in style and content that a single author may have composed both; or at least one strongly influenced the other. The author of *Huwidagman* may have been Mar Ammo, one of Mani's chief disciples. Mar Ammo was the principal apostle of Manichaeism to the Parthians, chosen for this task because of his knowledge of their language. He was with Mani during the last days of the prophet's life, and subsequently became the subject of many legends. Mar Ammo's authorship would place the composition of *Huwidagman* late in the third century A.D.

The hymns consist of elegaic unrhymed verses divided into *handams*, or "limbs." They employ various mnemonic devices: frequent repetition, the use of stock phrases, alliteration, and much pictorial imagery. They are dramatic in form: the soul, which has just left the body, engages in dialogue with the Saviour. Presumably the hymns were sung at the funerals of the Manichaean "Elect." But they cannot have been intended to speed the soul on its way to paradise. According to Manichaean doctrine, the soul is rewarded only according to its own knowledge and virtue; the efforts of persons left behind cannot help.

The two cycles follow a common pattern. They begin with a soul in distress, tormented by doubts and demons, beseeching the Saviour for aid. The Saviour arrives; the demons leave; and the soul is promised redemption. The Saviour is not named—perhaps intentionally, so that any of the saviours recognized by Manichaeism could be suggested. It is taken for granted that the soul must be reborn many times before it can finally be liberated. Its ultimate destination is mentioned only in general terms. But other Manichaean sources indicate that the soul was believed to sojourn for a while in the New Paradise—the Saviour's own kingdom—before attaining the highest realm of Light.

FROM HUWIDAGMAN

IVa

1 Who will release me from all the pits and prisons, in which are gathered (?) lusts that are not pleasing?

2 Who will take me over the flood of the tossing sea—the zone of conflict in which there is no rest?

3 Who will save me from the jaws of all the beasts who destroy and terrify (?) one another without pity?

4 Who will lead me beyond the walls and take me over the moats, which (are) full of fear and trembling from ravaging demons?

5 Who will lead me beyond rebirths, and free me from (them) all—and from all the waves, in which there is no rest?

6 I weep for (my) soul, saying: May I be saved from this, and from the terror of the beasts who devour one another!

From *The Manichaean Hymn-Cycles in Parthian,* ed. by Mary Boyce, London: Oxford University Press, 1954, pp. 81-3, 101-5, 139-41, 155-61. Reprinted by permission of Oxford University Press, with one change requested by Professor Boyce.

7 The bodies of men, and of birds of the air, of fish of the sea, and four-footed creatures and of all insects—
8 who will take me beyond these and save me from (them) all, so that I shall not turn and fall into the perdition of those hells?
9 so that I shall not pass through defilement in them, nor return in rebirth, wherein all the kinds of plants (are) taken out in . . . ?
10 Who will save me from the swallowing heights (and?) the devouring deeps, which are all hell and distress?

VIc

1 I shall take (thee) eagerly and soar up upon wings, high over all the (Dark) Powers and rebellious Princes.
2 I shall lead (thee) into the primeval calm of that land;[1] and I shall show (thee) the Fathers, my (?) own divine entity (?).
3 Thou shalt rejoice in gladness, in blissful praises. Thou shalt be without grief and . . . shalt forget distress.
4 Thou shalt put on a radiant garment, and gird on Light; and I shall set on thy head the diadem of sovereignty.
5 [Thou shalt] . . . through . . . brilliant jewel . . .beneficent . . .

[Four verses missing]

10 By a spiritual invocation[2] [there was built ?] on that [structure ?] the fortress,[3] high and vast, of the noble Em[peror].
11 A palace is the dominion of the primeval First-born,[4] for in it he clothes himself in gladness and binds on the diadem of sovereignty.
12 And all (his) friends—he binds the diadem upon them, and clothes their bodies in the garment of gladness.

1. The paradise.
2. Literally, "by a spiritual mouth." The paradise is created by God's "word."
3. I.e., the New Paradise.
4. The First Man.

13 And all the believers and the pious Elect he clothes in praise, and binds on them the diadem.

14 They reign (now) in gladness, even as (once they had) been fettered for (their mere) name,[5] and (had) undergone anguish at the hands of (their) foes.

15 And [he makes ?] them . . . with all . . . through that apparition . . .

[Four verses missing]

20 [The return from] the . . . Depth was obtained out of the Victory; [for] the enemies are subdued, and the Height (lies) in front!

21 . . . [is] the day when He will reveal his form, [the] beneficent [Father], the Lord of the Aeons of Light.

22 [He will show that radiant shape] and brilliant, glorious form [to all the gods] who shall dwell there.

[End of this fragment of the sixth canto]

FROM ANGAD ROŠNAN

VI

1 When I had said these words, with soul a-tremble, I beheld the Saviour as he shone before me.

2 I beheld the sight of all the Helmsmen,[6] who had descended with him to array my soul.

3 I lifted up my eyes toward that direction, and saw all deaths were hidden by the Envoy.[7]

4 All ravages had become remote from me, and grievous sickness, and the anguish of their distress.

5 The sight of them was hidden, their darkness had fled away. All (was divine) nature, without peer.

6 [There shone forth] Light, elating and lovely [and full] of gladness, pervading all my mind.

5. I.e., as Manichaeans, members of a persecuted sect.
6. The helmsmen who guide the ships of Light.
7. Perhaps the Messenger, one of the "Great Ones" of Manichaeism.

7 In joy unbounded he spoke with me, raising up my soul from deep affliction (?).
8 To me he sayeth, Come, spirit! fear not. I am thy Mind,[8] thy glad tidings of hope.
9 And thou art the . . . garment of my body, which brought dismay to the Powers (of Darkness) . . .
10 I am thy Light, radiant, primeval, thy Great Mind and complete hope.

VII

1 Come, spirit, fear no more! Death has fallen, and sickness fled away.
2 The term of troubled days is ended, its terror departed amid clouds of fire.
3 Come, spirit, step forth! Let there be no desire for the house of affliction,
4 which is wholly destruction and the anguish of death. Truly thou wast cast out from thy native abode.
5 And all the pangs thou hast suffered in hell[9] thou hast undergone for this, in the outset and beginning.
6 Come yet nearer, in gladness without regret; lie not content in the dwelling of death.
7 Turn not back, nor regard the shapes of the bodies, which lie (there) in wretchedness, they and (their) fellows.
8 See, they return through every rebirth, through every agony and every choking (?) prison.
9 See, they are reborn among all (kinds of) creatures, and their voice is heard in burning sighs.
10 Come yet nearer, and be not fond of this beauty that perishes in all (its) varieties.
11 It falls and melts as snow in sunshine. There is no abiding for any fair form.
12 It withers and fades as a broken rose, that wilts in the sun, whose grace is destroyed.
13 Yet come, thou spirit, and be not fond of the sum of hours and the fleeting days.

8. Mind sometimes takes the role of the Saviour in the Manichaean myth.
9. I.e., on earth.

14 Turn not back for every outward show. Desire[10] (is) death, and leads to destruction.

15 Hence, spirit, come! . . . I shall lead (thee) to the height, [to thy native abode].

16 I shall show (thee) the pledge (?) . . . the hope thou hast yearned for . . .

17 Remember, O spirit! look on the anguish (?) that (thou hast) borne through the fury of all (thy) ravagers.

18 Regard the world and the prison of creation; for all desires will be swiftly destroyed.

19 Terror, fire and ruin will overtake all those who dwell therein.

20 The height will be shattered with all (its) dwellings; all the heavens will fall down into the deep.

21 The trap of destruction will swiftly close upon those deceivers who brag therein.

22 The whole dominion, with the brilliance of all the stars —ruin will come upon them, and the pang of their indignity.

23 All the Princes and the border-rebels (will suffer) for ever in wretchedness within the blazing fire.

24 Every desire and every shining show will dissolve (?) through . . .

25 The whole of life, from every seed and [stem], will swiftly be wrecked and brought to perdition.

26 The whole of the lusts, gilded with all (their) charm . . . fire, will be heaped upon it.

27 . . . each mansion . . . which has been established—each will be broken open, and will tumble down upon them.

10. Desire for the things of this earth.

Introduction to the Psalms to Jesus

This eloquent hymn forms part of the collection of "Psalms to Jesus" included among the Coptic Manichaean papyri found at Medinet Madi in Egypt. It appears to be a funerary text; the first and last several lines suggest that it commemorates the death of one of the Manichaean "Elect." It begins with an appeal to the Saviour—in this case Jesus—and concludes with the soul's triumphant ascent to paradise.

Psalm 246 employs many of the standard Manichaean similies. The earth is the abode of demonic powers—wild beasts who oppress the pure and innocent soul. The soul is a stranger in the world; its existence is a burden to it; and death is welcomed as the escape from Darkness into Light. The hymn regards the soul as an individual entity, but also as a representative of the entire exiled Light. The soul is a passive part of a grandiose and mighty machine; its fate is bound up with the fate of the universe.

FROM THE PSALMS TO JESUS

CCXLVI

Come to me, my kinsman, the Light, my guide.
. . . my soul, bear up: thou hast thy Saviour: [thy] defence is Christ, for he will receive thee into his Kingdom.
Since I went forth into the darkness I was given a water to drink which . . . .[1] me. I bear up beneath a burden which is not my own.[2]
I am in the midst of my enemies, the beasts surrounding me; the burden which I bear is of the powers and principalities.[3]

From *A Manichaean Psalm-Book,* Part 2, ed. by C. R. C. Allberry, Stuttgart: W. Kohlhammer Verlag, 1938, pp. 54-5. Reprinted by permission of W. Kohlhammer Verlag.

1. Water was one of the evil sons of Darkness. The missing word may be something like "benumbed," "poisoned," etc.
2. I.e., the burden of the entire universe.
3. I.e., the demonic rulers of the world.

They burned (?) in their wrath, they rose up against me, they ran to . . . . me, like sheep that have no shepherd.
Matter[4] and her sons divided me up amongst them, they burnt (?) me in their fire, they gave me a bitter likeness.
The strangers with whom I mixed, me they know not; they tasted my sweetness, they desired to keep me with them.
I was life to them, but they were death to me; I bore up beneath them, they wore me as a garment upon them.
I am in everything, I bear the skies, I am the foundation, I support the earths, I am the Light that shines forth, that gives joy to souls.
I am the life of the world: I am the milk that is in all trees: I am the sweet water that is beneath the sons of Matter.
. . . . I went forth to the . . . .
. . . the Aeons[5] . . . they sent me forth to the . . . . .
[I] bore these things until I had fulfilled the will [of my Father]; the First Man is my father whose [will] I have carried out.
[Lo,] the Darkness I have subdued; lo, the fire of the fountains [I have extinguished] it, as the Sphere[6] turns hurrying round, as [the sun] receives the refined part of life.[7]
O soul, raise thy eyes to the height and contemplate thy bond . . . . thou hast reached it; lo, thy Fathers are calling thee.
[Now] go aboard the Ships of Light[8] and receive thy [garland of glory and return to thy kingdom and rejoice with all the Aeons].
Glory and honour to our Lord Mani [and his holy Elect and the soul of the blessed Mary.]

4. Matter (*Hyle*) was Darkness or evil personified. Its sons were smoke, fire, wind, water, and darkness.
5. The sons of Darkness are called Aeons.
6. The sphere of the heavens.
7. The portion of Light-substance which was least contaminated by Matter.
8. The sun and the moon.

III

Western Hellenism

LANDS OF THE WESTERN MEDITERRANEAN

McNEILL & SEDLAR (III)
"Classical Mediterranean World"

Introduction to Lucretius

Lucretius Carus is one of the greatest poets who ever wrote in the Latin language; and his masterpiece, *De Rerum Natura* ("On the Nature of Things") is the fullest surviving exposition of the thoughts of the Greek philosopher Epicurus (d. 270 B.C.). Nonetheless, our knowledge of the poet's life rests upon only two brief references in all ancient literature. His great poem has come down to us in a single copy, discovered in the fifteenth century by the Renaissance scholar Poggio Bracciolini.

The dates for Lucretius are uncertain, but probably his span of life covered the first half of the first century B.C. (*ca.* 99-55 B.C.). He thus experienced the years of civil strife between aristocrats and populace at Rome, and died shortly before the struggle between Caesar and Pompey for mastery of the Mediterranean world. No doubt the unrest of the times stimulated his adoption of Epicureanism. The system of Epicurus regarded individual happiness rather than common welfare as the chief good, and defined the goal of life as tranquillity, indifference, and independence of worldly concerns.

The basis of this ethic was the physics of the Greek Atomists, who taught that Nature is composed of an infinite number of parts. Like the sixth-century Ionians who had sought to explain the world in terms of a single element like fire or water, the Atomists too regarded Nature as reducible to an ultimate substance. But their basic entity, the atom—by being infinitely divisible and possessing the property of motion—seemed to explain the varied phenomena of the world better than any perceptible element could do. The atom they defined as a portion of matter—meaning that it occupied space. Each atom was surrounded by a void, or the absence of matter, through which it moved. Birth and growth occurred through the atoms' striking against one another and forming aggregates. Decay and death were the reverse of this process: the disintegration of atomic groups under the impact of other atoms.

Just as Epicurus' physics was reducible to the individual atom, so also his ethics was concerned with the individual man, who like the atom bore within himself his impulse to action. But though the Epicureans regarded personal happiness as the goal of human striving, they did not define happiness in the usual sense. Like Plato, they taught that the highest object of life ought to be insight into the ultimate nature of things. Such insight can free mankind from fears based upon error or superstition, such as the fear of the gods or of death. Reason makes it possible to distinguish between the transient and the permanent, the necessary and the superficial. The senses cannot give us a true picture of the world (for the atoms are invisible, intangible, and silent); sense-pleasures are fleeting, and the happy man will not rely upon them.

In an age when books were scarce and few could read, poetry was a better vehicle of communication than prose; for verses more easily stick in the memory. Lucretius tells us that he tried to set forth the doctrine of his master in "sweet melody" and "touch it with the honeyed language of the Muses" in order to hold the listener's attention to the serious study of the universe. That he managed to present a complex philosophical system in a masterpiece of the poetic art is only one measure of his skill. To a considerable extent he was obliged even to create his own terminology; for the Latin language of his day—well suited to deal with matters of war and government—lacked a philosophic and scientific vocabulary. His poem, composed of about 7500 lines arranged into six books, shows certain signs of incompleteness, leading some authorities to speculate that he died before finishing it. Nonetheless, *On the Nature of Things* became a model for the heroic poetry of a later age, and remains one of the principal works of Latin literature.

LUCRETIUS: FROM ON THE NATURE OF THE UNIVERSE

Book II

Therefore do not be deterred by mere novelty:
do not reject True Reason[1] from your mind, but ponder it

From *On the Nature of the Universe* (*De Rerum Natura*), trans. by James H. Mantinband, New York: Frederick Ungar, 1965, pp. 63-7, 91-5, 98. Reprinted by permission of Frederick Ungar Publishing Company.

1. I.e., the Epicurean doctrine.

keenly and thoughtfully, and if it seems to be true,
admit you are beaten, but if it is false, prepare to fight.
For since the universe[2] is infinite beyond
the walls of heaven, the intellect[3] tries to seek out
those distant spaces where the mind[4] longs to explore
and where the liberated spirit[5] flies of itself.

First of all, around our world in all directions
on either side, above and below through the universe,
there is no limit, as I have shown and the facts proclaim,
and the nature of boundless space illuminates.
And since there is infinite space in all directions,
and atoms infinite in number, countless in sum
and forever flying about in perpetual motion,
it cannot by any stretch of the imagination
be thought that ours is the only earth and sky created,
and that all those other atoms have nothing at all to do;
especially since the world was made by Nature:[6] the atoms
of their own accord, colliding with each other,
combining in all sorts of ways, without intention,
without volition, and some of these combinations
in each case, could become the beginnings of all things:[7]
of earth and sea and sky and races of living creatures.
And so I say again and again: you must confess
that elsewhere there are other combinations of matter
such as this which the ether[8] holds in its firm embrace.
And besides, since abundant material is on hand
and plenty of space, and nothing at all is there to prevent it,
these things then must certainly be done and accomplished.
And if there is such a great abundance of these atoms
that our whole span of life would not suffice to count them,

2. The universe, or "sum of things," includes all the worlds, not just our earth and the heavenly bodies surrounding it.

3. Or "rational soul."

4. *Mens*, a word sometimes translated as "intellect."

5. *Anima*, sometimes also translated as "soul."

6. I.e., not by the gods.

7. I.e., certain combinations of atoms produce the motions which result in the formation of a world.

8. Ether was a hypothetical substance thought to pervade space and serve as the medium of motion within space.

and if the same power and the same nature is there,
able to throw the atoms together in any place
in the same way as they have been thrown together here,
you must admit that other worlds in other places
exist, and other races of men and animals.
Moreover, nothing in the universe is unique,
and grows up as the only specimen of its kind,
without being one of a species and similar to others.
First of all, direct your mind to the animals:
you see that this is true of the mountain-wandering beasts,
and of the twofold race of men,[9] and the scaly fishes
swimming in silence, and of all the flying creatures.
Therefore you must confess the same for sky and earth,
and sun and moon and sea, and everything in existence:
that they are not unique, but of a countless number,
inasmuch as a fixed limit[10] is set for them
and they are just as mortal as any of the species
that are found in such abundance here on earth.[11]
Now, if you hold to these convictions, Nature is seen
free and untrammeled, rid of her haughty overlords,
doing all of her own accord without the gods.
For, by the holy hearts of the gods, in tranquil peace
living their placid ages and their life serene,[12]
who can rule the universe, who hold in his hand
the mighty reins of the unfathomable ocean?
Who can revolve the heavens all at the same time
and warm the fruitful lands with his ethereal fires?
Or be at all times present, and in all places too,
making darkness with clouds and shaking the placid sky
with thunderbolts, and hurling lightnings that destroy
his own temples, and passing away into the desert,

9. Male and female.
10. A limited span of life.
11. Lucretius seems to be arguing that an eternal body might conceivably be unique; but since the heavenly bodies are destructible like everything else, they must be composed of atoms.
12. Lucretius views the gods as living in some distant place and indifferent to human affairs.

throw his missiles in his rage, which spare the guilty
and slay instead the innocent and undeserving?
And since the world's[13] first birthday, since the dawn of time,
when the sea and earth and sun first came into being,
many bodies have been added from outside,[14]
and many seeds[15] which the great Sum has brought together
in its revolutions, whence the sea and land
might be increased, and the sky might amplify its space
and raise the vault of heaven and make the air arise.
For all bodies are being dispersed abroad by impacts
from all places, and each goes back to its own kind;
liquid to liquid, the earth grows by the elements
of earth, and fire struck from fire, and air from air,
until they reach the final limits of their growth,
when Nature, creator of all things, has done her task.
This happens when no more is added to the veins
of life, than that which ebbs away and passes back,
And at this time the life of all things comes to a standstill,
for this is when the power of Nature curbs their growth.
Whatever you see growing and increasing happily,
little by little climbing up the ladder of life,
assimilates more atoms than it gives away,
as long as food is easily taken into its veins
and while its spaces are not so wide that they must lose
a greater quantity of atoms than they feed on.
For we must surely see that many elements
ebb away and pass from things; but more flow in
until the pinnacle of growth has been attained.
After this, by slow degrees, age breaks the strength
and vigor of the body, and decay begins.
And indeed, the larger and wider a body is,
the more elements it scatters when growth has ended,
the more it sends off from its body in all directions.

13. Our earth.
14. From outside the earth; nothing can be outside of the universe.
15. Lucretius does not use the Greek word *atomoi;* ordinarily he speaks of "the seeds of things."

Nor is food sent so easily into the veins,
nor is there enough, in proportion to the floods
it loses, for replenishments to be effected.
For it is food that must renew and recreate;
food replenishes, and food sustains all things,
but to no avail, since the veins can no longer hold
enough, and Nature cannot supply as much as is needed.
And so things die away, made meager by the loss
of atoms, since all things succumb to external blows,
inasmuch as nourishment fails with advancing age.
Nor is there anything that the bombarding bodies
cannot shatter and break up with their fatal impacts.
  And even heaven's mighty walls shall be besieged,
and they too shall collapse and fall in utter ruin.
Even today the earth's power is being broken,
and now she hardly can produce the tiniest creatures,
who once made all the generations of huge beasts.
For, I think, it is not true that the races of men
were lowered down from heaven by a golden chain,
nor did they spring from the pounding surf upon the rocks,
but the earth, who nourishes them, gave them their birth.
Furthermore, of her own accord she first created
the shining grain and smiling vineyards for mankind.
She herself produced sweet fruits and fertile pastures,
which now can scarce grow anything, for all our toil.
And we exhaust our oxen and our farmers' strength,
we wear out plowshares in the fields that barely feed us,
so much do they begrudge their fruits and increase our labor.
And now the agèd plowman shakes his head and sighs
again and again, to see his labors come to naught,
and he compares the present age to days gone by,
often praising the erstwhile fortunes of his father,
and groans to think of the good old days, when men were pious.
and life was easily supported on smaller farms;
since each man's bit of ground was formerly much less.
The gloomy grower of the old and withered vines
sadly curses the times he lives in, and wearies heaven,

not realizing that all is gradually decaying,
nearing the end, worn out by the long span of years.[16]

End of Book II.

Book III

Therefore death is nothing to us,[17] for it matters not,
since the nature of the mind[18] is known to be mortal;
and just as, in the days of old, we felt no distress
when Carthaginians were pouring in to do battle,
and when the entire world, shaken by war's dread tumult,
reeled and trembled under the lofty vault of heaven,
and all men were in doubt, not knowing to which empire
all humanity on land and sea would be subject:—
so, when we shall be no more, when body and spirit,[19]
by whose union we exist, have been separated,
nothing more will be able to touch us, who shall not be,
nothing at all will be able to affect our senses,
not though earth were fused with sea or sea with sky.
And even granted that the nature of mind and spirit[20]
still had the power to feel, when torn away from the body,
that is nothing to us, who are brought into existence
by the wedlock of body and spirit, joined and made one.[21]
And even if the atoms that compose our body
were reassembled by time and brought to their present arrangement,
and to this arrangement the light of life were given[22]—

16. In Greek and Roman times it was generally believed that the Golden Age lay sometime in the distant past and was followed by progressive decline. Elsewhere Lucretius defends the Epicurean view that mankind has been making steady progress in the arts and sciences.
17. I.e., to those of us living today.
18. Again, *anima* or "soul."
19. Body and soul (*anima*).
20. The nature of soul and souls (*animi natura animaeque*).
21. Since our individual consciousness is the product of a particular combination of a body and a soul, consciousness disappears with the disintegration of this union.
22. The Epicureans rejected the Stoic belief that things must return to their

even that would not be any concern of ours,
once the chain of memory had been snapped and broken.
We, who are now, are not concerned with ourselves that were
in any previous time, nor touched by former sufferings.
For when you look back at all the tremendous expanse
of unmeasured time, and think how many and varied
are the atoms' movements, then you might believe with ease
that these same atoms that now compose us, have been arranged
many times before in the same combinations.
But our mind cannot recall or remember this:
for a break in life has intervened, and the atoms' motions
all have wandered far astray from any sensation.[23]
For if the future holds misery and woe for a man,
then he himself will have to exist in that future time
in order to suffer. But death removes us from this fate,
denying existence to the self that would suffer thus;
so we may be sure we have nothing to fear in death:
one who no longer is, cannot be miserable,
or differ at all from one who never has been born,
when immortal death has taken mortal life away.
And therefore when you see a man resenting his lot,
that after death his corpse will molder in the tomb,
or be destroyed by fire or the jaws of beasts,
you may be certain that his words do not ring true,
that deep in his heart there lurks some secret pang, although
he may deny the belief in sensation after death.
I think he does not admit what he professes, and why;
and he does not completely remove himself from life,
but unconsciously makes something of himself survive.
For when a living man anticipates the thought
that after death the birds and beasts will rend his body,
he pities himself: he does not distinguish between himself
and the outcast corpse; but imagines himself to be that object,
and, standing there, he projects his own feelings into it.

---

original state once a fixed cycle or time-period has elapsed, though they conceded that such a return might occur by chance.

23. I.e., their motions are very different from those motions which produce sensation.

And so he resents having been born mortal: he does not see
that in real death there will not be another self
to mourn his own departure or to stand by and suffer
with the agony of being mangled or cremated.
For if it is a bad thing after death to be mauled
by wild beasts' jaws, why should it not be just as painful
to be roasted in the blazing flames on a funeral pyre,
or to lie embalmed in honey, suffocated
and stiff with cold upon a slab of chilly marble,
or to be crushed beneath a heavy load of earth?
"No longer now your happy home and your good wife
shall welcome you, nor your sweet children come a-running
to win the first kiss, touching your heart with silent joy!
No more prosperity, no protection for your family.
Alas, unhappy wretch!" men say, "one fatal day
has cheated you of all the blessings of this life!"
But they do not go on to add: "And now no yearning
for all these lost delights can touch you any more."
If they could clearly see, and spoke accordingly,
they would rid their hearts of weighty fears and torments!
"Yes, you are now at peace in the quiet sleep of death
and will remain so forever, free of pain and grief;
but we, beside you as you burn on the dreadful pyre,
we have wept insatiably for you, and no day
shall ever come to lift the load of grief from our hearts."
Of such a man we should ask, why all this bitterness,
if a body returns to sleep and peaceful repose,
what reason to pine and weep with everlasting sorrow?
Thus, again, men speak, when they recline at the banquet
with goblets in their hands and garlands on their brows—
they say in their hearts: "How short the enjoyment for us poor mortals!
Soon it will be gone and it can never return!"
As if in death the chief calamity for them
will be that they are parched and shrivelled by burning thirst,
or tormented by the longing for anything.
For no one misses himself, nor does he long for life,
when mind and body alike are peacefully asleep.

And even if that sleep should be made everlasting,
no longing for ourselves would torment us at all.
And yet the vital atoms dispersed throughout the body
are not wandering far away from the sensory motions,
when a man wakes up from sleep and collects his wits.[24]
Death, then, must be thought to be even less than sleep,
if anything can be less than what we see to be nothing:
for there is a greater dispersion of the disturbed matter
once we are dead, nor can anyone awake and arise
whom once the chilly end of life has overtaken.

Suppose that Nature herself should suddenly find a voice
and reprimand some one of us in such words as these:
"What grieves you, mortal, making you indulge yourself
in all these lamentations? Why weep and wail at death?
For if your life until this moment has been pleasant,
if all your blessings have not flowed away like water
in a leaky vase, and been wasted and unenjoyed,
why not, O foolish man, retire, as a dinner guest
who has had his fill, and take your rest in peace and quiet?
But if all your blessings have been spilt and lost,
if life is odious to you, why seek to prolong it,
when you will only be a prey to future misfortunes?
Why not rather make an end of life and affliction?[25]
For I have no new invention or contrivance
that can please you: everything remains the same.
If your body is not already worn out with years
and your limbs decrepit, still nothing new can happen,
even though you should outlive all generations,
even though you never were to die at all."
What could we answer Nature, except that she is right,
and the argument she sets forth is a valid one?
But suppose some aged person should complain
—some miserable man bewailing imminent doom—
would she not be right to scold him all the more:

24. In sleep the atoms assume slightly different motions from those which cause sensation; when the sleeper awakes they resume their normal activity. Lucretius discusses sleep at greater length in Book IV of the poem.

25. Like the Stoics, the Epicureans regarded suicide as permissible in certain circumstances.

"Away with tears, you villain! Cease your lamentations!
Before you withered, you tasted all the joys of life;
but since you always want what you haven't and scorn what you have,
your life has slipped away unblessed and unfulfilled.
And death is standing by your head, without your knowledge,
before you can retire, sated, from the banquet.
But come now, and dismiss what is not meet for your years.
Depart: make room for your children, since you have no choice."
She would be right, in my opinion, thus to reproach.
For the old is always thrust aside to make a place
for the new; one thing is built from the wreckage of another.
But there is no black pit of Hell awaiting us:
atoms are needed for future generations' growth,
and when they have lived their lives they will follow you.
Earlier generations have gone, and future ones
will do the same: one thing will always grow from another.
No man has life in freehold:[26] we all are merely tenants.
Look back at all the ages that passed before our birth
and see how utterly they count to us as nothing.
This is the mirror Nature is holding up for us
to see the time that is to come when we are dead.
Is this so terrible? Is it so very depressing?
Is it not more tranquil than the deepest sleep?

. . . .

What is this evil lust for life that holds us in fear
and makes us slaves to such anxiety and danger?
There is a definite end of life for mortal men.
Death cannot be avoided: everyone must die.
Besides, we live our lives the same from day to day;
nor can we create new pleasures by living longer;
as long as we lack what we desire, it seems more precious
than anything else; but when we have it, we want something different.
One long unchanging thirst for life keeps us always gasping.
We never know what fortune the years to come will bring,

26. I.e., as a permanent possession.

what lies in store for us, or what the end will be.
By prolonging life we do not take away one bit
from the duration of our death; we cannot diminish
the time we shall be dead after we leave the earth.
However many generations you may live,
the same eternal death will still be waiting for you.
The time of Non-existence will be no less for him
who made an end of life at sunset yesterday,
than for him who perished many months and years before.

End of Book III.

Introduction to Caesar Augustus

Beginning as a small city-state along the Tiber, Rome in the third century B.C. gradually became the master of Italy. Three long wars with Carthage (264-146 B.C.) eliminated her chief rival to hegemony in the western Mediterranean. Spain, then Greece and north Africa, became Roman provinces. In the century before Christ, Roman rule advanced northward into Gaul (France), eastward into Asia Minor and Syria. By the time of Augustus, the boundaries of the Roman empire were the Atlantic, the Rhine, and the Danube in Europe, the Euphrates and the Arabian desert in Asia, the Sahara in Africa. Subsequent wars would only round out the frontiers and defend what had already been won.

For nearly five centuries prior to Julius Caesar, Rome had possessed a republican form of government—a delicate balance of forces between an oligarchical Senate and several popular Assemblies, with various elected magistrates serving as checks on each other's powers. But the spoils of conquest, the influence of cheap grain and slaves, and the growth of large farms disrupted the agrarian society on which the Republic was based. A turbulent urban proletariat arose, demanding its share of political power. Already shaken by internal conflicts, the Roman Republic fell victim to its own victorious generals. Pompey, the conqueror of Syria and much of Asia Minor, lent his support to one party; Caesar, the conqueror of Gaul, upheld the claims of the rival faction. Eventually, the issue was joined on the battlefield. Caesar defeated Pompey; and in 44 B.C. the cowed Senate elected him dictator for life. But a group of his own associates, incensed at this betrayal of republican principles, assassinated him on the floor of the Senate.

This murder inaugurated a fourteen-year struggle for power in which the leading protagonists were Caesar's former lieutenant, Antony; his chief assassins, Brutus and Cassius; and his nephew and heir, Octavian, later to be called Augustus. Nineteen years old at Caesar's death and with slight experience in government and war, Octavian nonetheless played his hand well. He joined forces with Antony and Lepidus to form a triumvirate which defeated the armies collected by Brutus and Cassius. A provisional division of the empire among the victorious triumvirs led to further rivalry, culminating in the battle of Actium in 31 B.C. This battle left Octavian the undisputed master of the Roman world, and marked the beginning of two centuries of nearly unbroken peace within the boundaries of the empire.

The following inscription was composed only a few years before the death of Augustus in 14 A.D. Accurate as far as it goes, it is necessarily partisan in nature and glosses over the less attractive aspects of the emperor's career. The marble temple on which it appears was erected at Ancyra (Ankara) in present-day Turkey by some of the cities of Roman Asia in gratitude for Augustus' beneficence toward them—grants of money, relief from tribute, and the construction of public works. Dedicated to the emperor himself, it testifies that the worship of Augustus had begun even in his own lifetime.

CAESAR AUGUSTUS: THE ANCYRA INSCRIPTION

1 When I was nineteen I collected an army on my own account[1] and at my own expense,[2] by the help of which I restored the republic to liberty,[3] which had been enslaved by the

Trans. by Evelyn Shuckburgh in *Augustus, The Life and Times of the Founder of the Roman Empire*, London: T. Fisher Unwin, 1903, pp. 293-301.

1. Octavian had no legal authority to raise an army and exercise military command.
2. With funds bequeathed to him by Julius Caesar.
3. "Republic" generally refers to the constitutional arrangements prevailing at Rome between 508 B.C. and 49 B.C., although the emperors utilized various republican institutions.

tyranny of a faction;[4] for which services the Senate,[5] in complimentary decrees, added my name to the roll of their House in the consulship[6] of Gaius Pansa and Aulus Hirtius (B.C. 43), giving me at the same time consular precedence in voting; and gave me imperium.[7] It ordered me as pro-praetor[8] "to see along with the consuls that the republic suffered no damage." Moreover, in the same year, both consuls having fallen, the people elected me consul and a triumvir[9] for revising the constitution.

2 Those who killed my father[10] I drove into exile, after a legal trial,[11] in punishment of their crime, and afterwards when these same men rose in arms against the republic[12] I conquered them twice in a pitched battle.[13]

3 I had to undertake wars by land and sea, civil and foreign, all over the world, and when victorious I spared all citizens who asked for pardon.[14] Those foreign nations, who could safely

4. I.e., the Senatorial party which included the assassins of Julius Caesar and which wished to restore the republican constitution.

5. The principal governing body under the Republic, composed of members of the most prominent families of Rome, former magistrates holding life tenure.

6. The consuls were the highest elective officials at Rome. Their duties included execution of the laws, administration of justice, and command in war.

7. "Imperium" meant supreme civil and military power, formerly granted for a limited time only to meet an emergency.

8. Under the Republic the praetors were the highest judicial authorities, next in rank to the consuls.

9. A triumvir was any one of three supreme commissioners. Augustus refers to the triumvirate which he formed in 43 B.C. to oppose the Senatorial party led by Brutus and Cassius.

10. Julius Caesar, his uncle and adoptive father.

11. The assassins were granted amnesty by the Senate, though most of them were soon forced to leave Rome. The chief assassins, Brutus and Cassius, were deprived of their offices as governors of Macedonia and Syria and given the lesser governorships of Crete and Cyrene.

12. Brutus and Cassius refused to accept demotion, but returned to their former provinces to raise troops for the expected struggle with Antony and Octavian.

13. At Philippi in Thrace.

14. Although the survivors of Brutus' and Cassius' armies were spared after Philippi, Augustus fails to mention the notorious "proscriptions" (lists) published at the same time by which the Triumvirs declared more than two thousand of the most prominent men of Rome to be outside the protection of the laws. At least half of these were actually murdered and their properties confiscated.

be pardoned, I preferred to preserve rather than exterminate. About 500,000 Roman citizens took the military oath to me.[15] Of these I settled out in colonies[16] or sent back to their own towns, after their terms of service were over, considerably more than 300,000; and to them all I assigned lands purchased by myself or money in lieu of lands. I captured 600 ships not counting those below the rating of triremes.[17]

4 I twice celebrated an ovation,[18] three times curule triumphs,[19] and was twenty-one times greeted as imperator.[20] Though the Senate afterwards voted me several triumphs I declined them. I frequently also deposited laurels in the Capitol[21] after performing the vows which I had taken in each war. For successful operations performed by myself or by my legates under my auspices by land and sea, the Senate fifty-three times decreed a supplication to the immortal gods. The number of days during which, in accordance with a decree of the Senate, supplication was offered amounted to 890. In my triumphs there were led before my chariot nine kings or sons of kings. I had been consul thirteen times at the writing of this, and am in the course of the thirty-seventh year of my tribunician power (A.D. 13-14).

5 The Dictatorship[22] offered me in my presence and absence

15. An oath of allegiance to the person of Augustus.
16. Veterans were frequently rewarded for their services by the grant of lands in selected towns in Italy or the provinces—lands which sometimes were confiscated from political opponents.
17. The trireme was the standard war-galley in Greek and Roman times. Recent research suggests that it was rowed not with three superimposed banks of oars, but by a single line of oars arranged in groups of three.
18. A minor triumph (see note 19) granted for a victory in which fewer than five thousand of the enemy were slain.
19. The triumph was a procession of floats and wagons full of captives and spoils, held in honor of a general who had won a victory in which more than five thousand of the enemy were killed. "Curule" designated the highest class of magistrates, including consul, praetor, dictator, and censor.
20. This word originally meant commander of an army, and only later acquired the significance of "emperor."
21. A large, magnificent temple at Rome.
22. Supreme and undivided authority, not subject to veto or appeal. Under the Republic dictatorial powers were usually granted for periods of about six months to meet a specific crisis. Julius Caesar was the first to be voted dictator for life.

by the Senate and people in the consulship of Marcus Marcellus and Lucius Arruntius (22 B.C.) I declined to accept. I did not refuse at a time of very great scarcity of corn the commissionership of corn supply, which I administered in such a way that within a few days I freed the whole people from fear and danger. The consulship—either yearly or for life—then offered to me I declined to accept.

6 In the consulship of M. Vinicius and Q. Lucretius (19 B.C.), of P. and Cn. Lentulus (18 B.C.), and of Paullus Fabius Maximus and Q. Tubero (11 B.C.), when the Senate and people of Rome unanimously agreed that I should be elected overseer of the laws and morals;[23] with unlimited powers and without a colleague,[24] I refused every office offered me which was contrary to the customs of our ancestors. But what the Senate at that time wished me to manage, I carried out in virtue of my tribunician power,[25] and in this office I five times received at my own request a colleague from the Senate.

7 I was one of the triumvirate[26] for the re-establishment of the constitution for ten consecutive years. I have been princeps senatus[27] up to the day on which I write this for forty years. I am Pontifex Maximus,[28] Augur,[29] one of the fifteen commissioners for religion, one of the seven for sacred feasts, and Arval brother,[30] a sodalis Titius,[31] a fetial.[32]

23. Or censor: an official chosen every fifth year to take the census, assess property for taxation, determine military status and oversee public morals.
24. It was common under the Republic to designate two persons for each office on the theory that each would act as a check on the other.
25. A tribune was originally one of two elected representatives of the plebs, empowered to veto any decision of the Senate.
26. See note 9.
27. Presiding officer of the Senate, "First on the roll call of the Senate," whose approval was necessary before new measures could be submitted. The word later acquired the meaning of "prince."
28. Chief priest, head of the college of priests.
29. The augurs were priests who studied the will of the gods. Theirs was the most influential of the priestly colleges at Rome.
30. Member of a brotherhood of priests who were especially concerned with the fertility of the earth. The emperor was always a member of their college.
31. The "Companions of Titus" were a minor priesthood at Rome. Nothing is known of them but their name.
32. Member of a priestly association which sanctified the ratification of treaties and declarations of war.

8 In my fifth consulship (29 B.C.) I increased the number of the patricians[33] by order of people and Senate. I three times made up the roll of the Senate,[34] and in my sixth consulship (28 B.C.) I took a census of the people with M. Agrippa[35] as my colleague. I performed the lustrum[36] after an interval of forty-one years; in which the number of Roman citizens[37] entered on the census roll was 4,063,000. A second time with consular imperium I took the census by myself in the consulship of Gaius Censorinus and Gaius Asinius (8 B.C.), in which the number of Roman citizens entered on the roll was 4,223,000. I took a third census with consular imperium, my son Tiberius Caesar[38] acting as my colleague, in the consulship of Sextus Pompeius and Sextus Appuleius (A.D. 14), in which the number of Roman citizens entered on the census roll was 4,937,000. By new laws passed I recalled numerous customs of our ancestors that were falling into desuetude in our time, and myself set precedents in many particulars for the imitation of posterity.

9 The Senate decreed that vows should be offered for my health by consuls and priests every fifth year. In fulfilment of these vows the four chief colleges of priests or the consuls often gave games[39] in my lifetime. Also individually and by townships the people at large always offered sacrifices at all the temples for my health.

10 By a decree of the Senate my name was included in the ritual of the Salii;[40] and it was ordained by a law that my per-

33. Persons of the highest-ranking social class.
34. I.e., changed the composition of the Senate.
35. Augustus' faithful friend and aide, a great engineer and builder, a general, the victor at the battle of Actium.
36. A solemn ceremony of national purification to maintain good relations with the gods.
37. Roman citizens were males above age 15 who were supposedly descended from one of the original tribes of Rome, or aliens who had been granted citizenship.
38. This was the future emperor Tiberius (reigned A.D. 14-37), the son of Augustus' wife Livia by her first husband, Tiberius Claudius Nero.
39. Athletic contests, including foot races, discus throwing, wrestling, boxing, and prize fighting.
40. Or "Leapers," one of the minor associations of priests who ushered in each New Year with a ritual dance to Mars.

son should be sacred[41] and that I should have the tribunician power for the term of my natural life.[42] I refused to become Pontifex Maximus in succession to my colleague[43] during his life, though the people offered me that sacred office formerly held by my father. Some years later I accepted that sacred office on the death of the man who had availed himself of the civil disturbance to secure it;[44] such a multitude flocking to my election from all parts of Italy as is never recorded to have come to Rome before, in the consulship of P. Sulpicius and C. Valgius (6 March, 12 B.C.).

11 The Senate consecrated an altar to Fortuna Redux,[45] near the temple of Honour and Virtue, by the Porta Capena, for my return, on which it ordered the Vestal Virgins[46] to offer a yearly sacrifice on the day on which in the consulship of Q. Lucretius and M. Vinucius (19 B.C.) I returned to the city from Syria, and gave that day the name Augustalia from my cognomen (15 Dec.).

12 By a decree of the Senate at the same time part of the praetors and tribunes of the plebs, along with the consul Q. Lucretius and leading nobles, were despatched into Campania[47] to meet me—an honour that up to this time has been decreed to no one else. When I returned to Rome from Spain and Gaul after successful operations in those provinces, in the consulship of Tiberius Nero and Publius Quintilius (13 B.C.), the Senate voted that an altar to Pax Augusta[48] should be consecrated for my return on the Campus Martius, upon which it ordered the magistrates and priests and Vestal Virgins to offer an annual sacrifice (30 Jan.).

41. Exceptional men were often regarded as gods in the ancient world and worshipped together with the household deities and the ancestors. Julius Caesar had been recognized as a god by the Senate two years after his assassination.
42. Under the Republic the tribune's term of office had been one year.
43. Marcus Lepidus, his colleague in the triumvirate, who died in 12 B.C.
44. The same Lepidus as in note 43.
45. The goddess of Fate.
46. A selected group of young women who tended the hearth of Vesta, goddess of fire.
47. Region of southwestern Italy around modern Naples.
48. "Augustan Peace," commemorating the fact that after 30 B.C. there were no major wars within the empire.

13 Whereas the Ianus Quirinus,[49] which our ancestors ordered to be closed when peace throughout the whole dominions of the Roman people by land and sea had been obtained by victories, is recorded to have been only twice shut before my birth since the foundation of the city, the Senate three times voted its closure during my principate.

14 My sons Gaius and Lucius Caesar, whom fortune snatched from me in their early manhood,[50] in compliment to me, the Senate and Roman people designated consuls in their fifteenth year[51] with a proviso that they should enter on that office after an interval of five years. From the day of their assuming the toga virilis[52] the Senate decreed that they should take part in public business. Moreover, the Roman equites[53] in a body gave each of them the title of Princeps Iuventutis,[54] and presented them with silver shields and spears.

15 To the Roman plebs[55] I paid 300 sesterces[56] per head in virtue of my father's will; and in my own name I gave 400 apiece in my fifth consulship (29 B.C.) from the sale of spoils of war; and a second time in my tenth consulship (24 B.C.) out of my own private property I paid a bounty of 400 sesterces per man, and in my eleventh consulship (23 B.C.) I measured out twelve distributions of corn, having purchased the grain from my own resources. In the twelfth year of my tribunician power (11 B.C.), I for the third time gave a bounty of 400 sesterces a head. These largesses of mine affected never less than 250,000 persons. In the eighteenth year of my tribunician power and my twelfth consulship (5 B.C.) I gave 320,000 of the urban

49. Janus was the god of the cottage door, the city gate, the day, year, or any beginning; he had two faces, one turned in each direction.
50. These were actually Augustus' grandsons, the sons of his daughter Julia by his general and friend Marcus Agrippa, subsequently adopted by the emperor as his sons. Gaius died in A.D. 4, Lucius in A.D. 2.
51. I.e., long before the usual age for assuming such an office.
52. The garment assumed at about age 14 to mark the transition from boyhood to manhood.
53. The equites were the second-ranking class in Roman society, below the patricians, one of the two orders admitted to the Senate.
54. "Young prince."
55. The plebs were the general body of Roman citizens, ranking below patricians and equites.
56. A sesterce was equal to one-fourth of a denarius.

plebs sixty denarii[56] a head. In the colonies of my soldiers, in my fifth consulship (29 B.C.) I gave from the sale of spoils of war 1,000 sesterces a head; and among such settlers the number who received that triumphal largess amounted to about 120,000 men. In my thirteenth consulship (2 B.C.) I gave 60 denarii apiece to the plebeians then in receipt of public corn; they amounted to somewhat more than 200,000 persons.

16 The money for the lands, which in my fourth consulship (30 B.C.), and afterwards in the consulship of M. Crassus and Cn. Lentulus the augur (14 B.C.), I assigned to the soldiers, I paid to the municipal towns. The amount was about 600,000,000 sesterces, which I paid for lands in Italy, and about 260,000,000 which I disbursed for lands in the provinces.

I was the first and only one within the memory of my own generation to do this of all who settled colonies in Italy and the provinces. And afterwards in the consulship of Tib. Nero and Cn. Piso (7 B.C.), and again in the consulship of C. Antistius and D. Laelius (6 B.C.), and of C. Calvisius and L. Pasienus (4 B.C.), and of L. Lentulus and M. Messalla (3 B.C.), and of L. Caninius and Q. Fabricius (2 B.C.), to the soldiers, whom after their terms of service I sent back to their own towns, I paid good service allowances in ready money; on which I expended 400,000,000 sesterces as an act of grace.

17 I four times subsidised the aerarium[57] from my own money, the sums which I thus paid over to the commissioners of the treasury amounting to 150,000,000 sesterces. And in the consulship of M. Lepidus and L. Arruntius (A.D. 6), to the military treasury, which was established on my initiative for the payment of their good service allowance, to the soldiers who had served twenty years or more, I contributed from my own patrimony 170,000,000 sesterces.

18 From and after the year of the consulship of Gnaeus and Publius Lentulus (18 B.C.), whenever the payment of the revenues were in arrear, I paid into the treasury from my own patrimony the taxes, whether due in corn or money, sometimes of 100,000 persons, sometimes of more.

57. The national Treasury, one of two coffers for the receipt of taxes at Rome, controlled by the Senate. The other was the imperial Treasury controlled and managed by the emperor.

19 I built the curia[58] and Chalcidicum[59] adjoining it, and the temples of Apollo[60] on the Palatine[61] with its colonnades, the temple of the divine Iulius,[62] the Lupercal,[63] the colonnade at the Flaminian circus,[64] which I allowed to be called Octavia, from the name of the builder of the earlier one on the same site, the state box at the Circus Maximus,[64] the temples of Jupiter Feretrius[65] and of Jupiter Tonans[66] on the Capitol, the temple of Quirinus,[67] the temples of Minerva[68] and of Juno the Queen,[69] and of Iupiter Libertas[70] on the Aventine,[71] the temple of the Lares[72] at the head of the via Sacra,[73] the temple of divine Penates[74] in the Velia,[75] the temple of Youth, the temple of the Mater Magna[76] on the Palatine.

20 The Capitolium[77] and the Pompeian theatre—both very costly works—I restored without any inscription of my own name. Water-conduits in many places that were decaying from age I repaired; and I doubled the aqueduct called the Aqua Marcia, by turning a new spring into its channel.

58. The Senate house.
59. The entrance-hall to a public building, an annex or addition to a basilica.
60. The god of light, the life-giver and enemy of darkness.
61. One of the seven hills on which Rome was built.
62. Augustus' uncle, Julius Caesar.
63. A structure sacred to the god Lupercus, who protected the flocks from wolves.
64. Flaminian Circus and Circus Maximus: the two great amphitheatres at Rome where admission was free to all citizens. The costs of performances were paid by political candidates.
65. Probably: Jupiter the Striker (of those who violated oaths).
66. Jupiter the Thunderer.
67. Quirinus was one of Rome's favorite gods, identified with Romulus, one of the city's founders.
68. The goddess of wisdom, handicrafts, and guilds, actors, musicians, and scribes.
69. The wife of Jupiter, protector of women, marriage, and maternity.
70. Jupiter as the personification of liberty.
71. Another of Rome's seven hills.
72. The guardian spirits of buildings, fields, and the household.
73. The Sacred Way leading up to the temples of Jupiter and Saturn on the Capitoline hill.
74. Gods who protected storerooms and barns.
75. Ordinarily: the city of Elea in southern Italy, though here the context indicates a place in Rome.
76. Cybele, the "Great Mother" goddess of Asia Minor whose worship gained popularity in Rome under the Empire. She was primarily a goddess of fertility, but also a healer of disease and protector in war.
77. A rich and magnificent temple.

The Forum Iulium[78] and the basilica,[79] which was between the temple of Castor[80] and the temple of Saturn,[81] works begun and far advanced by my father, I completed; and when the same basilica was destroyed by fire, I began its reconstruction on an extended plan, to be inscribed with the names of my sons, and in case I do not live to complete it I have ordered it to be completed by my heirs.

In my sixth consulship (28 B.C.), I repaired eighty-two temples of the gods in the city in accordance with a decree of the Senate, none being omitted which at that time stood in need of repair. In my seventh consulship (27 B.C.) I constructed the Flaminian road from the city to Ariminum,[82] and all the bridges except the Mulvian and Minucian.

21 On ground belonging to myself I built a temple to Mars Ultor[83] and the Forum Augustum,[84] with money arising from sale of war spoils. I built a theatre adjoining the temple of Apollo, on ground for the most part purchased from private owners, to be under the name of my son-in-law Marcus Marcellus.[85] Offerings from money raised by sale of war-spoil I consecrated in the temple of Apollo, and in the temple of Vesta, and in the temple of Mars Ultor, which cost me about 100,000,000 sesterces. Thirty-five thousand pounds of gold, crown money contributed by the municipia and colonies of Italy for my triumphs, I refunded in my fifth consulship (29 B.C.), and subsequently, as often as I was greeted Imperator, I refused to receive crown money, though the municipia and colonies had decreed it with as much warmth as before.

22 I three times gave a show of gladiators[86] in my own name,

78. A forum was a large public square surrounded by monumental buildings. The Forum Iulium was built by Julius Caesar to relieve the congestion of the older Forum Romanum.
79. A rectangular roofed hall serving as a social or commercial meeting place. The basilica style was later used for many Christian churches.
80. Castor and Pollux were the protector gods of Rome.
81. Saturn was the god of sowing, who was supposed to have reigned over Rome in a mythical Golden Age in the distant past.
82. Town on the Adriatic, now Rimini.
83. Mars "the Avenger."
84. The new forum built by Augustus.
85. Son of Augustus' sister Octavia, later the husband of his daughter Julia.
86. Armed men, usually slaves or war prisoners, who engaged in public combats in an arena with other men or animals, using swords or other weapons.

and five times in the name of my sons and grandsons; in which shows about 10,000 men contended. I twice gave the people a show of athletes collected from all parts of the world in my own name, and a third time in the name of my grandson. I gave games in my own name four times, as representing other magistrates twenty-three times. In behalf of the quindecimviri,[87] and as master of the college, with M. Agrippa as colleague, I gave the Secular games[88] in the consulship of C. Furnius and C. Silanus (17 B.C.). In my thirteenth consulship (2 B.C.), I gave for the first time the games of Mars which, since that time, the consuls have given in successive years. I gave the people wild-beast hunts, of African animals, in my own name and that of my sons and grandsons, in the circus and forum, and the amphitheatres twenty-six times, in which about 3,500 animals were killed.

23 I gave the people the spectacle of a naval battle on the other side of the Tiber, in the spot where now is the grove of the Caesars, the ground having been hollowed out to a length of 1,800 feet, and a breadth of 1,200 feet, in which thirty beaked ships, triremes or biremes, and a still larger number of smaller vessels contended. In these fleets, besides the rowers, there fought about three thousand men.

24 In the temples of all the states of the province of Asia, I replaced the ornaments after my victory, which he with whom I had fought[89] had taken into his private possession from the spoilation of the temples. There were about eighty silver statues of me, some on foot, some equestrian, some in chariots, in various parts of the city. These I removed, and from the money thus obtained I placed golden offerings in the temple of Apollo in my own name and in that of those who had honoured me by the statues.

25 I cleared the sea of pirates. In that war I captured about 30,000 slaves, who had run away from their masters, and had borne arms against the republic, and handed them back to their owners to be punished. The whole of Italy took the oath to me

87. A group of fifteen men who paid for public games.
88. Three days of ceremonies, contests and spectacles, religious ritual and song celebrating the return of Saturn's Golden Age.
89. Marc Antony.

spontaneously, and demanded that I should be the leader in the war in which I won the victory of Actium.[90] The provinces of the Gauls, the Spains, Africa, Sicily, Sardinia, took the same oath. Among those who fought under my standards were more than seven hundred Senators, eighty-three of whom had been, or have since been consuls up to the time of my writing this, 170 members of the sacred colleges.

26 I extended the frontiers of all the provinces of the Roman people, which were bordered by tribes that had not submitted to our Empire. The provinces of the Gauls, and Spains and Germany, bounded by the Ocean from Gades[91] to the mouth of the river Elbe, I reduced to a peaceful state. The Alps, from the district near the Adriatic to the Tuscan sea, I forced to remain peaceful without waging unprovoked war with any tribe. My fleet sailed through the Ocean from the mouth of the Rhine towards the rising sun, up to the territories of the Cimbri,[92] to which point no Roman had penetrated, up to that time, either by land or sea. The Cimbri, and Charydes, and Semnones and other peoples of the Germans, belonging to the same tract of country, sent ambassadors to ask for the friendship of myself and the Roman people. By my command and under my auspices, two armies were marched into Aethiopia and Arabia, called Felix,[93] nearly simultaneously, and large hostile forces of both these nations were cut to pieces in battle, and a large number of towns were captured. Aethiopia was penetrated as far as the town of Nabata, next to Meroe. Into Arabia the army advanced into territories of the Sabaei as far as the town Mariba.

27 I added Egypt to the Empire of the Roman people.[94] When I might have made the Greater Armenia[95] a province after the assassination of its king Artaxes, I preferred, on the

90. The battle which finally determined that Augustus would be the sole ruler of the Roman empire, fought in 31 B.C. in the Ionian Sea between the forces of Augustus and Marc Antony.
91. City on the west coast of Spain, now Cadiz.
92. A Germanic tribe which threatened Italy.
93. Arabia was believed to be rich in gold and jewels.
94. Before Actium, Marc Antony had ruled Egypt together with the Egyptian queen, Cleopatra.
95. The area south of the Caucasus Mountains between the Caspian and the Black Sea.

precedent of our ancestors, to hand over that kingdom to Tigranes, son of King Artavasdes, grandson of King Tigranes, by the hands of Tiberius Nero,[96] who was then my stepson. The same nation being afterwards in a state of revolt and rebellion, I handed over to the government of King Ariobarzanes, son of Artabazus, king of the Medes, after it had been reduced by my son Gaius; and after his death to his son Artavasdes, upon whose assassination I sent Tigranes, a member of the royal family of the Armenians, into that kingdom. I recovered all the provinces on the other side of the Adriatic towards the East and Cyrenae,[97] which were by this time for the most part held by various kings, and before them Sicily and Sardinia which had been overrun by an army of slaves.

28 I settled colonies of soldiers in Africa, Sicily, Macedonia, both the Spains, Achaia,[98] Asia, Syria, Gallia Narbonensis,[99] Pisidia.[100] Italy has twenty-eight colonies established under my auspices, which have in my lifetime become very densely inhabited and places of great resort.

29 A large number of military standards, which had been lost under other commanders, I recovered, after defeating the enemy from Spain and Gaul and the Dalmatians. I compelled the Parthians[101] to restore the spoils and standards of three Roman armies, and to seek as suppliants the friendship of the Roman people. These standards I laid up in the inner shrine belonging to the temple of Mars Ultor.

30 The tribes of the Pannonii,[102] which before I was princeps an army of the Roman people never reached, having been subdued by Tiberius Nero, who was then my stepson and legate (11 B.C.), I added to the Empire of the Roman people, and I extended the frontier of Illyricum[103] to the bank of the river Danube. And when an army of the Daci[104] crossed to the south

96. See note 38.
97. Region of north Africa between Tunisia and Tripolitania.
98. The northern Peloponnesus.
99. Narbonese Gaul, the area of southeastern France and northwestern Italy.
100. Province on the southern coast of Asia Minor, just west of Cilicia.
101. Rome's imperial neighbor on the east.
102. Tribes from the region of present-day Hungary and northern Croatia.
103. The area between the Adriatic, Alps, and Danube.
104. Tribes living in Transylvania (now western Rumania).

of that river it was conquered and put to flight under my auspices; and subsequently an army, being led across the Danube, forced the tribes of the Daci to submit to the orders of the Roman people.

31 To me there were often sent embassies of kings from India, who had never before been seen in the camp of any Roman general. By ambassadors the Bastarnae[105] and the Scythians[106] and the kings of the Sarmatians,[107] who live on both sides of the river Don, and the king of the Albani[108] and of the Hiberi[108] and of the Medes,[109] sought our friendship.

32 Kings of the Parthians—Tiridates, and afterwards Phrates, son of King Phrates—fled to me for refuge; of the Medes Artavasdes; of the Adiabeni[110] Artaxares; of the Britons Dumnobellaunus and Tim. . . ; of the Marcomanni[111] and Suebi. . .[111] . . . Phrates, king of the Parthians, son of Orodes,[112] sent all his sons and grandsons to me in Italy, not because he had been overcome in war, but seeking our friendship by means of his own sons as pledges. And a very large number of other nations experienced the good faith of the Roman people while I was princeps, with whom before that time there had been no diplomatic or friendly intercourse.

33 The nations of the Parthians and the chief men of the Medes by means of embassies sought and accepted from me kings of those peoples—the Parthians Vonones, son of King Phrates, grandson of King Orodes; the Medes Ariobarzanes, son of King Artavasdes, grandson of King Ariobarzanes.

34 In my sixth and seventh consulships (28,27 B.C.), when I had extinguished the flames of civil war, having by universal

105. A roving tribe, probably Germanic, which is first recorded as occupying the lower Danube region.
106. A people living between the Carpathian Mountains and the Don River in southern Russia.
107. An Indo-European nomadic tribe closely related to the Scythians.
108. Warlike tribes from the Caucasus region of northern Iran.
109. Inhabitants of the province of Media in western Iran.
110. A people from the upper Tigris region.
111. The Marcomanni and Suebi were both Germanic tribes.
112. Orodes II, the king of Parthia who occupied most of Roman Asia after Crassus' defeat at Carrhae (Harran) in 53 B.C., was subsequently defeated by Antony in 38 B.C.

consent become possessed of the sole direction of affairs, I transferred the republic from my power to the will of the Senate and people of Rome. For which good service on my part I was by decree of the Senate called by the name of Augustus,[113] and the door-posts of my house were covered with laurels in the name of the state, and a civic crown was fixed up over my door, and a golden shield was placed in the Curia Iulia,[114] which it was declared by its inscriptions the Senate and people of Rome gave me in recognition of valour, clemency, justice, piety. After that time I took precedence of all in authority (*auctoritate*), but of power I had nothing more than those who were my colleagues in the several magistracies.

35 While I was administering my thirteenth consulship (2 B.C.), the Senate and equestrian order and the Roman people with one consent greeted me as FATHER OF MY COUNTRY, and decreed that it should be inscribed in the vestibule of my house, and in the Senate house, and in the Forum Augustum, and under the chariot which was there placed in my honour in accordance with a senatorial decree.

When I wrote this I was in my seventy-sixth year (A.D. 13-14).

113. A word hitherto applied to holy objects and places or to certain creative divinities; it gave the bearer an air of sanctity.
114. The new Senate house begun by Julius Caesar.

Introduction to Juvenal

Juvenal (Decimus Juvenalis, *ca.* A.D. 60-140) was the greatest satiric poet produced by Rome, and the most bitter. In savage and brilliant epigrams he lashed out at the corruption and depravity of Roman society as he observed it. Rome for Juvenal was the overcrowded, parasitical metropolis of an empire, swarming with foreigners, full of intrigue and moral license. Roman society was polarized between the arrogant rich and the debased poor, all dependent upon the fiat of an emperor who was above the law. For what were probably compelling reasons of personal safety, Juvenal veiled his criticism of current abuses by using historical themes. This presumably had something to do with the extraordinary fact that one of Rome's greatest poets spent his lifetime in obscurity.

Juvenal's biography can be only tentatively reconstructed; for he spoke rarely of himself and passed almost unnoticed in the writings of his contemporaries. He does tell us that he was born a Roman citizen in the small Italian town of Aquinum. Various allusions in his poems suggest that he was familiar with court life in the time of the emperor Domitian (reigned A.D. 80-96). Quite possibly he was then a young and ambitious army officer, growing ever angrier at the dishonest ways by which promotions were gained and at the incompetent sycophants who gained them. In any event, an abrupt break in his career occurred about A.D. 93. He does not tell us exactly what it was; but certain allusions suggest that Domitian sent him into exile in retaliation for a lampoon on a court favorite. A remote frontier post in Egypt was probably the place of banishment, where, after the fashion of Roman political exiles, he must have lived in isolation and discomfort under the supervision of the garrison commander. Following the assassination of Domitian and the accession of the emperor Nerva in A.D. 96, Juvenal was recalled to Rome.

No doubt he was filled with bitterness at the injustice with which he had been treated. His property confiscated, he now lived as a hanger-on of rich patrons—the only alternative to sinking down into the working class. The patrons were greedy and arrogant, with an insatiable appetite for flattery. The seeker after favors had to wait endlessly in outer rooms, always in formal dress, bribe servants, and fawn, all in the hope of some handout or being asked to dinner. Juvenal's poems leave no doubt that he felt strongly the humiliation and disgrace of such an existence, and resented those who were more successful sycophants than he. To a Roman conscious of his ancestry, the idea of being out-maneuvered by foreigners was particularly galling.

Anti-foreignness was not ordinarily a Roman trait. Some of Rome's most distinguished authors and statesmen had come from distant provinces; anyone who spoke Latin and acquired Roman customs was accepted in polite society regardless of his origins. Nonetheless, a degree of hostility was always present between Romans and Greeks. The Greeks were not ignorant provincials eager to accept Roman civilization; they considered their own attainments superior, and despised the Romans as crude. Greek was the unquestioned language of culture and thought; knowledge of Greek was the mark of an educated man. The Romans, the conquerors and rulers of an empire, resented this. And Juvenal had a special reason for disliking Greeks. He competed with them for the patronage of the rich and well born, the largesse which allowed him to retain a modicum of gentility. In this rivalry for favors, the versatility and quick minds of the Greeks gave them an advantage.

The following lines from the Third Satire deal with the poet's feelings about Greeks. The theme of the poem as a whole is the vileness of Rome, the discomforts and hazards of living there, and the superiority of life in the country. The piece is set in the form of a farewell to Rome by Juvenal's friend Umbricius, who is leaving the city to settle in the country for good. The poet snarls at all the things he detests about Rome: its crookedness and corruption, the difficulty of being poor there, the money-worship, the din, the overcrowded slums ready to collapse, the danger of robbery and assault in the streets. The Greeks, of course, are just one of many undesirable elements on Juvenal's list of the things which make Rome unlivable.

JUVENAL: FROM SATIRE III

. . . .

"Then, too, the manners dearest to our rich.
I hate them, and I swear it's no small bitch.
I can't stand, Quirites,[1] that Rome of Greeks,

"nor that proportion of our scum that's Greek.
For years the Syrian springs poured in our Tiber
bringing new slang, new manners, harps, and flutes,
weird timbrels and the circus prostitutes.[2]
Now dam those foreign whores in their own cinctures,
unmask their painted cheek.

From *Satires*, trans. by Jerome Mazzaro, Ann Arbor: University of Michigan Press, 1965, pp. 38-40. Reprinted by permission of the University of Michigan Press.

1. I.e., native Romans. The Quirites were the earliest inhabitants of Rome.

2. Syrian girl-harpists and timbrel players were well known in Rome; often they became prostitutes.

Dining, the country fops trip in Greek sandals
and anchor jewelry on their necks and clothes.
From lofty Sicyon[3] or from breezy Andros,[4]
they make their ways into our finest stables.

"They work their ways in homes they learn to rule.
Quick-witted, impudent as the Assyrian
Isaeus,[5] only stormier in speech.
Whatever role you want, they're quick to don.
They'll paint or prophesy or even teach,
be priest as well, or fool,
astrologer, physician, confidant.
They know all and will do the tasks you will.
They're like no Moor, Samaritan, or Pole[6]
but like that Daedalus[7] our tales recount.

"Shouldn't I flee such men? Should they come first
and rest upon a better couch than I,
who're blown here by the winds that bring our plums?[8]
Is this the end one's heritage becomes?
I, who am born beneath a Roman sky?
Like spring their praises burst.
They praise illiterates for speech, the lame for leg,
compare one's scrawny neck to that praised girth
when Hercules brought Antaeus to earth,[9]
or go in raptures hearing some fop brag

3. A town in the northeastern Peloponnesus.

4. An island of the Aegean Sea.

5. A noted professional orator and teacher of rhetoric at Rome.

6. The translator has taken liberties with the Latin for the sake of English rhyme. The Latin reads: "Moor, Sarmatian (*not* Samaritan!), or Thracian." Sarmatia was the region between the Vistula and the Volga Rivers, now part of Poland and the Soviet Union.

7. Daedalus was an Athenian known both for inventiveness and for treachery. In Greek mythology he was the noted architect and inventor who built the Labyrinth at Cnossus in Crete. He then betrayed the secret of its design to the nymph Ariadne, who guided Theseus through the maze to kill the Minotaur dwelling inside.

8. I.e., blown in from Syria.

9. In Greek mythology, the giant Antaeus was invincible as long as he maintained contact with his mother Earth; but Hercules lifted him off the ground and strangled him.

"melodious as roosters crow at hens.
Of course, we praise them, too, but they're believed!
Could any actor match them playing Thais,
a matron or a slut or girl enslaved?[10]
You'd not believe men's manners were like this!
You'd swear they're women's.[11]
Yet home, these Greeks would be thought second-rate
beside those actors playing their theaters,
for they're a race and country of poseurs.
Just smile and watch; a Greek's sides nearly split.

"Shed one tear and he weeps, though not with grief.
In winter build a fire, and he's cold, too.
Be warm and sweatbeads dot his nose's ridge.
You're never equals. He must have the edge,
ready by day or night to take his cue
to wrench his hands or laugh
if you but belch, piss, shit, or just guffaw
or your tipped chamber pot begins to gurgle.
And, too, nothing's more sacred than his goal,
not mother, daughter, would-be son-in-law,

"or even his own son, or lacking these,
he'll try to rape his best friends' grandmothers
to learn more dirt or frame his next intent.
And since I'm on the Greeks, I'll leave the others,
and mention crimes of philosophic bent.
A stoic who betrays
his friend,[12] born where that Gorgon's horse was lost,
at Tarsus,[13] right along that fearsome river.[14]

10. In Greek-style comedies there were three types of feminine role: the courtesan, the matron, and the maid or slave-girl. Thais (a character in a play by Terence) was the first type.

11. Women's roles on the stage were played by men. Juvenal is suggesting that real men could not imitate women so successfully.

12. The stoic was Publius Celer, who accused his friend Soranus to the Emperor Nero.

13. In Greek mythology, Pegasus was the winged horse who sprang from the blood of the slain Gorgon, Medusa. The hero Bellerophon fell off the horse at Tarsus.

14. The Cydnus, an exceptionally cold stream.

There's no room left for Romans where Greeks are.
The shrewd Greek-minded cocks must rule the roost.

Introduction to Marcus Aurelius

Stoicism, like Epicureanism, was the product of a society in disintegration. Both schools of thought originated in Greece in the late fourth century B.C., when social upheavals and corrupt governments had rendered an ethic of public service and city patriotism out of date. For both schools, the goal of life was the tranquillity and inner peace of the individual. Virtue was defined as indifference toward the affairs of life and as freedom from emotion—the overcoming of the world within rather than without.

But unlike the Epicureans with their atomistic physics, the Stoics regarded the universe as a kind of harmony governed by Providence. The cosmos to them was a type of machine composed of interrelated parts; mankind belongs to the whole, which is the city of the world. Man ought thus to live in accordance with the laws of the universe, or Nature. Nature is identical with reason: the same power which regulates the cosmos also forms the raw sense-perceptions of the individual into order and unity. This world-Reason, or *logos,* the Stoics also called God.

Stoicism was a philosophy particularly well suited to the Romans of the late empire. Its emphasis on the patient endurance of adversity rather than on positive creativity, on duty rather than pleasure, appealed especially to the governing class. Perhaps no single figure embodies the Stoic ideal more completely than Marcus Aurelius, adopted son of the emperor Antoninus Pius, who ruled the empire in the last years of the "Roman Peace" (A.D. 161-80). Ancient and modern historians agree in praising the wisdom of his government and the purity of his life. Retiring by nature, and preferring philosophy to war, he was forced by his position into the center of public affairs. He had the misfortune to reign in a period of monumental disasters. Invading barbarians from the north threatened the imperial frontiers in Europe and even Italy itself; the Parthians challenged Roman hegemony in the East; the plague brought back by the legions from Asia decimated Roman society and played its part in the gradual decline of the empire. A general in spite of himself, Marcus spent much of his reign in fighting the northern barbarians, and died, worn out, in his camp on the Danube. The *Meditations,* by which posterity chiefly remembers him, were composed in the intervals of war. Written in the Greek language, they are a kind of diary of often disconnected thoughts; the "you" to whom he speaks is himself.

MARCUS AURELIUS: FROM THE MEDITATIONS

Book IV

1 The attitude of that which rules within us[1] toward outside events, if it is in accord with nature, is ever to adapt itself easily to what is possible in the given circumstances. It does not direct its affection upon any particular set of circumstances to work upon, but it starts out toward its objects with reservations,[2] and converts any obstacle into material for its own action, as fire does when it overpowers what is thrown upon it. A small flame might be quenched by it, but a bright fire very rapidly appropriates to itself whatever is put upon it, consumes it and rises higher because of these obstacles.

2 Let no action be done at random, or in any other way than in accordance with the principle which perfects the art.

3 Men seek retreats for themselves in country places, on beaches and mountains, and you yourself are wont to long for such retreats, but that is altogether unenlightened when it is possible at any hour you please to find a retreat within yourself. For nowhere can a man withdraw to a more untroubled quietude than in his own soul, especially a man who has within him things of which the contemplation will at once put him per-

1. The directing power (*igemonikon*) or divine reason within man produces (conscious) sensations and acts of will out of raw, undefined sense-impressions.

2. I.e., one should not set one's heart on any particular aim, but adjust to circumstances and make each new situation the occasion for the practice of reason.

fectly at ease, and by ease I mean nothing other than orderly conduct.[3] Grant yourself this withdrawal continually, and refresh yourself. Let these be brief and elemental doctrines which when present will suffice to overwhelm all sorrows and to send you back no longer resentful of the things to which you return.

For what is it you resent? The wickedness of men? Reflect on the conclusion that rational beings are born for the sake of each other, that tolerance is a part of righteousness, and that men do not sin on purpose. Consider how many men have been hostile and suspicious, have hated and waged war, and then been laid out for burial or reduced to ashes. Desist then. Do you resent the portions received from the whole? Consider the alternatives afresh, namely "Providence or atoms,"[4] and how many proofs there are that the universe is like a city community.[5] Are you still affected by the things of the body? Reflect that the mind, once it has freed itself and come to know its own capacities, is no longer involved in the movements of animal life,[6] whether these be smooth or tumultous. For the rest, recall all you have heard about pain and pleasure, to which you have given assent.

Does paltry fame disturb you? Look how swift is the forgetting of all things in the chaos of infinite time before and after, how empty is noisy applause, how liable to change and uncritical are those who seem to speak well of us, how narrow the boundaries within which fame is confined. The whole earth is but a point in the universe, and how small a part of the earth is the corner in which you live. And how many are those who there will praise you, and what sort of men are they?

From now on keep in mind the retreat into this little territory within yourself. Avoid spasms and tensions above all; be free and look at your troubles like a man, a citizen and a mortal creature. Among the foremost things which you will look into are these two: first, that external matters do not affect the soul but stand quietly outside it, while true disturbances come from

3. I.e., behavior according to the principles of reason.
4. I.e., either the universe is ruled by Providence (Necessity), as Marcus and the Stoics believed, or by the chance encounter of atoms which scatter again when the body dies.
5. *Polis.*
6. I.e., of the *pneuma*, or "breath of life."

the inner judgment; second, that everything you see has all but changed already and is no more. Keep constantly in mind in how many things you yourself have witnessed changes already. The universe is change, life is understanding.

4 If we have intelligence in common, so we have reason which makes us reasoning beings, and that practical reason which orders what we must or must not do; then the law too is common to us[7] and, if so, we are citizens; if so, we share a common government; if so, the universe is, as it were, a city—for what other common government could one say is shared by all mankind?

From this, the common city, we derive our intelligence, our reason and our law—from what else? Just as the dry earth-element in me has been portioned off from earth somewhere, and the water in me from the other element, the air or breath from some other source and the dry and fiery from a source of its own (for nothing comes from what does not exist or returns to it), so also then the intelligence comes from somewhere.

5 Death, like birth, is a mystery of nature. The one is a joining together of the same elements into which the other is a dissolving. In any case, it is nothing of which one should be ashamed, for it is not incompatible with the nature of a rational being or the logic of its composition.

6 Their nature inevitably required that they behave in this way. He who wants this not to be wants a fig tree not to produce its acrid juice. In any case remember this: within a very short time both you and he will have died, and soon not even your name will survive.

7 Discard the thought of injury, and the words "I have been injured" are gone; discard the words "I have been injured," and the injury is gone.

8 What does not make a man[8] worse does not make his life worse, and does him no injury, external or internal.

9 The nature of the universally beneficial[9] has inevitably brought this about.

7. Not the statutory law of a particular place, but the universal norms of behavior.

8. His character.

9. I.e., Providence.

10 "Everything which happens, is right." Examine this saying carefully and you will find it so. I do not mean right merely in the sense that it fits the pattern of events, but in the sense of just, as if someone were giving each his due. Examine this then as you have begun to do, and, whatever you do, do it as a good man should, as the word good is properly understood. Safeguard this goodness in your every action.

. . . .

12 You should always be ready for two things, first, to do only what reason, as embodied in the arts of kingship and legislation, perceives to be to the benefit of mankind; second, to change your course if one be present to put you right and make you abandon a certain opinion. Such change, however, should always result from being convinced of what is just and for the common good, and what you choose to do must be of that nature, not because pleasure or fame may result from it.

. . . .

14 You exist but as a part of the Whole. You will disappear into the Whole which created you, or rather you will be taken up into the creative Reason when the change comes.

15 Many grains of incense on the same altar; one was cast earlier, the other later, but it makes no difference.

. . . .

17 Live not as if you had ten thousand years before you. Necessity is upon you. While you live, while you may, become good.

18 How much ease he gains who does not look at what his neighbor says or does or thinks, but only at what he himself is doing in order that his own action may be just, pious, and good. Do not glance aside at another's black character but run the straight course to the finishing line, without being diverted.

19 The man who thrills at the thought of later fame fails to realize that every one of those who remember him will very shortly die, as well as himself. So will their successors, until all memory of him is quenched as it travels through the minds of men, the flame of whose life is lit and then put out. But suppose those who will remember you to be immortal and the memory of you everlasting; even so, what is it to you? And I do not

mean that praise is nothing to you when dead, but what is it to you while you live, except insofar as it affects your management of affairs? For now you inopportunely neglect nature's gift of virtue while you cling to some other concern.

20 All that has any beauty at all owes this to itself, and is complete in itself, but praise is no part of it. Nothing becomes either better or worse for being praised, and I mean this to apply also to things more commonly called beautiful, such as works of nature or works of art. As for the truly beautiful, it has no need of anything further, any more than does law, or truth, or kindness or reverence. Which of these things is made beautiful by praise or destroyed by censure? Does an emerald become less beautiful if it is not praised? What of gold, ivory, purple, a lyre, a dagger, a little flower or a bush?

. . . .

22 Do not wander aimlessly, but give every impulse its just due, and in every sensation preserve the power of comprehension.

23 Everything which is in tune with you, O Universe, is in tune with me. Nothing which happens at the right time for you is early or late for me. Everything, O Nature, which your seasons produce is fruit to me. All things come from you, exist in you, and will return to you. If he could say: "Beloved city of Cecrops,"[10] will you not say: "Beloved city of Zeus"?

24 "Do but little, if you would have contentment."[11] Surely it is better to do what is necessary, as much as the reason of one who is by nature a social creature demands, and in the manner reason requires it to be done. This will not only bring the contentment derived from right conduct, but also that of doing little, since most of our words and actions are unnecessary and whoever eliminates these will have more leisure and be less disturbed. Hence one should on each occasion remind oneself: "Surely this is not one of the necessary actions?" One should

10. I.e., Athens. Cecrops was the mythological founder of Athens, who was supposed to have introduced civilization there. The phrase is from a play of Aristophanes.

11. A saying of the Greek Atomist philosopher Democritus (*ca.* 460-362 B.C.).

eliminate not only unnecessary actions but also unnecessary imaginings, for then no irrelevant actions will follow.

25 Make trial of how the life of the good man turns out for you, of the man who is glad of the share he receives from the Whole and satisfied if his own action be just and his own disposition kindly.

26 You have seen those things; look also at these: do not disturb yourself, achieve simplicity in yourself. Someone does wrong? The wrong is to himself. Something has happened to you? It is well. From the beginning all that happens has been ordained and fated for you as your part of the Whole. In a word, life is short; we must therefore derive benefit from the present circumstances with prudence and with justice. Be sober and relaxed.

27 Either a universe with order and purpose or a medley thrown together by chance, but that too has order. Or can there be order of a kind in your inner world, but no order in the Whole, especially as all things are distinguished from one another, yet intermingle, and respond to each other?

. . . .

29 If the man who does not understand the truths embodied in the universe is a stranger in it, no less a stranger is he who does not understand what happens in the world of sense. An exile is he who flees from social principle; blind, who keeps the eye of his mind closed; a beggar, who has need of another and does not possess within himself all that is of use in life. A tumor on the universe is he who cuts himself off in rebellion against the logic of our common nature because he is dissatisfied with his lot, for it is that nature which brought it about, as it also brought you about. He is but a splinter off the community who separates his own soul from that of all rational beings, which is one.

. . . .

31 Treasure what little you have learnt and find refreshment in it. Go through what remains of your life as one who has wholeheartedly entrusted all that is his to the gods and has not made himself either despot or slave to any man.

32 Consider, for the sake of argument, the times of Vespa-

sian;[12] you will see all the same things: men marrying, begetting children, being ill, dying, fighting wars, feasting, trading, farming, flattering, asserting themselves, suspecting, plotting, praying for the death of others, grumbling at their present lot, falling in love, hoarding, longing for consulships and kingships. But the life of those men no longer exists, anywhere. Then turn to the times of Trajan;[13] again, everything is the same; and that life too is dead. Contemplate and observe in the same way the records of the other periods of time, indeed of whole nations: how many men have struggled eagerly and then, after a little while, fell and were resolved into their elements. But above all call to mind those whom you yourself have witnessed vainly struggling because they would not act in accord with their own nature and cling to it, and be satisfied with it. It is necessary thus to remind ourselves that every action requires the attention we give it to be measured according to its value, for if you do not dwell more than is fitting upon things of lesser importance, you will not impatiently give up the struggle.

. . . .

34 Surrender yourself willingly to Clotho[14] to help her spin whatever fate she will.

35 All is ephemeral, the one remembering and the one remembered.

36 Observe continually all that is born through change, and accustom yourself to reflect that the nature of the Whole loves nothing so much as to change existing things and to make similar new things. All that exists is in a sense the seed of what will be born from it, but you regard as seeds only those which are cast into the earth or the womb. But that is too unenlightened.

. . . .

40 One should continually think of the universe as one living being, with one substance and one soul—how all it contains falls under its one unitary perception, how all its actions derive

12. Roman emperor, reigned A.D. 69-79.
13. Roman emperor, reigned A.D. 98-117.
14. One of the three Fates (goddesses of human destiny). Clotho spins the thread of life; Lachesis determines its length; Atropos cuts it off.

from one impulse, how all things together cause all that happens, and the nature of the resulting web and pattern of events.

41 You are a little soul carrying a corpse, as Epictetus says.[15]

42 There is no evil in things in process of change, nor any good in things resulting from change.

43 Time is a river of things that become, with a strong current. No sooner is a thing seen than it has been swept away, and something else is being carried past, and still another thing will follow.

44 Everything that happens is as customary and understandable as the rose in springtime or the fruit in summer. The same is true of disease, death, slander and conspiracy, and all the things which delight or pain foolish men.

45 What happens next is always intimately related to what went before. It is not a question of merely adding up disparate things connected by inevitable succession, but events are logically interdependent. Just as the realities are established in tune with one another, so, in the world of sense, phenomena do not occur merely in succession, but they display an amazing affinity with one another.

46 Always remember the words of Heraclitus[16] that "the death of earth becomes water and the death of water becomes air, and that of air, fire, and so back again." Remember also what he says about the man who has forgotten whither the road leads. And "men are at odds with that with which they are in most constant touch, namely the Reason" which governs all; and again, "those things seem strange to them which they meet every day"; and "we must not act and speak as if asleep," for even then we seem to act and speak. And that one should not accept things "like children from parents" simply because they have been handed down to us.

47 If a god were to tell you that you will die tomorrow, or at any rate the day after, you would not make much of the difference between the day after and tomorrow—not unless you were altogether ignoble, for how short is the time between!

15. Roman Stoic philosopher, lived *ca.* A.D. 60-120.
16. Greek philosopher (flourished *ca.* 500 B.C.) who asserted that fire is the ultimate nature of things.

So now consider that the difference between the last possible year and tomorrow is no great matter.

. . . .

49 Be like a rock against which the waves of the sea break unceasingly. It stands unmoved, and the feverish waters around it are stilled.

"I am unfortunate because this has happened to me." No indeed, but I am fortunate because I endure what has happened without grief, neither shaken by the present nor afraid of the future. Something of this sort could happen to any man, but not every man can endure it without grieving. . . . What has happened can then in no way prevent you from being just, great-hearted, chaste, wise, steadfast, truthful, self-respecting and free, or prevent you from possessing those other qualities in the presence of which man's nature finds its own fulfillment. Remember in the future, when something happens which tends to make you grieve, to cling to this doctrine: this is no misfortune, but to endure it nobly is good fortune.

. . . .

Introduction to Augustine

The future Saint Augustine was born in A.D. 354 in the Roman province of Numidia in North Africa. Numidia at that time was the home of a heterogeneous mixture of peoples: remnants of the old Phoenicians who had ruled Carthage in its heyday, and who still spoke their Semitic tongue; native Africans, the ancestors of the present-day Berbers; and the offspring of Roman settlers. The province was likewise a battleground of many faiths: Manichaeism, Christianity, Donatism (the Christian heresy which sought to separate the African Church from Rome), and various pagan cults. Augustine himself was a product of this diverse environment. Born to a Christian mother and a pagan father, he was a Manichaean for nine years before turning to Christianity.

Nothing in Augustine's early career marked him as a future Christian saint. The son of a native African family of modest means, he received an elementary education in grammar and classical literature, and at age seventeen went to Carthage for further schooling. There he studied the usual classical subjects: rhetoric, mathematics, and philosophy, though he never mastered Greek. After finishing his formal education he became a professional teacher of rhetoric, and by his own account, led a licentious life. At twenty-nine he left Carthage for Italy, where he accepted the post of municipal instructor in rhetoric at Milan. There he also studied Plato and Plotinus and associated with Neo-Platonist circles; probably some of the Neo-Platonist coloring in his later theology goes back to this period.

But despite his professional successes, Augustine was tormented by religious doubts. While still at Carthage, he had rejected the Christian faith taught him by his mother and become an adherent of Manichaeism. He tells us that Manichaeism then seemed to him superior to other religions in its ability to explain the order of the universe and prove its beliefs by reason. The *Confessions* do not specify by what arguments he became convinced that this was not the case; apparently he attributed that insight to the grace of God. Subsequently he wrote books against the Manichaeans, though it is still arguable that his conviction of the overwhelming power of evil owed something to their influence.

In A.D. 387 Augustine was baptized by St. Ambrose, the Christian bishop of Milan. Shortly afterward he returned to Africa, where with some of his friends he founded a monastic community. Ordained a priest in 391, he became an administrative assistant to the bishop of Hippo (now Bône), a modest seaport town not far from Carthage. There his combination of religious fervor with subtle intellect attracted attention; and when the old bishop retired in 395, Augustine was chosen to succeed him. For thirty-four years he remained bishop of Hippo, active in teaching, preaching, and administering the diocese, and in defending orthodoxy against Manichaeism and Donatism.

But Augustine's great influence upon later Christianity rests not on his activities as bishop, but on his voluminous writings. Two of his works have become classics of world literature. The *Confessions,* which are addressed to God himself, record the spiritual struggles which led to the saint's conversion. Composed with mature reflection some twelve years after his baptism, Augustine's portrait of himself is astonishingly frank. He spares no words in denouncing his former sins: pride in worldly success, sexuality, and above all, his rejection of the true God. No doubt the searing remembrance of those early torments contributed to his emphasis on the sinfulness of sex which so influenced Christian attitudes, and to his conviction that personal effort alone is insufficient for salvation.

The *City of God* was Augustine's answer to the sack of Rome by the Visigoths in A.D. 410, an event which profoundly shocked the Christian world. Many speculated that the old Roman gods, angry at their displacement by Christianity as the official faith of the empire, had caused the disaster. Augustine argued that Rome's own sins of corruption and indecency were responsible. Rome, however magnificent, is only an earthly city; but there exists a higher city, which is God's. The city of God was founded by angels; it includes past, present, and future believers in Christ; those who live in it will reign eternally with God. The earthly city arose through Satan's rebellion against God; its inhabitants are condemned to perpetual torment. Augustine conceded that the city of God was not entirely identical with the Christian Church; the Church has temporal as well as spiritual interests and some of its members are sinful. But his theory of the two cities passed into the medieval assertion of the supremacy of Church to state, and was employed to justify a whole series of Roman popes in their quarrels with national kings.

Augustine is by common consent one of the greatest theologians of all time. His views on sin, grace, and free will dominated the Western Church down to the thirteenth century. He is also the father of Western monasticism, for which his own little community formed a prototype. Even the Aristotelian Thomas Aquinas admired him; and in the sixteenth century the Protestant reformers regarded their movement as to some extent a return to his ideas.

But Augustine's popularity is probably due as much to his intense conviction and personal vision of God as to his theological views. The *Confessions* ranks among the most widely read books in history. In that uniquely honest document, Christians for over fifteen hundred years have found a reflection of their own inward life.

AUGUSTINE: FROM THE CONFESSIONS

Book V, Chapter 6

For about nine years, in my mental aberration, I was a disciple of the Manichees, and for nearly all of this time I had been waiting with a kind of boundless longing for the coming of this man Faustus.[1] For the other Manichees whom I met and who failed to produce any answers to the questions I was raising on these subjects were always putting forward his name and promising me that as soon as Faustus arrived and I was able to discuss matters with him, all these difficulties of mine, together with any more weighty questions that I might care to ask, would be very easily dealt with and very lucidly explained. Well, he did arrive, and I found him a charming man with a very pleasant choice of words; he came out with exactly the same things as the others are always saying, but he did it much more elegantly.

However, my thirst could not be relieved by expensive drinking vessels and a well-dressed waiter. My ears were full already of this stuff, and the arguments themselves did not appear to me to be any better simply because they were better expressed; eloquence did not make them true; nor could I consider the soul wise because the face was attractive and the words well chosen. And as to those who promised me so much of him, they were not good judges of things. Their reason for thinking him wise and intelligent was simply that his way of speaking gave them pleasure.

I have had experience too of a quite different kind of person, the sort who will bring truth itself into suspicion and refuse to assent to it, if it is expressed in a good and ordered style. But you, my God, had already taught me in wonderful and hidden ways, and I believe that it was you who taught me because it is

1. A bishop of the Manichaeans famed for his learning and eloquence.

the truth and apart from you there is no other teacher of the truth, wherever or however it may be revealed. I had now learned this from you: that a thing is not necessarily true for being expressed eloquently, nor necessarily false if the sounds made by the lips are imperfectly pronounced; nor, on the other hand, is a thing true simply because it is expressed in a rough and ready way, nor false because it is uttered in a fine style. For with wisdom and folly the same thing holds good as with wholesome and unwholesome food. You can have silver or earthenware dishes on the table, just as you can have a decorated or undecorated use of language; either kind of food can be served in either kind of dish.

So those eager feelings of mine, with which I had so long been waiting for this man, were certainly gratified when I saw the way he carried himself and the way he behaved in a discussion, and when I saw how readily he found just the right words for expressing his thought I was delighted, and with many others, indeed more than most, I praised him and spoke highly of him. But I was upset when I found that, with all his disciples around him, I was not allowed to put a question to him and communicate to him the perplexities which troubled me by talking to him as man to man with each of us speaking in turn.[2] In the end I did get a chance to do this and, with some friends of mine, was able to engage his attention at a time when it was not incorrect for him to discuss matters by means of question and answer. I put forward some of the things which were disturbing me and at once discovered that this man was not educated in any of the liberal sciences except literature, and even here his learning was of a very conventional kind. He had read some of Cicero's[3] speeches, a very few books by Seneca,[4] some poetry, and those volumes written by people of his own persuasion which were in Latin and were neatly constructed; he also had daily practice in making speeches, and all this was the source of his eloquence, which was made the more agreeable

2. It was customary for students freely to ask questions of their teachers; Augustine was troubled that Faustus did not follow this procedure.

3. Roman statesman, orator, and philosopher, lived 106-43 B.C.

4. Roman author of tragic dramas, statesman and Stoic, lived 4 B.C.–A.D. 65.

and charming by being directed by a good intelligence and expressed with a kind of grace which was natural to the man.

Is it not so, as I remember it, Lord my God, judge of my conscience? My heart and my memory are open before you, and you in the hidden secrecy of your providence were working upon me then and setting in front of my face those shameful errors of mine, so that I might see them and hate them.

Chapter 7

For after it became quite clear to me that he was ignorant of those subjects in which I had thought him to be so particularly learned, I began to lose hope in his being able to solve my perplexities and explain to me the questions that troubled me—though, as I see now, he could have been ignorant of all this and still held the truth of piety, if only he had not been a Manichee. The books of the Manichees are indeed full of lengthy fables about the heaven and the stars and the sun and the moon, and I now thought that he could not possibly give me a reasoned answer to what I wanted to know, which was whether, after comparing all this with the calculations I had read of elsewhere, the facts were as stated in the books of Manes,[5] or if, at any rate, some explanation equally good could be discovered in these books. When I put forward this question as something to be considered and discussed he behaved with great modesty and would not venture to take up the burden. He knew that he was ignorant of these things and was not ashamed to admit it. He was not one of those talkative people (I had had to put up with a great many of them) who attempted to instruct me in these subjects but had no instruction to give. Indeed he had a heart which, while not right toward you, was quite well prepared to look after himself. He was not altogether ignorant of his own ignorance, and he had no wish to get rashly involved in a controversy which he could not possibly win and from which he would find it difficult to retire. For this too I liked him all the better; for there is more beauty in the modesty of a mind that admits its faults than in the knowledge that I was seeking for.

5. Mani.

So I found him too when it came to all the more difficult and subtle questions.

As a result of this I lost the enthusiasm which I had had for the writings of Manes, and I had all the less confidence in the other Manichaean teachers after I found that the famous Faustus had shown up so badly in many of the questions which perplexed me. However I began to spend much time with him because of his own kind of enthusiasm, which was for literature, and it was literature which I, as professor, was at that time teaching to the young at Carthage. I used to read with him what he wanted to have read or what I considered right for his kind of intelligence. But all the ambition I had had to go far in that sect simply collapsed once I had got to know the man. Not that I broke completely with the Manichees. It was simply that, not being able to find anything better than the course on which I had somehow or other become set, I had decided to stay as I was for the time being, unless something else should happen to appear which seemed preferable. So this Faustus, who to many people had been a real snare of death, now began, without willing it or knowing it, to unloosen the snare in which I had been caught. Your hands, my God, in the secrecy of your providence never abandoned my soul; from the blood of my mother's heart, by the tears which she shed day and night, sacrifice for me was offered to you, and in wonderful ways you dealt with me. It was your doing, my God: for *the steps of a man are ordered by the Lord, and He shall dispose his way*. Or how shall we find salvation except by your hand's remaking what you made?

Chapter 8

You acted upon me in such a way that I was persuaded to set out for Rome to teach there the same subjects as I had been teaching in Carthage. How it was that I came to be persuaded to do this must not be passed over in my confession to you; here too I must ponder over and openly declare the deep secrecy of your ways and your mercy which is always so close to us. I wanted to go to Rome not only because of the higher earnings and the greater reputation which my friends, who persuaded me to go, thought I would get there, though these reasons did have some weight with me at that time; in fact, however, my main and almost my only reason for going was that I heard that in Rome the young men followed their studies in a more orderly manner and were controlled by a stricter discipline. They were not allowed, for instance, insolently and at their own pleasure to come rushing into the school of a man who was not their own teacher; in fact they were not allowed to enter the school at all without the master's permission.

At Carthage, on the other hand, the students are disgracefully out of control. They come breaking into a class in the most unmannerly way and, behaving almost like madmen, disturb the order which the master has established for the good of his pupils. They commit a number of disorderly acts which show an incredible stupidity and which ought to be punished by law. However, custom protects them, and this is a fact which makes their state even more wretched, because the things they do appear to them permissible, though by your eternal law such things can never be permitted, and they imagine that they are getting away scot-free with what they do, whereas the very blindness with which they act is their punishment, and the harm which they do to themselves is incomparably worse than what they do to others. When I was a student myself I refused to become one of those who behaved in this way, though when I became a teacher I had to put up with this behavior from other people, and so the reason why I wanted to go to Rome was that all who knew about it told me that there these things were not done. But you, my hope and my portion in the land of the living, were urging me to change countries for the salvation of my soul. In Carthage you prepared goads for me, so that I should be driven from the place, and at Rome you provided attractions which would draw me there, and in both cases you made use of men who were in love with this deathly life; on the one side were people acting like lunatics and on the other people who promised me mere vanities. So, to reform my ways, you secretly made use both of their perversity and of my own. For those who were disturbing my peace were blinded by a disgraceful frenzy, and those who urged me to go elsewhere savored of earth. And I, hating my real misery in Carthage, looked for a false happiness in Rome.

. . . .

Chapter 10

. . . In Rome, I associated myself with those false and deceiving "saints," not only with the "hearers"[6] (one of whom was the man in whose house I had been ill and had recovered), but also with the ones whom they call "the elect." For I was still of the opinion that it is not we ourselves who sin, but some other nature which is in us; it gratified my pride to think that I was blameless and, if I did something wrong, not to confess that I had done it, so that you might heal my soul, because my soul had sinned against you. Instead I liked to excuse myself and accuse something else—something that was in me, but was not really I. But in fact I was wholly I and it was my impiety which had divided one me from another me. My sin was all the more incurable because I imagined that I was not a sinner, and it was most execrable wickedness in me that I preferred that you, you, Almighty God, should be overcome in me to my destruction rather than that I should be overcome by you for my salvation.

You had not yet *set a watch before my mouth and a door of safekeeping around my lips, that my heart might not turn aside to wicked speeches, to make excuses of sins, with men that work iniquity*. And for this reason I was still in the fellowship of their Elect. However, I saw no prospect of being able to go far in that false doctrine, and I began to have less and less interest in and enthusiasm for even those principles of theirs with which I had decided to be content, if I could find nothing better.

The thought occurred to me that those philosophers who are called the Academics[7] were wiser than the rest, because they held that everything should be considered doubtful and had come to the conclusion that no truth could be comprehended by

6. Or: "Elect" and laymen (of Manichaeism).

7. The Academics were the philosophical descendants of Plato. Evidently they contented themselves in public with refuting others' errors, thus giving rise to the opinion that they were sceptics.

man. For it seemed to me quite clear that this (as is the general belief) was the view they held, though in fact I had not yet even grasped what they were driving at. Certainly I quite openly persuaded this man in whose house I was staying not to have such excessive faith, which I could see that he had, in all those fables of which the books of Manes are full. Yet I still lived on more friendly terms with the Manichees than with others not of that heresy. I was no longer defending it with my old fervor, but my friendship with those people (and Rome shelters a great many of them) made me slower to look for some other belief, especially since, Lord of heaven and earth, Creator of all things visible and invisible, I had no hope of finding the truth in your Church. For they had turned me against it, and I thought it most unseemly to believe that you had the shape of our human flesh and were bounded by the bodily outlines of our limbs. When I wanted to think of my God, I did not know how to think of him except as a mass of bodies,[8] for it seemed to me that what was not this was nothing. And this was the chief, indeed almost the only, cause of my inevitable error.

Because of this I believed that evil also was some such a kind of substance, with its own foul and hideous bulk, which might be either gross (which they called earth) or thin and subtle like the body of air; for they imagine it to be a kind of malignant mind creeping through the earth. And because this strange form of piety of mine led me to believe that a good God had never created any evil nature, I came to the conclusion that there were two masses in opposition to each other, both infinite, but the evil one more contracted and the good one more expansive. And from this pestilent beginning other sacrilegious notions followed naturally.

When my mind tried to revert to the Catholic faith, it was driven back again, because I had a false idea of what the Catholic faith really was. It seemed to me more reverent to believe that you, God (to whom I now confess your mercies done in me), were infinite in all parts except one—for I should be forced to confess that you were finite in respect to that part

8. Heavenly bodies, stars, etc.

where the mass of evil was set in opposition to you—rather than to hold the view that you were in all your parts finitely contained in the shape of a human body.[9] And it seemed better to believe that you had created no evil than to believe that what I conceived to be the nature of evil was from you,[10] and evil seemed to me in my ignorance to be not only a substance, but actually a physical substance; for I could not even think of mind except as a rarified form of body with extension in space. And I thought of our Saviour Himself, your Only-begotten Son, as if He were for our salvation stretched out to us, as it were, from the mass of your bright and shining substance, and as a result I could believe nothing of Him except what would fit in with my empty imagination. I considered that such a nature could not possibly be born of the Virgin Mary, unless it were mingled with her flesh, and I could not see how the nature which I had imagined to myself could be mingled without being defiled.[11] Thus I was afraid to believe that He was born in the flesh lest I should be forced to believe that He was defiled by the flesh. I know that your spiritual ones will be smiling at me, though kindly and lovingly, if they read the story of these confusions of mind. But this was what I was like at that time.

. . . .

Chapter 12

I started at once to do what I had come to do, namely to teach rhetoric at Rome. First of all I collected a few pupils at my house and by means of them I began to become known. I soon found out that things went on in Rome which I had not had to put up with in Africa. True enough I discovered that in Rome there was none of that subversive behavior which I knew on the part of the worst types of young men; but, so I was told, "in order to avoid paying their fees to the professor, a number of young men form a conspiracy and suddenly go off to study under another professor, thus breaking their pledged words and

9. I.e., in Christ.
10. Since the Manichaeans believed that both good and evil had existed from all eternity, God in their system was not responsible for evil.
11. To the Manichaeans, flesh (matter) was the embodiment of evil.

showing that to them justice is cheap compared with the love of money." I hated them too in my heart, though the hatred I felt was not a perfect hatred. I think that I hated them more because of what I was likely to suffer from them personally than because of the wrong they did to everyone concerned. Such people, however, are certainly vile characters; they fornicate against you in loving the fleeting mockeries of time and the filthy lucre which soils the hand that holds it and in embracing this fleeting world and in despising you who abide and who call them back to you and who give pardon to the adulterous soul of man when it returns to you. I still hate wicked and depraved people of this sort, though I love the thought of their being corrected and taught to love learning more than money and to love you, God, the truth and fullness of certain good, and the purest peace, more than learning. But at that time I was more anxious not to have to put up with their evil ways for my own sake than that they should learn good for your sake.

Chapter 13

So when the prefect of the city in Rome received a message from Milan, asking him to provide them with a professor of rhetoric and promising to pay the expenses of his journey out of public funds, I applied for the post myself. My application was supported by those very people who were intoxicated with the vanities of Manichaeism, and it was just to be rid of these people that I was going—though neither they nor I realized the fact. So I had the opportunity to make a speech on a set subject; Symmachus, who was then prefect, approved of it, and I was sent to Milan. And at Milan I came to Bishop Ambrose,[12] who had a worldwide reputation, was a devout servant of yours and a man whose eloquence in those days gave abundantly to *Thy people the fatness of Thy wheat, the gladness of Thy oil and the sober intoxication of Thy wine.* Though I did not realize it, I was led to him by you so that, with full realization, I might be led to you by him. That man of God welcomed me as a father and, in his capacity of bishop, was kind enough to

12. The later Saint Ambrose, bishop of Milan A.D. 374-398.

approve of my coming there. I began to love him at first not as a teacher of the truth (for I had quite despaired of finding it in your Church) but simply as a man who was kind and generous to me. I used to listen eagerly when he preached to the people, but my intention was not what it should have been; I was, as it were, putting his eloquence on trial to see whether it came up to his reputation, or whether its flow was greater or less than I had been told. So I hung intently on his words, but I was not interested in what he was really saying and stood aside from this in contempt. I was much pleased by the charm of his style, which, although it was more learned, was still, so far as the manner of delivery was concerned, not so warm and winning as the style of Faustus. With regard to the actual matter there was, of course, no comparison. Faustus was merely roving around among Manichaean fallacies, while Ambrose was healthily teaching salvation. But salvation is far from sinners of the kind that I was then. Yet, though I did not realize it, I was drawing gradually nearer.

Chapter 14

For although my concern was not to learn what he said but only to hear how he said it (this empty interest being all that remained to me, now that I had despaired of man's being able to find his way to you), nevertheless, together with the language, which I admired, the subject matter also, to which I was indifferent, began to enter into my mind. Indeed I could not separate the one from the other. And as I opened my heart in order to recognize how eloquently he was speaking it occurred to me at the same time (though this idea came gradually) how truly he was speaking. First I began to see that the points which he made were capable of being defended. I had thought that nothing could be said for the Catholic faith in the face of the objections raised by the Manichees, but it now appeared to me that this faith could be maintained on reasonable grounds—especially when I had heard one or two passages in the Old Testament explained, usually in a figurative way, which, when I had taken them literally, had been a cause of death to me. So, after a number of these passages had been explained to me in their spiritual sense, I began to blame that despairing attitude of mine which had led me to believe that the Law and the Prophets could not possibly stand up to hostile and mocking criticism. However, I did not feel that I ought to take the way of the Catholics simply because they too could produce learned men to maintain their belief and to answer objections skillfully and without absurdity; nor did I think that the faith which I held should be condemned simply because the Catholics were just as well able to defend theirs. So, though the Catholic cause did not seem to me defeated, it did not yet seem to me to have won.

Then indeed I began to bend my mind earnestly to the question: Could I find any sure proofs by which to convict the Manichees of falsehood? If only I had been able to form the idea of a substance that was spiritual, all their strongholds would have collapsed at once and been thrown out of my mind. But I could not.

However, with regard to the body of this world and the whole of nature that is within the reach of our bodily senses, I considered, after much consideration and frequent comparisons, that very many of the philosophers held views which were much more probable than those of the Manichees. So, in what is assumed to be the manner of the Academics, while doubting everything and wavering between one thing and another, I did at least decide that I must leave the Manichees. For even in this period of doubt, I did not consider that I ought to remain in that sect when I already thought more highly of some of the philosophers than of the Manichees. Though still I absolutely refused to allow these philosophers to take care of my sick soul, because they were without the saving name of Christ. I decided, therefore, to be for the time being a catechumen in the Catholic Church (the Church which my parents had encouraged me to join) until I should see some certain light by which to steer my course.

Book VIII, Chapter 6

Now, Lord, my helper and my redeemer, I shall tell and confess to your name how it was that you freed me from the bondage of my desire for sex, in which I was so closely fettered, and from my slavery to the affairs of this world. I was leading my usual life; my anxiety was growing greater and greater, and every day I sighed to you. I went often to your Church, whenever I had time to spare from all that business under the weight of which I was groaning.

. . . .

Chapter 7

. . . Many years (at least twelve) of my own life had gone by since the time when I was nineteen and was reading Cicero's *Hortensius* and had been fired with an enthusiasm for wisdom. Yet I was still putting off the moment when, despising this world's happiness, I should give all my time to the search for that of which not only the finding but merely the seeking must be preferred to the discovered treasures and kingdoms of men or to all the pleasures of the body easily and abundantly available. But I, wretched young man that I was—even more wretched at the beginning of my youth—had begged you for chastity and had said: "Make me chaste and continent, but not yet." I was afraid that you might hear me too soon and cure me too soon from the disease of a lust which I preferred to be satisfied rather than extinguished. And I had gone along evil ways, following a sacrilegious superstition—not because I was convinced by it, but simply preferring it to the other doctrines into which I never inquired in a religious spirit, but merely attacked them in a spirit of spite.

I had thought that the reason why I was putting off from day to day the time when I should despise all worldly hopes and follow you alone was because I could see no certainty toward which I could direct my course. But now the day had come when in my own eyes I was stripped naked and my conscience cried out against me: "Can you not hear me? Was it not this that you used to say, that you would not throw off the burden of vanity for a truth that was uncertain? Well, look. Now the truth is certain, and you are still weighed down by your burden. Yet these others, who have not been so worn out in the search and not been meditating the matter for ten years or more, have had the weight taken from their backs and have been given wings to fly."

. . . .

Chapter 10

Let them perish from your presence, God, as perish empty talkers and seducers of the soul, who, having observed that there are two wills in the act of deliberating, conclude from this that we have in us two minds of two different natures, one good and one evil.[13] They themselves are truly evil, when they hold these evil opinions, and they are just as capable of becoming good if they will realize the truth and agree with the truth, so that your apostle may say to them: *Ye were sometimes darkness, but now light in the Lord.* But these people, by imagining that the nature of the soul is what God is, want to be light, not in the Lord, but in themselves, and the result is that they have become an even deeper darkness, since in their appalling arrogance they have gone further away from you—from you, *the true Light that enlighteneth every man that cometh into the world.* Take heed what you say, and blush for shame: *draw near unto Him and be enlightened, and your faces shall not be ashamed.*

As to me, when I was deliberating about entering the service of the Lord my God, as I had long intended to do, it was I who willed it, and it was I who was unwilling. It was the same "I" throughout. But neither my will nor my unwillingness was whole and entire. So I fought with myself and was torn apart by myself. It was against my will that this tearing apart took place, but this was not an indication that I had another mind of a different nature; it was simply the punishment which I was suffering in my own mind. It was not I, therefore, who caused it, but *the sin dwells in me*, and, being a son of Adam, I was suffering for his sin which was more freely committed.

. . . .

Chapter 11

So I was sick and in torture. I reproached myself much more bitterly than ever, and I turned and twisted in my chain till

13. The Manichaean opinion.

I could break quite free. Only a little of it still held me, but it did still hold me. And you, Lord, in the secret places of my soul, stood above me in the severity of your mercy, redoubling the lashes of fear and shame, so that I should not give way once more and so that that small weak piece of chain which still remained should not instead of snapping grow strong again and tie me down more firmly than before. I was saying inside myself: "Now, now, let it be now!" and as I spoke the words I was already beginning to go in the direction I wanted to go. I nearly managed it, but I did not quite manage it. Yet I did not slip right back to the beginning; I was a stage above that, and I stood there to regain my breath. And I tried again and I was very nearly there; I was almost touching it and grasping it, and then I was not there, I was not touching it, I was not grasping it; I hesitated to die to death and to live to life; inveterate evil had more power over me than the novelty of good, and as that very moment of time in which I was to become something else drew nearer and nearer, it struck me with more and more horror. But I was not struck right back or turned aside; I was just held in suspense.

Toys and trifles, utter vanities had been my mistresses, and now they were holding me back, pulling me by the garment of my flesh and softly murmuring in my ear: "Are you getting rid of us?" and "From this moment shall we never be with you again for all eternity?" and "From this moment will you never for all eternity be allowed to do this or to do that?" My God, what was it, what was it that they suggested in those words "this" or "that" which I have just written? I pray you in your mercy to keep such things from the soul of your servant. How filthy, how shameful were these things they were suggesting! And now their voices were not half so loud in my ears; now they no longer came out boldly to contradict me face to face; it was more as though they were muttering behind my back, stealthily pulling at my sleeve as I was going away so that I should turn and look at them. Yet still they did hold me back as I hesitated to tear myself away and to shake them off and to take the great step in the direction where I was called. Violence of habit spoke the words: "Do you think that you can live without them?"

But by now it spoke very faintly. In the direction toward which I had turned my face and still trembled to take the last step, I could see the chaste dignity of Continence; she was calm and serene, cheerful without wantonness, and it was in truth and honor that she was enticing me to come to her without hesitation, stretching out to receive and to embrace me with those holy hands of hers, full of such multitudes of good examples. With her were so many boys and girls, so much of youth, so much of every age, grave widows and women grown old in virginity, and in them all was Continence herself, not barren, but *a fruitful mother of children*, her joys, by you, Lord, her husband. She smiled at me and there was encouragement in her smile, as though she were saying: "Can you not do what these men and these women have done? Or do you think that their ability is in themselves and not in the Lord their God? It was the Lord God who gave me to them. Why do you try and stand by yourself, and so not stand at all? Let him support you. Do not be afraid. He will not draw away and let you fall. Put yourself fearlessly in His hands. He will receive you and will make you well."

And I was blushing for shame, because I could still hear the dim voices of those vanities, and still I hung back in hesitation. And again she seemed to be speaking: "Stop your ears against those unclean members of yours, so that they may be mortified. They tell you of delights, but not of such delights as the law of the Lord your God tells."

So went the controversy in my heart—about self, and self against self. And Alypius[14] stayed close by me, waiting silently to see how this strange agitation of mine would end.

Chapter 12

And now from my hidden depths my searching thought had dragged up and set before the sight of my heart the whole mass of my misery. Then a huge storm rose up within me bringing with it a huge downpour of tears. So that I might pour out all these tears and speak the words that came with them I rose up

14. Augustine's younger friend and former student; his faithful follower.

from Alypius (solitude seemed better for the business of weeping) and went further away so that I might not be embarrassed even by his presence. This was how I felt and he realized it. No doubt I had said something or other, and he could feel the weight of my tears in the sound of my voice. And so I rose to my feet, and he, in a state of utter amazement, remained in the place where we had been sitting. I flung myself down on the ground somehow under a fig tree and gave free rein to my tears; they streamed and flooded from my eyes, an *acceptable sacrifice to Thee.* And I kept saying to you, not perhaps in these words, but with this sense: "*And Thou, O Lord, how long? How long, Lord; wilt Thou be angry forever? Remember not our former iniquities.*" For I felt that it was these which were holding me fast. And in my misery I would exclaim: "How long, how long this 'tomorrow and tomorrow'? Why not now? Why not finish this very hour with my uncleanness?"

So I spoke, weeping in the bitter contrition of my heart. Suddenly a voice reaches my ears from a nearby house. It is the voice of a boy or a girl (I don't know which) and in a kind of singsong the words are constantly repeated: "Take it and read it. Take it and read it." At once my face changed, and I began to think carefully of whether the singing of words like these came into any kind of game which children play, and I could not remember that I had ever heard anything like it before. I checked the force of my tears and rose to my feet, being quite certain that I must interpret this as a divine command to me to open the book and read the first passage which I should come upon. For I had heard this about Antony:[15] he had happened to come in when the Gospel was being read, and as though the words read were spoken directly to himself, had received the admonition: *Go, sell all that thou hast, and give to the poor, and thou shalt have treasure in heaven, and come and follow me.* And by such an oracle he had been immediately converted to you.

So I went eagerly back to the place where Alypius was sit-

15. Saint Anthony (A.D. 251-356?), the founder of Egyptian monasticism. His reputation for extreme austerities and sanctity was widespread throughout Christendom.

ting, since it was there that I had left the book of the Apostle when I rose to my feet. I snatched up the book, opened it, and read in silence the passage upon which my eyes first fell: *Not in rioting and drunkenness, not in chambering and wantonness, not in strife and envying: but put ye on the Lord Jesus Christ, and make not provision for the flesh in concupiscence.* I had no wish to read further; there was no need to. For immediately I had reached the end of this sentence it was as though my heart was filled with a light of confidence and all the shadows of my doubt were swept away.

Before shutting the book I put my finger or some other marker in the place and told Alypius what had happened. By now my face was perfectly calm. And Alypius in his turn told me what had been going on in himself, and which I knew nothing about. He asked to see the passage which I had read. I showed him and he went on further than the part I had read, nor did I know the words which followed. They were these: *Him that is weak in the faith, receive.* He applied this to himself and told me so. He was strengthened by the admonition; calmly and unhesitatingly he joined me in a purpose and a resolution so good, and so right for his character, which had always been very much better than mine.

The next thing we do is to go inside and tell my mother. How happy she is! We describe to her how it all took place, and there is no limit to her joy and triumph. Now she was praising you, *Who art able to do above that which we ask or think;* for she saw that with regard to me you had given her so much more than she used to ask for when she wept so pitifully before you. For you converted me to you in such a way that I no longer sought a wife nor any other worldly hope. I was now standing on that rule of faith, just as you had shown me to her in a vision so many years before. And so you had changed her mourning into joy, a joy much richer than she had desired and much dearer and purer than that which she looked for by having grandchildren of my flesh.